The International Relations of Eastern Europe

INTERNATIONAL RELATIONS INFORMATION GUIDE SERIES

Series Editor: Garold W. Thumm, Professor of Government and Chairman of the Department, Bates College, Lewiston, Maine

Also in this series:

ARMS CONTROL AND MILITARY POLICY—*Edited by Donald F. Bletz**

ECONOMICS AND FOREIGN POLICY—*Edited by Mark R. Amstutz*

THE EUROPEAN COMMUNITIES—*Edited by J. Bryan Collester**

INTELLIGENCE, ESPIONAGE, COUNTERESPIONAGE, AND COVERT OPERA-TIONS—*Edited by Paul W. Blackstock and Frank Schaf, Jr.*

INTERNATIONAL AND REGIONAL POLITICS IN THE MIDDLE EAST AND NORTH AFRICA—*Edited by Ann Schulz*

INTERNATIONAL ORGANIZATIONS—*Edited by Alexine Atherton*

LATIN AMERICA—*Edited by John J. Finan**

THE MULTINATIONAL CORPORATION—*Edited by Helga Hernes*

POLITICAL DEVELOPMENT—*Edited by Arpad von Lazar and Bruce Magid**

SOUTH ASIA—*Edited by Richard J. Kozicki**

SOUTHEAST ASIA—*Edited by Richard Butwell**

THE STUDY OF INTERNATIONAL RELATIONS—*Edited by Robert L. Pfaltzgraff, Jr.*

SUB-SAHARAN AFRICA—*Edited by W.A.E. Skurnik*

U.S. INVOLVEMENT IN VIETNAM—*Edited by Allan W. Cameron**

*in preparation

The above series is part of the
GALE INFORMATION GUIDE LIBRARY

The Library consists of a number of separate series of guides covering major areas in the social sciences, humanities, and current affairs.

General Editor: Paul Wasserman, Professor and former Dean, School of Library and Information Services, University of Maryland

Managing Editor: Denise Allard Adzigian, Gale Research Company

The International Relations of Eastern Europe

A GUIDE TO INFORMATION SOURCES

Volume 8 in the International Relations Information Guide Series

Robin Alison Remington

*Associate Professor of
Political Science
University of Missouri
Columbia*

Gale Research Company
Book Tower, Detroit, Michigan 48226

Library of Congress Cataloging in Publication Data

Remington, Robin Alison.
    The international relations of Eastern Europe.

    (International relations information guide
series ; v. 8)
    Bibliography: p. 273
    Includes index.
    1. Europe, Eastern—Foreign relations—
Bibliography. I. Title.
Z6465.E853R45   [DJ49]   016.32747   73-17512
ISBN 0-8103-1320-0

For my grandmother Edith Therrien,
who taught me the value of books
For my mother Mabelle Therrien Poynter,
who taught me the importance of sharing
and for my daughter Lisa,
who continues the tradition

VITA

Robin Alison Remington is associate professor of political science at the University of Missouri (Columbia) and research affiliate of the Massachusetts Institute of Technology Center for International Studies. She is also a member of the Executive Council of the American Association for Southeast European Studies. Her books include WINTER IN PRAGUE: DOCUMENTS ON CZECHOSLOVAK COMMUNISM IN CRISIS (1969) and THE WARSAW PACT: CASE STUDIES IN COMMUNIST CONFLICT RESOLUTION (1971). She has done field work in Yugoslavia, Czechoslovakia, and Poland and has published widely on East European foreign policy.

CONTENTS

Contents

viii

ACKNOWLEDGMENTS

Any bibliography of this sort is of necessity a collective effort or it never gets beyond the original disorganized mountain of file cards. My debts are many. I appreciate the seemingly endless checking and rechecking of research assistants Nancy Hearst and Rada Vlajinac at the MIT Center for International Studies when the project began. Having moved to the University of Missouri (Columbia) political science faculty in 1974, their task was taken up by Christopher Hamilton, Pamela Smith Ingram, and, in the final agony, by Donna Marie Walker. I am grateful to my colleagues for keeping me abreast of their more recent research, for the politeness of many nameless editors when I resorted to the telephone for information about forthcoming volumes, and for the constant assistance and courtesy of librarians at the MIT Dewey Library, the Harvard Russian Research Center Library, and Ellis Library at the University of Missouri, Columbia. The manuscript was typed by Patricia L. Marden, copyedited by Ester Allweiss, typed in final camera-ready form by Barbara N. Stire, and guided through the publication process by Denise Allard Adzigian and Claudia Dembinski.

The publication of this volume has been made possible by the patience of our series editor G.W. Thumm whose encouragement overcame the many delays and frustrations inherent in such a project. However, neither Professor Thumm nor any of those whose assistance was so valuable are responsible for the annotations or the inevitable errors. That responsibility is mine alone.

Robin Alison Remington
Columbia, Missouri

INTRODUCTION

The study of East European international relations is a tricky business in which nothing can be taken for granted. In this area academic boundaries are as unstable as the region's historical borders. Deciding what is Eastern Europe depends on the criteria used. Ideological and geographical boundaries are not the same. The once-perceived unity of the Soviet bloc has so visibly cracked that even the most dogmatic observers have trouble justifying Eastern Europe as a unified concept when Yugoslavia, Albania, and Rumania are taken into consideration. East Germany, the smaller half of a truncated nation that has become an economic success story in its own right, presents a unique problem. There is growing, if at times reluctant, recognition among scholars that perhaps the most salient characteristic of Eastern Europe is the area's progressive differentiation and fragmentation. As Korbonski has pointed out, in some cases cross-system differences between Communist and non-Communist European nations appear smaller than those between Communist countries themselves.[1] In the future it might well be more useful to compile such a bibliography on the Balkans or Central Europe without making ideological distinctions.

Perhaps most importantly, such decisions are increasingly recognized as being arbitrary. This selected bibliography focuses on Communist Eastern Europe for three reasons. First, the definition of a region is always largely based on custom and habit of scholarship concerning that area. Thus, despite contemporary trends to the contrary, post-World War II scholarly and journalistic works devoted to Eastern Europe for the most part use ideological boundaries. Secondly, the regional alliance structures, core parts of the international relations of member states, have ideologically determined membership in practice, if not in principle. Thirdly, there is the question of how to serve the needs of potential users of this bibliography, and in my judgment, the largest number of students and scholars will be benefited by taking a modified, ideologically defined, area studies approach. Therefore, the bibliography is divided into two parts: Eastern Europe as a region based on the above criteria, and also country-specific sources relating to Albania, Bulgaria, Czechoslovakia, East Germany, Hungary, Poland, Rumania, and Yugoslavia.

Yet having located "our" Eastern Europe, there remains a fundamental difficulty of distinguishing between the domestic and foreign policy of the countries in question. East European postwar political systems were explicitly based on a foreign model, and tinkering with domestic preferences for expanding participation and/or economic reform had, and has, direct impact on these nations' relationships with the Soviet Union and other East European countries. In these circumstances, to treat international relations as separate from the domestic political process is to perpetuate a fiction. Nor do separate bodies of scholarship exist. According to Triska and Johnson: "The most significant variable in explaining political system stability and change in Eastern Europe is thus Soviet security."[2] All scholars might not go so far. Nonetheless, key works dealing with domestic political change in Eastern Europe usually have sections devoted to foreign policy. Even when this is not the case, there may be significant implications of such a work for the international relations of Eastern Europe. For example, a study by R. Barry Farrell, ed. POLITICAL LEADERSHIP IN EASTERN EUROPE AND THE SOVIET UNION (1970), has valuable insights for students struggling with the question of to what extent the Soviet model continues to influence East European patterns.[3] Thus, this selection is based on the assumption that there is a symbiotic relationship between East European domestic developments and international relations. Internal developments have been included when they can be considered a variable influencing international policies, with an understanding that at least some part of the concern for East European international relations comes from scholars seeking to add an external variable as a predictor of system change within Eastern Europe.

Another consideration had to be the placing of Eastern Europe within the context of comparative communism. To what extent are the international relations of Eastern Europe influenced by the fact that these nations share a common ideology and what Modelski has identified as a Communist political culture, "embodied in its own prolific literature, (with) ... its own distinct language and symbols, its own history, and its own heroes, villains, and martyrs, and its own ritual behavior?"[4] This is not identical with the myth of a united Communist foreign policy. Rather, it points to the more subtle influence of the perception of belonging to a "family of socialist nations" within which there are behavioral expectations that do not apply to outsiders. Such a perception merits investigation as a potential input to foreign policy decision making within Eastern Europe. For students and scholars working with this dimension, as well as for those concerned with cross-system comparisons and lacking familiarity with Communist and/or East European studies per se, the basic theoretical works dealing with comparative communism have been included. In order to assist those trying to make distinctions between Communist political culture and historical political cultures of the region, there are also works dealing with general historical background both for the interwar years and before. These include general studies, like Hugh Seton-Watson's EASTERN EUROPE BETWEEN THE WARS: 1918-1941 (1962), and recent reexaminations of specific periods, such as Anna M. Cienciala's POLAND AND THE WESTERN POWERS 1938-1939: A STUDY OF THE INTERDEPENDENCE OF EASTERN AND WESTERN EUROPE (1968).

This bibliography has been compiled primarily with undergraduate and graduate students in mind. It has been organized to be useful to those emphasizing an area study approach as well as to those students of comparative and international politics interested in issue-oriented East European data; hence, the inclusion of subdivisions dealing with the institutional approach, comparative approach, and nationalism as an alternative. There is, however, an underlying assumption that "student" implies a much broader audience than individuals attending colleges and universities. Therefore, considerable thought was given in annotating to indicate those works that are more appropriate for a general reader than for a potential specialist. It was my hope that high school as well as college students would find this work useful, and that an adult with interests related to ethnic origin might use this as a starting point for further exploration. That hope contributed to my including a variety of journalistic and memoir accounts, which is not to discount the potential academic value of such books. I kept cross-referencing to a minimum.

In considering the years since 1945 that provide the major focus of the following selections, it becomes clear that the study of Eastern Europe has been closely related to American foreign policy; sometimes reflecting, sometimes anticipating assumptions in Washington. Bluntly, ever since World War II Eastern Europe has been a low priority headache for U.S. policy makers. Deciding what to do about the area severely complicated Soviet-American relations at the end of the war, leading the then Secretary of State Cordell Hull to wistfully comment in his memoirs that if Great Britain and Russia would only agree on a solution, Washington would gladly go along. Former President Ford's first "plain talk" to the nation in 1974 in which he referred to our relations with Western Europe, Japan, Latin America, China, and the Soviet Union--but not Eastern Europe--indicated a certain continuity of preference for benign neglect.

Yet, despite this reluctance to have a coherent East European policy, Eastern Europe continued and continues to intrude into other vital areas of American national interest. The area covers eight countries; 1,264,438 square kilometers; and roughly 120 million in population. It has systematically impacted on U.S.-Soviet relations, been a consideration in Washington's West European policy, influenced NATO strategies, become ever more important vis-à-vis the Middle East, and even played a not insignificant role in the presidential campaign of 1976. In short, Eastern Europe is hard to ignore.

With the cold war of the 1950s, Hull's desire to avoid the complications of relating to East European nations directly had become a convenient policy simplification of "collective treatment," symbolized by demands for "roll-back" and liberation. Eastern Europe was perceived as a part of the package of U.S.-Soviet hostilities. It was assumed by Washington that the area could be treated as a unit, important primarily as a potential pressure point to be used in confrontation with the Russians. As a corollary, there was the assumption that the object was to split the Soviet bloc; that once Moscow's hold weakened (or if an East European Communist regime fell, such as during the Hungarian uprising of 1956) more liberal, pluralistic, and automatically more desirable substitutes would arise.

Thus, during the early postwar period and throughout the cold war years, the study of East European international relations focused on "satellite states," emphasizing Soviet iron-fisted domination, and the rape of Eastern Europe. Such studies were often written by journalists, those who had suffered most from postwar chaos and political change, and East European emigré scholars. This is not to discount their version of reality, but rather to point to the result: the assumption of gray uniformity as a characteristic of postwar Eastern Europe. In the literature, it meant emphasis on that which was the same in the Soviet Union and Eastern Europe in terms of internal political dynamics, on Soviet hegemony in foreign policy, on possible opposition to and potential breakdowns in the pattern of Communist consolidation. There are many books devoted to Communist crises, such as the Soviet-Yugoslav dispute of 1948, the Hungarian uprising and the Polish October of 1956, and the 1968 invasion of Czechoslovakia. Attention has tended to focus on challengers to Moscow's domination rather than on the perceived solid citizens of the Soviet bloc. That pattern was in part a problem of access, which is beginning to change. If the number of books written about Yugoslavia as compared to other East European countries is considered, the result is clear.

These were interesting, important arenas of study. In retrospect, it might be said that the cold war perceived realities were not the only realities; the academic focus of that period was not only areas of East European development. Why, for instance, were the most avid East European watchers caught flatfooted by the Prague Spring of 1968? The invasion came as a surprise to many; for our purposes, it is more important that the Czechoslovak behavior that led up to the use of troops was equally unpredictable. Even in the 1950s, Eastern Europe was not as uniform as it appeared. Stalin died in 1953. With him died whatever validity there may have been for "collective treatment" of Eastern Europe either as a policy or an academic approach. However, policies and intellectual habits alike are hard to change.

The Soviet Union in the 1960s became a "limited adversary" rather than the enemy. The complexity of international politics as the cold war began to be seen in less than total terms had both total and academic spin-offs with respect to Eastern Europe. As the bipolar international system faded into infinitely more fluid, decentralized patterns, the implications of detente and open conflicts between the Soviet Union and a number of East European Communist regimes led to reassessments. There came to be an appreciation of the importance of Brzezinski's point that there was no intrinsic reason why the initial diversity among East European regimes ended so abruptly in 1948.[5]

In summary, attention began to be paid in the 1960s to the fact that for twenty-plus years Communist regimes highly conscious of their national boundaries had existed in Eastern Europe and that the relationship of these countries to Moscow was increasingly complicated. Gradually, scholars began to think in terms of "client states" rather than "satellites." More and more, each country is considered as a distinct political unit with its own historical, cultural, and political inputs into both domestic and foreign policy. This is not to say that Soviet hegemony is no longer a reality; rather, that it is evaluated as one variable, and not necessarily the deciding one.

This change in perspective has brought with it changes in both the substance of studies dealing with Eastern Europe and methodology. With respect to substance, there is more interest in differences between both East European systems and the Soviet Union and within Eastern Europe, than in what is the same. Although it is obviously possible to go too far in this direction, to my mind it is a useful corrective. As for methodology, studies are increasingly interdisciplinary and cross-national in approach, such as Sylva Sinanian's collection, EASTERN EUROPE IN THE 1970'S (1972). Increasingly, there is a need to combine knowledge from political science, economics, sociology, history, and philosophy in attempting to overcome problems of cultural baggage that hinder the understanding of East European data just as such problems plague the study of any foreign society and culture. Moreover, there is also recognition of the value of cross-national cooperation in such efforts, cooperation that includes contributions by East European scholars who frequently have both better understanding and access to their societies than do outsiders. Thus, the methodological framework within which East European international relations is studied has broadened significantly.

As Gati put it, the states of Eastern Europe are "not the pawns they used to be, nor as autonomous as most would like to be. . . ."[6] They are increasingly seen as largely independent political actors living with pressures, options, and restraints not so different from those of other small- and medium-sized nations. While the vision is not as poetic as "eagles in cobwebs"[7]--it may be more useful for analysis.

NOTES

1. Andrzej Korbonski, "The Prospects for Change in Eastern Europe," SLAVIC REVIEW: AMERICAN QUARTERLY OF SOVIET AND EAST EUROPEAN STUDIES 2 (June 1974): 219.

2. Jan F. Triska and Paul M. Johnson, "Political Development and Political Change," in COMPARATIVE SOCIALIST SYSTEMS: ESSAYS ON POLITICS AND ECONOMICS, ed. Carmelo Mesa-Lago and Carl Beck (Pittsburgh, Pa.: United Center for International Studies, 1975), p. 282.

3. Sarah Meiklejohn Terry, "External Influences on Political Change in Eastern Europe: A Framework for Analysis," in POLITICAL DEVELOPMENT IN EASTERN EUROPE, ed. Jan F. Triska and Paul [M.] Cocks (New York: Praeger, 1977), pp. 277-314.

4. George Modelski, THE COMMUNIST INTERNATIONAL SYSTEM (Princeton, N.J.: Princeton University Center for International Studies Monograph, 1960), p. 45.

5. Z[bigniew].K. Brzezinski, THE SOVIET BLOC: UNITY AND CONFLICT (Cambridge, Mass.: Harvard University Press, 1971), p. 51.

6. Charles Gati, ed., THE INTERNATIONAL POLITICS OF EASTERN EUROPE (New York: Praeger, 1976), p. 14.

7. Taken from the title of Paul Lendvai's book EAGLES IN COBWEBS: NATIONALISM AND COMMUNISM IN THE BALKANS (London: Macdonald, 1969).

Part I

EASTERN EUROPE AS A REGION

Chapter I
BIBLIOGRAPHIES, REFERENCES, BASIC TEXTS

1 Bako, Elemer. GUIDE TO HUNGARIAN STUDIES. 2 vols. Stanford, Calif.: Hoover Institution Press, 1973. xv, 1,218 p.

2 Benes, Vaclav [L.], et al. EASTERN EUROPEAN GOVERNMENT AND POLITICS. New York: Harper and Row, 1966. viii, 247 p.

An introductory text, excluding Bulgaria and Albania. Historical, institutional approach.

3 Brzezinski, Zbigniew K. THE SOVIET BLOC: UNITY AND CONFLICT. Rev. ed. Cambridge, Mass.: Harvard University Press, 1971. xviii, 599 p. Paperbound.

Classic overview of the relationships between the USSR and East European states from 1945 to the late 1960s. Comprehensive statement of the impact of intra-Communist crisis and the diversity of developments both domestically and in the foreign policy. Excellent reference bibliography for the beginning student.

4 Burks, R.V. THE DYNAMICS OF COMMUNISM IN EASTERN EUROPE. Princeton, N.J.: Princeton University Press, 1961. xii, 244 p.

Emphasis on the importance of the peasantry rather than the proletariat in the development of East European communism. Also considers impact of industrialization in the West on the backward economies of the East.

5 Byrnes, Robert Francis. BIBLIOGRAPHY OF AMERICAN PUBLICATIONS ON EAST CENTRAL EUROPE 1945-1957. Slavic and East European Series, no. 12. Bloomington: Indiana University Publications, 1958. xxx, 213 p.

6 Davies, Norman. POLAND PAST AND PRESENT: A SELECT BIBLIOGRAPHY OF WORKS IN ENGLISH. Newtonville, Mass.: Oriental Research Partners, 1977. xxi, 185 p. Paperbound.

7   Fischer-Galati, Stephen Z. RUMANIA: A BIBLIOGRAPHIC GUIDE. New
     York: Arno Press, 1968. viii, 75 p.

     Reprinted from 1963 Library of Congress edition.

8   Hirsch, Gisela, comp. A BIBLIOGRAPHY OF GERMAN STUDIES, 1945-
     1971: GERMANY UNDER OCCUPATION, FEDERAL REPUBLIC OF GER-
     MANY, GERMAN DEMOCRATIC REPUBLIC. Bloomington and London:
     Indiana University Press, 1972. xvi, 603 p.

9   Horecky, Paul L., ed. EAST CENTRAL EUROPE: A GUIDE TO BASIC
     PUBLICATIONS. Chicago: University of Chicago Press, 1969. xxv,
     56 p.

     An annotated bibliography of books on Czechoslovakia, Hun-
     gary, Poland, and East Germany.

10   _____. SOUTHEASTERN EUROPE: A GUIDE TO BASIC PUBLICATIONS.
     Chicago: University of Chicago Press, 1969. xxii, 755 p.

     Both areawide and country-by-country breakdown.

11   Horecky, Paul L., chief ed., and Kraus, David H., assoc. ed. EAST
     CENTRAL AND SOUTHEAST EUROPE. Santa Barbara, Calif.: ABC-Clio
     Press, 1976. xii, 467 p.

     A guide to major collections on the political and socioeconomic
     developments in Eastern Europe in research libraries, archives,
     and special institutions in the United States and Canada.

12   Horton, John J. YUGOSLAVIA. World Bibliographical Series, no. 1.
     Santa Barbara, Calif.: ABC-Clio Press, 1977. xvi, 194 p.

13   Kanet, Roger E. SOVIET AND EAST EUROPEAN FOREIGN POLICY:
     A BIBLIOGRAPHY OF ENGLISH AND RUSSIAN LANGUAGE PUBLICA-
     TIONS 1967-1971. Santa Barbara, Calif., and Oxford: ABC-Clio Press,
     1974. xvi, 208 p.

     A valuable reference for scholars.

14   Kolarz, Walter. BOOKS ON COMMUNISM. London: Ampersand, 1963.
     viii, 568 p.

     Part 2 includes sections on individual East European countries
     as well as the Berlin rising of 1953 and Hungarian revolution
     (October 1956).

15   Kraus, David [H.], ed., and Mavon, Anita R., assoc. ed. THE AMERICAN
     BIBLIOGRAPHY OF SLAVIC AND EAST EUROPEAN STUDIES. Prepared

by the Library of Congress for the American Association for the Advancement of Slavic Studies. Washington, D.C.: 1966-- . Annual.

A bibliography which covers books and articles by American authors published in the United States or abroad. Includes doctoral dissertations.

16   Petrovich, Michael B. YUGOSLAVIA: A BIBLIOGRAPHIC GUIDE. Washington, D.C.: Library of Congress, 1974. xi, 270 p.

17   Price, Arnold H., comp. EAST GERMANY: A SELECTED BIBLIOGRAPHY. Washington, D.C.: Library of Congress, 1967. viii, 133 p.

18   Pundeff, Marin V. BULGARIA: A BIBLIOGRAPHIC GUIDE. Washington, D.C.: Library of Congress, 1965. ix, 98 p.

19   Rakowska-Harmstone, Teresa, and Gyorgy, Andrew, eds. THE GOVERNMENTS AND POLITICS OF EASTERN EUROPE. Bloomington: Indiana University Press, forthcoming 1978.

Includes analyses of the dilemmas of economic integration and East European international relations as well as relevent foreign policy analysis in the country-specific chapters.

20   Rothschild, Joseph. COMMUNIST EASTERN EUROPE. New York: Walker, 1964. vi, 168 p.

Country-by-country survey for introductory students or general readers. Useful reference section by Rudolf L. Tokes on East European Communist parties, biographical information, key leaders, and economic developments.

21   Skilling, H. Gordon. THE GOVERNMENTS OF COMMUNIST EASTERN EUROPE. New York: Thomas Crowell, 1966. xii, 259 p. Paperbound.

One of the better introductory texts. Written from a comparative perspective with sections on constitutional forms, parties, leadership cadres, decision-making patterns, legal systems, and interbloc relations. Concludes with emphasis on evolution in intra-Communist state relations. Unfortunately, now dated.

22   Staar, Richard F. THE COMMUNIST REGIMES IN EASTERN EUROPE. Rev. ed. Stanford, Calif.: Hoover Institution on War, Revolution, and Peace, 1977. 302 p. Paperbound.

A general, country-by-country treatment of postwar Eastern Europe. Sees little change in the Soviet-East European relationship over time and is not optimistic about a lessening

hardline influence in Moscow. Chapter 11 is on interbloc relations. Translated into Chinese, Korean, and German.

23 _____, ed. YEARBOOK ON INTERNATIONAL COMMUNIST AFFAIRS.
Stanford, Calif.: Hoover Institution Press, 1966-- .

Country-by-country profiles of individual Communist parties.

24 Sturm, Rudolf. CZECHOSLOVAKIA: A BIBLIOGRAPHIC GUIDE. Washington, D.C.: Library of Congress, 1967. xii, 157 p.

25 Vigor, Peter, ed. BOOKS ON COMMUNISM AND COMMUNIST
COUNTRIES. London: Ampersand, 1971. 444 p.

A useful, annotated, selected bibliography with references to
Eastern Europe on a country-by-country basis.

26 Whetten, Lawrence L. CURRENT RESEARCH IN COMPARATIVE COM-
MUNISM: AN ANALYSIS AND BIBLIOGRAPHIC GUIDE TO THE SOVIET
SYSTEM. New York: Praeger, 1976. vii, 159 p.

A useful reference though a misleading title. Includes bibliography of the USSR and Eastern Europe minus Albania but with
Yugoslavia. Divided into substantive economic, political, and
sociological categories rather than country-specific subsections.

27 Winkels, Dale R., comp. A SUBJECT GUIDE TO SLAVIC AND EAST
EUROPEAN SERIALS. Pittsburgh, Pa.: Book Center University of Pittsburgh, 1975. ii, 108 p. Paperbound.

Based on the University of Pittsburgh Hillman Library holdings
in the humanities and social sciences.

Chapter II

INSTITUTIONAL APPROACH

28   Brzezinski, Zbigniew K. "The Soviet Alliance System." In his THE SOVIET BLOC: UNITY AND CONFLICT, pp. 456-84. Cambridge, Mass.: Harvard University Press, 1971.

29   Cary, Charles D. "Patterns of Soviet Treaty Making with Other Communist Party-States." In COMMUNIST PARTY-STATES: COMPARATIVE AND INTERNATIONAL STUDIES, edited by Jan F. Triska, pp. 135-59. Indianapolis, Ind.: Bobbs-Merrill, 1969.

30   Gawenda, J.A.B. THE SOVIET DOMINATION OF EASTERN EUROPE IN LIGHT OF INTERNATIONAL LAW. Richmond, Va.: Foreign Affairs Publishing Co., 1974. 220 p.

31   Gryzbowski, Kazimierz. THE COMMONWEALTH OF SOCIALIST NATIONS: ORGANIZATIONS AND INSTITUTIONS. New Haven, Conn.: Yale University Press, 1964. xvii, 300 p.

        A standard scholarly study of East bloc institutions. Separate chapters on the Council for Mutual Economic Assistance (CMEA) and the Warsaw Pact.

32   Jamgotch, Nish, Jr. SOVIET-EAST EUROPEAN DIALOGUE: INTERNATIONAL RELATIONS OF A NEW TYPE? Stanford, Calif.: Hoover Institution on War, Revolution, and Peace, 1968. 165 p. Paperbound.

        A brief study of organizational and institutional dynamics among East European Communist states. Considers Eastern Europe as the core of the international Socialist system and never quite answers the question posed in the title.

33   Meissner, Boris. "The Soviet Union's Bilateral Pact System in Eastern Europe." In EASTERN EUROPE IN TRANSITION, edited by Kurt London, pp. 237-57. Baltimore, Md.: Johns Hopkins Press, 1966. Paperbound.

        A detailed discussion of the treaty infrastructure between

Eastern Europe and the Soviet Union. Useful reference for
students focusing on an institutional approach.

34   Remington, Robin Alison. "The Growth of Communist Regional Organization, 1949-1962." Ph.D. dissertation, Indiana University, 1966. 360 p.

35   Sharp, Samuel L. NEW CONSTITUTIONS IN THE SOVIET SPHERE.
Washington, D.C.: Foundation for Foreign Affairs, 1950. vi, 114 p.

Texts. Useful for traditional, legal comparisons.

36   Triska, Jan F., ed. CONSTITUTIONS OF COMMUNIST PARTY STATES.
Stanford, Calif.: Stanford University Press for the Hoover Institution,
1968. xiii, 541 p.

Collection of texts of the past and present constitutions of
Communist-governed states. Valuable reference, particularly
with respect to Soviet influence on East European constitutions.

Chapter III
COMPARATIVE APPROACH

37   Almond, Gabriel A. "Toward a Comparative Politics of Eastern Europe."
      STUDIES IN COMPARATIVE COMMUNISM 4 (April 1971): 71-78.

> Almond's response to an attempt of East European specialists to
> apply his model of comparative politics to Eastern Europe. Re-
> plies to specific criticism, emphasizing that the value of his
> approach rests on its intellectual background.

38   Barton, Allen H., et al., eds. OPINION-MAKING ELITES IN YUGO-
      SLAVIA. Foreword by Firdus Dzinic. New York; Washington, D.C.;
      London: Praeger, 1973. xii, 344 p.

> A valuable contribution to elite studies based on Yugoslav data
> collected in connection with an International Study of Opinion-
> Makers carried out through a series of national projects. The
> Yugoslav team published the results of its studies in Serbo-
> Croatian in four volumes in 1969. Deals with elite interview-
> ing, social background, recruitment, mobility, and political
> activity of elites.

39   Bass, Robert. "East European Communist Elites: Their Character and
      History." JOURNAL OF INTERNATIONAL AFFAIRS 20, no. 1 (1966):
      106-17.

40   Bauman, Zygmunt. "East Europe and Soviet Social Science: A Case of
      Stimulus Diffusion." In THE INFLUENCE OF EAST EUROPE AND THE
      SOVIET WEST ON THE USSR, edited by Roman Szporluk, pp. 91-116.
      New York: Praeger, 1975.

41   Beck, Carl. "Bureaucracy and Political Development in Eastern Europe."
      In BUREAUCRACY AND POLITICAL DEVELOPMENT, edited by Joseph La
      Palombara, pp. 268-300. Princeton, N.J.: Princeton University Press,
      1963.

42   Beck, Carl, et al., eds. COMPARATIVE POLITICAL LEADERSHIP.
New York: David McKay, 1973. xi, 319 p. Paperbound.

A study of leadership attributes in Eastern Europe, emphasizing
increased bureaucratization and the importance of political and
economic modernization. Includes relationship of changes in
political leaders and internal stability.

43   Benjamin, Roger W., and Kautsky, John H. "Communism and Economic
Development." AMERICAN POLITICAL SCIENCE REVIEW 62 (March
1969): 110-23.

Theoretical analysis. Not specifically oriented toward East
Europe, but with significant comparative implications.

44   Bertsch, Gary K. NATION-BUILDING IN YUGOSLAVIA: A STUDY OF
POLITICAL INTEGRATION AND ATTITUDINAL CONSENSUS. Beverly
Hills, Calif., and London: Sage Publications, 1971. 48 p.

Provocative model for scholars dealing with the prospects for
multiethnic societies, both Communist and non-Communist.

45   _____. VALUE CHANGE AND POLITICAL COMMUNITY: THE MULTI-
NATIONAL CZECHOSLOVAK, SOVIET, AND YUGOSLAV CASES.
Beverly Hills, Calif., and London: Sage Publications, 1974. 60 p.

46   Bruhns, F.C.; Cazzola, F.; and Wiatr, J[erzy].J., eds. LOCAL POLI-
TICS, DEVELOPMENT, AND PARTICIPATION. Pittsburgh, Pa.: Pittsburgh
University Center for International Studies, 1974. xv, 329 p. Paper-
bound.

A collection of papers from the First International Round Table
of the Research Committee on the Comparative Study of Local
Government and Politics, International Political Science Association, held in Taormina, Sicily in September 1971. Polish
and Yugoslav social scientists were among the contributors.
Particularly interesting for students of either development or
participation.

47   Burghardt, Andrew E., ed. DEVELOPMENT REGIONS IN THE SOVIET
UNION, EASTERN EUROPE AND CANADA. New York: Praeger, 1975.
xii, 192 p.

Contrasts Socialist experience with Canadian attempts to estab-
lish development regions.

48   Burks, R.V. TECHNOLOGICAL INNOVATION AND POLITICAL CHANGE
IN COMMUNIST EASTERN EUROPE. Santa Monica, Calif.: RAND
Memorandum RM-6051-PR, August 1969. 74 p.

Concludes that the widening technological gap is forcing East European Communist states to modify both their economic systems and their philosophy. In the more radical cases this could potentially lead to economic and political pluralization.

49 Clark, Cal. "The Study of East Europe on Integration: A 'Political' Perspective." EAST CENTRAL EUROPE 2, part 2 (1975): 132-45.

A provocative attempt to apply integration theory to Eastern Europe, underlining some problems of neofunctionalist and communications models.

50 Clark, Cal, and Farlow, Robert L. COMPARATIVE PATTERNS OF FOREIGN POLICY AND TRADE: THE COMMUNIST BALKANS IN INTERNATIONAL POLITICS. Bloomington, Ind.: International Development Research Center, 1976. xxi, 152 p.

A unique contribution using the linkage perspective with foreign trade as the empirical indicator testing assumptions about comparative Balkan foreign policy. Country-specific chapters re Yugoslavia, Rumania, Albania, and Bulgaria.

51 Cocks, Paul [M.]. "Bureaucracy and Party Control." In COMPARATIVE SOCIALIST SYSTEMS: ESSAYS ON POLITICS AND ECONOMICS, edited by Carmelo Mesa-Lago and Carl Beck, pp. 215-48. Pittsburgh, Pa.: University of Pittsburgh Center for International Studies, 1975.

52 Cohen, Lenard J., and Shapiro, Jane P. COMMUNIST SYSTEMS IN COMPARATIVE PERSPECTIVE. Preface by Zbigniew [K.] Brzezinski. New York: Doubleday, 1974. xii, 530 p. Paperbound.

A collection of essays by well-known scholars in the field dealing with both domestic and international aspects of Communist systems. Utilizes East European as well as Russian and Chinese examples.

53 Cornell, Richard. "Comparative Analysis of Communist Movements." JOURNAL OF POLITICS 30 (February 1968): 66-89.

Evaluates the growing literature in comparative communism.

54 Dallin, Alexander, and Breslauer, George W. POLITICAL TERROR IN COMMUNIST SYSTEMS. Stanford, Calif.: Stanford University Press, 1970. xi, 172 p.

Treats "terror" as a phenomenon that can be rationally analyzed. The authors study the impact of terror on the authority, ideology, and morale in Communist systems and the function of terror in revolutionary goals.

55   Eckstein, Alexander. "Economic Development and Political Change in
      Communist Systems." WORLD POLITICS 22 (July 1970): 475-95.

      A provocative, theoretical article. Not specifically directed
      toward Eastern Europe but with important implications for schol-
      ars interested in the relation of domestic resource allocation
      to defense posture and conduct of foreign policy.

56   Enloe, Cynthia H. ETHNIC CONFLICT AND POLITICAL DEVELOPMENT.
      Boston: Little, Brown, 1973. xvii, 282 p. Paperbound.

      Well-written, provocative study. Particularly useful to stu-
      dents of comparative politics, development, and federalism.
      Extensive use of Yugoslav examples, especially in the chapter
      devoted to systems in structural transition.

57   Farrell, R. Barry. "Foreign Policy Formation in the Communist Countries
      of Eastern Europe." EAST EUROPEAN JOURNAL, no. 1 (March 1967):
      39-74.

58   _____, ed. POLITICAL LEADERSHIP IN EASTERN EUROPE AND THE
      SOVIET UNION. Chicago: Aldine, 1970. xi, 359 p. Paperbound.

      A study of the theoretical questions inherent in Marxist theories
      of leadership, bureaucracy, and organization. Product of a
      conference held in November 1968 under the auspices of the
      comparative politics program at Northwestern University.

59   Finley, David D. "Integration among Communist Party-States: Compara-
      tive Case Studies." In COMMUNIST PARTY-STATES: COMPARATIVE
      AND INTERNATIONAL STUDIES, edited by Jan F. Triska, pp. 57-80.
      Indianapolis, Ind.: Bobbs-Merrill, 1969.

60   Fleron, Frederic J., Jr., ed. COMMUNIST STUDIES AND THE SOCIAL
      SCIENCES: ESSAYS ON METHODOLOGY AND EMPIRICAL THEORY.
      Chicago: Rand McNally, 1971. xiii, 481 p. Paperbound.

      An important contribution to comparative politics as well as
      comparative communism. Primarily concerned with methodology;
      however, any serious scholar of East European international re-
      lations cannot avoid taking these approaches into consideration,
      particularly in analyzing the fundamentals of Soviet-East Euro-
      pean interactions. Includes a chapter applying game theory
      to the Hungarian uprising of 1956.

61   Franck, Thomas M., and Weisband, Edward. WORD POLITICS: VERBAL
      STRATEGY AMONG THE SUPERPOWERS. New York: Oxford University
      Press, 1972. xiii, 176 p. Paperbound.

A provocative study of verbal behavior, system transformation, and crisis management based on comparing Soviet-East European relations with their U.S.-Latin American counterpart interactions. Considers the concept of "limited sovereignty" within both systems. Particularly useful to students of international relations and comparative foreign policy.

62   Gati, Charles, ed. THE POLITICS OF MODERNIZATION IN EASTERN EUROPE: TESTING THE SOVIET MODEL. New York: Praeger, 1974. xvii, 389 p.

One of the more exciting attempts to bring East European studies into the mainstream of political science. Useful to students of political development, comparative politics, modernization, and public administration. Part 6 deals explicitly with the international dimension of modernization both from the perspective of Soviet influence on East Europe and East European innovations as a force for change in the Soviet Union. Based on papers and discussion at a conference, "Eastern Europe: The Impact of Modernization," Columbia University, March 1973.

63   Gitelman, Zvi Y. "Beyond Leninism: Political Development in Eastern Europe." NEWSLETTER ON COMPARATIVE STUDIES OF COMMUNISM 5 (May 1972): 18-43.

A key article for students interested in political development and system change in Eastern Europe and the role played by Soviet-East European relations in that process.

64   _____. THE DIFFUSION OF POLITICAL INNOVATION: FROM EASTERN EUROPE TO THE SOVIET UNION. Beverly Hills, Calif.: Sage Publications, 1972. 59 p. Paperbound.

Discusses agents, clients, and the tactics of innovation as well as the relationship of innovation to political change in Communist Eastern Europe. Case studies: Yugoslavia, Czechoslovakia, and Hungary. Valuable to students of comparative politics both for content and methodology.

65   Godwin, Paul H.B. "Communist Systems and Modernization: Sources of Political Crises." STUDIES IN COMPARATIVE COMMUNISM 6 (Spring-Summer 1973): 107-34.

An attempt to provide a framework for comparative analysis of Communist systems, seen as one more variant of the more general phenomenon of modernizing systems. A useful methodological article. Uses Czechoslovak examples of linkages between economic development and political change that was to have important implications for Prague's foreign policy in both the East and West.

66   Goldman, Marshall I. COMPARATIVE ECONOMIC SYSTEMS: A READER.
      2d ed. New York: Random House, 1971. xiii, 476 p. Paperbound.

67   Gregory, Paul [R.]. SOCIALIST AND NON-SOCIALIST INDUSTRIALIZA-
      TION PATTERNS. New York: Praeger, 1970. xxvi, 209 p.

68   Griffith, William E. "Generational Change and Political Leadership in
      Eastern Europe and the Soviet Union." In POLITICAL GENERATIONS
      AND POLITICAL DEVELOPMENT, edited by Richard J. Samuels, pp. 125-
      34. Lexington, Mass.: Lexington Books, 1977.

69   Hammond, Thomas T., ed., and Farrell, Robert, assoc. ed. THE ANATO-
      MY OF COMMUNIST TAKEOVERS. Foreword by Cyril E. Black. New
      Haven, Conn., and London: Yale University Press, 1975. xviii, 667 p.
      Paperbound.

70   Heltai, George G. "Changes in the Social Structure of the East Central
      European Countries." JOURNAL OF INTERNATIONAL AFFAIRS 20, no.
      1 (1966): 165-71.

71   Hempel, K.S. "Comparative Research on Eastern Europe: A Critique of
      Hughes and Volgy's 'Distance in Foreign Behavior.'" AMERICAN JOUR-
      NAL OF POLITICAL SCIENCE 17 (May 1973): 367-93.

72   Herspring, Dale R., and Volgyes, Ivan, eds. CIVIL-MILITARY RELATIONS
      IN COMMUNIST SYSTEMS. Boulder, Colo.: Westview Press, 1978.

          Includes East European case studies to demonstrate key aspects
          of party-army relations, such as the military as an agent of
          political socialization and as a corporate interest group in
          Communist society. Also deals with Soviet-East European re-
          lations from the perspective of the dynamics of political auton-
          omy and military intervention.

73   Ionescu, Ghita. COMPARATIVE COMMUNIST POLITICS. London: Mac-
      millan, 1972. 64 p. Paperbound.

74   Jacob, Philip E., ed. VALUES AND THE ACTIVE COMMUNITY: A
      CROSS-NATIONAL STUDY OF THE INFLUENCE OF LOCAL LEADER-
      SHIP. New York: Free Press, 1971. xxxii, 416 p.

          An international study under the sponsorship of the International
          Social Science Council, Paris, involving academic research
          institutes in India, Poland, Yugoslavia, and the United States.
          Primarily concerned with local politics. Designed to determine
          the impact of values held by local political leaders on social
          change and development at the community level. Polish and
          Yugoslav studies relevant to scholars attempting to separate

local, political-cultural variables from the impact of the
Soviet model in Eastern Europe.

75   Janos, Andrew C., ed. AUTHORITARIAN POLITICS IN COMMUNIST
EUROPE: UNIFORMITY AND DIVERSITY IN ONE-PARTY STATES.
Institute of International Studies Research Series, no. 28. Berkeley:
University of California Institute of International Studies, 1976. xi, 196 p.

       Emphasis on the politics of change in the Communist societies
of the Soviet Union and Eastern Europe. Divided between a
general theoretical approach and country-specific analysis.

76   Johnson, Chalmers, ed. CHANGE IN COMMUNIST SYSTEMS. Stanford,
Calif.: Stanford University Press, 1970. xiii, 368 p. Paperbound.

       An excellent collection of essays stemming from a two-month
conference of top scholars in the field, sponsored by the American Council of Learned Societies. An example of the increasing integration of Communist studies into mainstream political
science and a valuable contribution to studies of comparative
communism.

77   Jowitt, Kenneth. "The Concepts of Liberalization, Integration and Ra-
tionalization in the Context of East European Development." STUDIES
IN COMPARATIVE COMMUNISM 4 (April 1971): 79-91.

       Application of political science concepts to East European
political processes with major implications for future policy
making, both domestic and foreign. Followed by comments by
three other scholars in the field.

78   _____. "An Organizational Approach to the Study of Political Culture
in Marxist-Leninist Systems." AMERICAN POLITICAL SCIENCE REVIEW
68 (September 1974): 1171-91.

       Relies heavily on Rumanian examples. Valuable theoretical
extension of earlier work.

79   _____. REVOLUTIONARY BREAKTHROUGHS AND NATIONAL DEVEL-
OPMENT: THE CASE FOR RUMANIA, 1944-1965. Berkeley and Los
Angeles: University of California Press, 1971. 317 p.

       Pioneering comparative analysis of the adaptability of "Leninist"
regimes in dealing with the nation-building process. Focuses
on relation of party to the Rumanian nation and the international Communist movement.

80   Kanet, Roger [E.]. "Integration Theory and the Study of Eastern Europe."
INTERNATIONAL STUDIES QUARTERLY 18 (September 1974): 368-92.

81   , ed. THE BEHAVIORAL REVOLUTION AND COMMUNIST STUD-IES: APPLICATIONS OF BEHAVIORALLY ORIENTED RESEARCH ON THE SOVIET UNION AND EASTERN EUROPE. New York: Free Press, 1971. xv, 375 p.

> Essential for graduate students of political science concerned with problems of methodology and research in Communist countries.

82   Kegley, Charles W., Jr. "The Transformation of Inter-Bloc Relations: Approaches to Analysis and Measurement." In THE FUTURE OF INTER-BLOC RELATIONS IN EUROPE, edited by Louis J. Mensonides and James A. Kuhlman, pp. 3-27. New York; Washington, D.C.; London: Praeger, 1974.

> Attempts to measure change in interbloc conflict as well as in the structure of interbloc behavior. Based on conceptualizing the region as a single subsystem.

83   Korbonski, Andrzej. "Leadership and Political Succession in Eastern Europe." STUDIES IN COMPARATIVE COMMUNISM IX, nos. 1 and 2 (Spring-Summer 1976): 3-22.

84   . "The Prospects for Change in Eastern Europe." SLAVIC REVIEW 33 (June 1974): 219-58.

> Analysis of current approaches emphasizing that the East Europeans are not unique but rather part "of the family" of modernizing, developing countries.

85   Lotarski, Susanne S. "Reform of Rural Administration: A Test of Managerial Solutions." CANADIAN SLAVONIC PAPERS 15 (Spring-Summer 1973): 108-21.

> Focuses on Polish reforms. Valuable for comparative local politics.

86   Matejko, Alexander. SOCIAL CHANGE AND STRATIFICATION IN EASTERN EUROPE. New York: Praeger, 1974. xviii, 272 p.

> A study of the relationship of stratification to social change based largely on Poland with some attempts to broaden its conclusions to other East European countries. Written by a Polish sociologist who left the country during the heightened tensions of 1968.

87   Mesa-Lago, Carmelo, and Beck, Carl, eds. COMPARATIVE SOCIALIST SYSTEMS: ESSAYS ON POLITICS AND ECONOMICS. Pittsburgh, Pa.: University of Pittsburgh Center for International Studies, 1975. xv, 441 p. Paperbound.

A cross-national, multidisciplinary study involving both political and economic analyses. Particularly valuable for those interested in methodologies combining theoretical approaches and empirical comparisons. Uneven.

88   Meyer, Alfred G. COMMUNISM. 3d ed. New York: Random House, 1967. viii, 241 p. Paperbound.

A theoretical analysis of communism as both an ideology and political movement. Well-written study for either a general reader or undergraduate class. Excellent background. Sections on communism since World War II and unity and diversity within the contemporary Communist movement most relevant to Eastern Europe. Author is a professor of political science at the University of Michigan, and a leading expert on communism and Marxist ideology.

89   _____. "The Comparative Study of Communist Political Systems." SLAVIC REVIEW 26 (March 1967): 3-12.

90   Mitchell, R. Judson. "A Theoretical Approach to the Study of Communist International Organizations." In COMMUNIST PARTY-STATES: COMPARATIVE AND INTERNATIONAL STUDIES, edited by Jan F. Triska, pp. 81-105. Indianapolis, Ind.: Bobbs-Merrill, 1969.

91   Montias, John Michael. "Modernization in Communist Countries: Some Questions of Methodology." STUDIES IN COMPARATIVE COMMUNISM 5 (Winter 1972): 413-22.

A valuable methodological discussion. Important for students of both comparative politics and political development. Implications for ability to measure external penetration as a factor in development.

92   "On Comparing East European Political Systems." STUDIES IN COMPARATIVE COMMUNISM 4 (April 1971): 30-70.

An explanation and discussion of the criteria used for comparative analysis of Eastern Europe. Introduction by the editor, Jan F. Triska, followed by specific comments regarding Rumania, Hungary, Czechoslovakia, and Yugoslavia. Particularly useful to scholars interested in the application of Gabriel A. Almond's comparative politics model.

93   Pirages, Dennis Clark. MODERNIZATION AND POLITICAL TENSION MANAGEMENT: A SOCIALIST SOCIETY IN PERSPECTIVE. CASE STUDY OF POLAND. New York: Praeger, 1972. xvi, 259 p.

A study of the impact of industrialization on Polish society.

Invaluable for students of comparative communism concerned
with the extent to which East European political-economic
development does or does not follow the Soviet model. Contribution to the empirical literature.

94 _____. "Socioeconomic Development and Political Access in Communist
Party-States." In COMMUNIST PARTY-STATES: COMPARATIVE AND
INTERNATIONAL STUDIES, edited by Jan F. Triska, pp. 249-81.
Indianapolis, Ind.: Bobbs-Merrill, 1969.

Relates level of modernization to nature of the political system.
Useful for cross-systems comparison including East European
data.

95 Pryor, Frederic L. PROPERTY AND INDUSTRIAL ORGANIZATION IN
COMMUNIST AND CAPITALIST NATIONS. Bloomington and London:
Indiana University Press, 1974. xviii, 513 p.

A study of comparative economic systems based on solid empirical content. Raises important questions about convergence
hypotheses.

96 Roskin, Michael. OTHER GOVERNMENTS OF EUROPE: SWEDEN, SPAIN,
ITALY, YUGOSLAVIA, AND EAST GERMANY. Englewood Cliffs, N.J.:
Prentice-Hall, 1977. x, 182 p.

Deals with Yugoslavia and East Germany in a comparative
European focus.

97 Rubinstein, Alvin Z. COMMUNIST POLITICAL SYSTEMS. Englewood
Cliffs, N.J.: Prentice-Hall, 1966. xvi, 399 p.

Particularly useful regarding takeover period in Eastern Europe.

98 Rush, Myron. HOW COMMUNIST STATES CHANGE THEIR RULERS.
Ithaca, N.Y.: Cornell University Press, 1974. 346 p.

Valuable addition to the literature of both comparative communism and elite studies. Considers the implications of succession crises in the USSR and those East European countries
where bureaucratic-institutional patterns largely determine the
outcome for foreign policy as being less drastic than they are
in those states still dominated by the personality of the charis-
matic leader who founded the party (i.e., Yugoslavia).

99 Shoup, Paul. "Eastern Europe and the Soviet Union: Convergence and
Divergence in Historical Perspective." In SOVIET SOCIETY AND POLI-
TICS IN THE 1970'S, edited by Henry W. Morton and Rudolf L. Tokes,
pp. 340-68. New York: Free Press, 1974.

An excellent analysis of both the relevance and the limits of relevance of the Soviet development model in Eastern Europe.

100 Sievers, Bruce R. "The Divided Nations: International Integration and National Identity." In COMMUNIST PARTY-STATES: COMPARATIVE AND INTERNATIONAL STUDIES, edited by Jan F. Triska, pp. 160-85. Indianapolis, Ind.: Bobbs-Merrill, 1969.

Deals with Germany, China, Vietnam, and Korea.

101 Simes, Dimitri K. "The Soviet Invasion of Czechoslovakia and the Limits of Kremlinology." STUDIES IN COMPARATIVE COMMUNISM 8 (Spring-Summer 1975): 174-80.

102 Sinanian, Sylva, et al., eds. EASTERN EUROPE IN THE 1970'S. New York: Praeger, 1972. ix, 260 p.

A cross-national, cooperative, and interdisciplinary approach indicative of the trend in East European studies to move away from cold war conceptions. Includes papers by experts from the United States, Canada, France, England, and West Germany as well as contributions from scholars of Eastern and South-eastern Europe. Based on a conference held at Columbia University, New York, on "New Perspectives in Understanding East Central Europe," December 3-5, 1971.

103 Skilling, H. Gordon. "Interest Groups and Communist Politics." WORLD POLITICS 18 (April 1966): 435-51.

Analyzes the literature, including contributions of Slovak and Yugoslav theorists.

104 Smolinski, Leon. "East European Influences on Soviet Economic Thought and Reforms." In THE INFLUENCE OF EAST EUROPE AND THE SOVIET WEST ON THE USSR, edited by Roman Szporluk, pp. 68-90. New York: Praeger, 1975.

Important for the study of innovation diffusion.

105 "Symposium on the Comparative Study of Communist Foreign Policies." STUDIES IN COMPARATIVE COMMUNISM 8 (Spring-Summer 1975): 3-65.

Experts in the field discuss methodology, conceptual frameworks, and utility of the study of comparative Communist foreign policies. Also deals with area studies and international relations as approaches. Essential for graduate students.

106 Szporluk, Roman, ed. THE INFLUENCE OF EAST EUROPE AND THE

SOVIET WEST ON THE USSR. New York: Praeger, 1975. x, 258 p.

Useful for students concerned with ideological and economic innovation transfer.

107 Tanter, Raymond. MODELLING AND MANAGING INTERNATIONAL CONFLICTS: THE BERLIN CRISES. Beverly Hills, Calif.: Sage Publications, 1974. 272 p.

See no. 843a.

108 Toma, Peter A. "The Case of Hungary." STUDIES IN COMPARATIVE COMMUNISM 4 (April 1971): 43-46.

Discussion of the author's attempt to apply Gabriel A. Almond's comparative politics model to Hungary. Originally presented at an American Political Science Association roundtable on comparing East European political systems, September 1970.

109 Tomasic, Dinko [A.]. PERSONALITY AND CULTURE IN EAST EUROPEAN POLITICS. New York: George W. Stewart, 1948. 249 p.

A dated but insightful sociological analysis of the political and social cultures of East European states.

110 Triska, Jan F., ed. COMMUNIST PARTY-STATES: COMPARATIVE AND INTERNATIONAL STUDIES. Indianapolis, Ind.: Bobbs-Merrill, 1969. xxxv, 302 p.

A collection of scholarly studies with emphasis on political and economic integration.

111 Triska, Jan F., and Cocks, Paul M., eds. POLITICAL DEVELOPMENT IN EASTERN EUROPE. New York: Praeger, 1977. xxiv, 374 p. Paperbound.

Examines ideological adaptation, institutions, and political organizations, elite-mass relationships and external influences on domestic politics.

112 Tucker, Robert C. "Communist Revolutions, National Cultures, and the Divided Nations." STUDIES IN COMPARATIVE COMMUNISM 7 (Autumn 1974): 235-45.

A stimulating contribution to comparative Communist studies, including a typology of Communist revolutions useful to students of both East European foreign policies and international relations. Analysis linking this typology to divided nations, particularly important to keep in mind regarding East German policy.

113 _____. "On the Comparative Study of Communism." WORLD POLITICS 19 (January 1967): 242-57.

114 _____. "Toward a Comparative Politics of Movement Regimes." AMERI-CAN POLITICAL SCIENCE REVIEW 55 (June 1961): 281-89.

115 Ulc, Otto. "The Case of Czechoslovakia." STUDIES IN COMPARATIVE COMMUNISM 4 (April 1971): 47-57.

   Discussion of Gabriel A. Almond's comparative politics model as applied to Czechoslovakia. Originally presented at an American Political Science Association roundtable in September 1970.

116 Volgyes, Ivan, ed. POLITICAL SOCIALIZATION IN EASTERN EUROPE, A COMPARATIVE FRAMEWORK. New York: Praeger, 1975. xiv, 199 p.

   Sets forth a general framework for analyzing agents of political socialization within Communist societies. Particularly useful to students of comparative politics and ideological transfer.

117 Weiner, Myron. "The Macedonian Syndrome: An Historical Model of International Relations and Political Development." WORLD POLITICS 23 (July 1971): 665-83.

   A stimulating contribution to international relations theory. Uses the factors involved in the long-disputed Macedonian question to formulate a model dealing with the impact of ethnic irredentism on international relations whether in Europe, Africa, Asia, or the Middle East.

118 Welsh, William A. "A Game-Theoretic Conceptualization of the Hungarian Revolt: Toward an Inductive Theory of Games." In COMMUNIST STUDIES AND THE SOCIAL SCIENCES: ESSAYS ON METHODOLOGY AND EMPIRICAL THEORY, edited by Frederic J. Fleron, Jr., pp. 420-66. Chicago: Rand McNally, 1971. Paperbound.

   A provocative attempt to apply contemporary game theory to the 1956 uprising in Hungary. More concerned with the U.S.-Soviet conflict during the incident than with the revolt itself, but is particularly useful for insight into external influences on intra-alliance crises.

119 Wesson, Robert G. COMMUNISM AND COMMUNIST SYSTEMS. Englewood Cliffs, N.J.: Prentice-Hall, 1978. x, 227 p. Paperbound.

   Considers East European systems among "Lesser Communist States."

120 Winner, Irene. A SLOVENE VILLAGE: ZEROVNICA. Providence, R.I.: Brown University Press, 1971. xiv, 267 p. Black and white illus.

A valuable addition to village studies for both anthropologists and political scientists. Section on the history of Zerovnica shows the differing impact of the village's international context on both development and attitude formation in the region.

121 Zimmerman, William. "The Transformation of the Modern State-System: The Exhaustion of Communist Alternatives." JOURNAL OF CONFLICT RESOLUTION 16 (September 1972): 303-17.

An analysis of the limitations of the Stalinist international system, Khrushchev's "resynthesis" and the problems inherent in that alternative. Concludes that as relations within the dominant international system are increasingly marked by flexible alignments and cross-cutting cleavages, the possibility for issue-related differentiation within Eastern Europe also rises. Primarily important for students of international relations theory.

Chapter IV

HISTORICAL BACKGROUND

122 Ainsztein, Reuben. JEWISH RESISTANCE IN NAZI–OCCUPIED EASTERN
EUROPE. New York: Barnes & Noble, 1975. xxviii, 970 p.

An exhaustively researched study intent on showing beyond
question that the East European Jews did defend themselves.

123 Auty, Phyllis, and Clogg, Richard, eds. BRITISH POLICY TOWARDS
WARTIME RESISTANCE IN YUGOSLAVIA AND GREECE. New York:
Barnes & Noble, 1975. xii, 308 p.

Readable and insightful.

124 Bannan, Alfred, and Edelenyi, Achilles. A DOCUMENTARY HISTORY
OF EASTERN EUROPE. New York: Twayne Publishers, 1970. 392 p.

A collection of significant documents and historical descriptions,
beginning with the first Slavic invasions during the medieval
period and ending with the Soviet invasion of Czechoslovakia
in 1968.

125 Berend, Ivan T., and Ranki, Gyorgy. ECONOMIC DEVELOPMENT IN EAST-
CENTRAL EUROPE IN THE 19TH AND 20TH CENTURIES. New York:
Columbia University Press, 1974. xiii, 402 p. Illus.

Good economic and historical background. Important for students of comparative politics and development.

126 Bishop, Robert, and Crayfield, E.S. RUSSIA ASTRIDE THE BALKANS.
New York: McBride, 1948. 287 p.

An early study of Communist takeover in the Balkans concen-
trating on the Soviet role. Written by members of American
and British intelligence communities in East Europe.

127 Black, C[yril].E., ed. CHALLENGE IN EASTERN EUROPE. Port Washington, N.Y., and London: Kennikat Press, 1954. xv, 276 p.

Twelve scholarly essays. Part 3 deals with the search for regional security.

128 Borkenau, Franz. WORLD COMMUNISM: A HISTORY OF THE COM-
MUNIST INTERNATIONAL. Introduction by Raymond Aron. Ann Arbor:
University of Michigan Press, 1962. 442 p. Paperbound.

A classic study of the Comintern. Most relevant for insights
into the formative period of East European Communist parties.
Contains chapters on the Hungarian dictatorship of Bela Kun
and the problems of Bulgarian communism also in the early
1920s.

129 Crampton, R.J. "The Decline of the Concert of Europe in the Balkans
1913-14." THE SLAVONIC AND EAST EUROPEAN REVIEW 52 (July
1974): 393-419.

Describes the decline of "Great Power" influence, illustrating
territorial and nationality issues at stake between the Balkan
states, the events surrounding the outbreak of war, and the
problems of attempting to dominate Balkan international relations.

130 Dallin, Alexander, et al. RUSSIAN DIPLOMACY AND EASTERN EUROPE
1914-1917. Introduction by Henry L. Roberts. New York: Kings Crown
Press, 1963. xviii, 305 p.

131 Deutscher, Isaac. STALIN: A POLITICAL BIOGRAPHY. 2d ed., rev.,
enl. New York: Oxford University Press, 1967. xvi, 603 p. Paperbound.

Sections dealing with Stalin's manipulation of the Comintern
as an arm of Soviet policy, his diplomacy concerning East
Europe during World War II, and the postscript dealing with
the dictator's last years, extremely useful for understanding
the impact of Soviet domestic considerations on Moscow's demands vis-à-vis Eastern Europe.

132 Fischer-Galati, Stephen [Z.], ed. MAN, STATE, AND SOCIETY IN
EASTERN EUROPEAN HISTORY. New York: Praeger, 1970. xlii, 343 p.

A selection of documents and articles reflecting the compati-
bility of Soviet dogmatism with East European historical tradi-
tions.

133 Foote, James. RUSSIAN AND SOVIET IMPERIALISM. Richmond, Va.:
Foreign Affairs Publishing Co., 1972. x, 272 p.

134 Halecki, Oscar. BORDERLANDS OF WESTERN CIVILIZATION: A HIS-

TORY OF EAST CENTRAL EUROPE. New York: Ronald Press, 1952. vii, 503 p.

> A classic political history of East Central Europe from the tenth century. Deals with the consequences of World War I with a chapter specifically on the international relations of the region during the interwar period. Excellent background to the contemporary international politics of Eastern Europe.

135 Jackson, George D. COMINTERN AND PEASANT IN EASTERN EUROPE. New York: Columbia University Press, 1966. ix, 330 p.

> Traces on a country-by-country basis the misunderstandings and erratic policies of the Comintern toward the agrarian parties and movements in interwar Eastern Europe.

136 Janos, Andrew [C.]. "The One-Party State and Social Mobilization: East Europe Between the Wars." In AUTHORITARIAN POLITICS IN MODERN SOCIETY: THE DYNAMICS OF ESTABLISHED ONE PARTY SYSTEMS, edited by Samuel P. Huntington and Clement H. Moore, pp. 204-36. New York: Basic Books, 1970.

137 Jelavich, Barbara. ST. PETERSBURG-MOSCOW. TSARIST AND SOVIET FOREIGN POLICY, 1814-1974. Bloomington and London: Indiana University Press, 1974. xii, 480 p. Paperbound.

> A diplomatic history emphasizing continuity from Tsarist to Soviet national interests as manifested in foreign policy toward Eastern Europe.

138 Jelavich, Charles, and Jelavich, Barbara. THE BALKANS. Englewood Cliffs, N.J.: Prentice-Hall, 1965. xi, 148 p.

> A history of the development of states in the Balkan area, especially focusing on diplomatic history, nationalisms, the interference and impact of great powers, with some attention to domestic situations.

139 _____, eds. THE BALKANS IN TRANSITION. Berkeley and Los Angeles: University of California Press, 1963. xvii, 451 p.

> Based on the proceedings of a conference at Berkeley, Calif., in June 1960. Essays on the development of Balkan life and politics since the eighteenth century. Emphasis primarily on the areas of similarity in the region--the influence of the West, the role of religion, nationalism, economic changes, problems of modernization and the difficulties of underdeveloped regions adapting to modern life and relations with the Soviet Union.

140   Kerner, Robert J., and Howard, Harry Nicholas. THE BALKAN CON-
       FERENCES AND THE BALKAN ENTENTE: A STUDY IN THE RECENT
       HISTORY OF THE BALKAN AND NEAR EASTERN PEOPLES. 1936. Rpt.
       Westport, Conn.: Greenwood Press, 1970. x, 271 p.

141   Kimmich, Christoph M. THE FREE CITY: DANZIG AND GERMAN FOR-
       EIGN POLICY 1919-1934. New Haven, Conn., and London: Yale Uni-
       versity Press, 1969. ix, 196 p.

       Important for discussion of interwar Polish-German relations.

142   Macartney, C.A., and Palmer, Alan W. INDEPENDENT EASTERN EU-
       ROPE: A HISTORY. London and New York: Macmillan and St. Martin's
       Press, 1962. vii, 499 p.

       A history of interwar Eastern Europe including an account of
       the Peace Conference and of diplomacy during the First World
       War. Chapter 6 devoted to East European international rela-
       tions from 1919-29.

143   Nollau, Gunter. INTERNATIONAL COMMUNISM AND WORLD REVO-
       LUTION: HISTORY AND METHODS. Translated by Victor Andersen.
       Foreword by Leonard Schapiro. New York: Praeger, 1961. xv, 357 p.

       Origin, development, and organization of the international
       Communist movement from the time of Marx's Communist Mani-
       festo (1848) until the 1960s. Most useful for scholars con-
       cerned with the concept of "proletarian internationalism" and
       its implications for Soviet-East European interparty relations.
       A good section on the Cominform. Written by a German
       scholar and lawyer, subsequently in the civil service in West
       Germany.

144   Palmer, Alan [W.]. THE LANDS BETWEEN: A HISTORY OF EAST-CENTRAL
       EUROPE SINCE THE CONGRESS OF VIENNA. New York: Macmillan,
       1970. ix, 405 p.

145   Pounds, Norman J.G. EASTERN EUROPE. Chicago: Aldine, 1969.
       xx, 920 p. Black and white illus.

       A classic geopolitical study by a professor of geography and
       history at Indiana University. Valuable reference, particularly
       for scholars interested in territorial irredentism as an element
       of East European international relations.

146   Ristelhueber, Rene. A HISTORY OF THE BALKAN PEOPLES. Edited and
       translated by Sherman David Spector. New York: Twayne Publishers,
       1971. xii, 470 p.

       Written by a French diplomat actively involved in the diplomacy of the Balkans. Served as French minister to Bulgaria in the late 1930s where he collected some of the material for this volume. A sensitive study of the impact of foreign imperialisms on Balkan politics.

147 Rothschild, Joseph. EAST CENTRAL EUROPE BETWEEN TWO WORLD WARS. Seattle: University of Washington Press, 1974. xvii, 240 p. Paperbound.

A solid contribution to organizing and interpreting the complicated affairs of these countries during the interwar years. Valuable background to understanding their subsequent foreign policies.

148 Roucek, Joseph S[labey]. BALKAN POLITICS: INTERNATIONAL RELATIONS IN NO MAN'S LAND. 1939. Rpt. Westport, Conn.: Greenwood Press, 1971. xiii, 298 p.

149 _____, ed. CENTRAL-EASTERN EUROPE: CRUCIBLE OF WORLD WARS. 1946. Rpt. Westport, Conn.: Greenwood Press, 1970. xii, 683 p.

150 Seton-Watson, Hugh. EASTERN EUROPE BETWEEN THE WARS: 1918-1941. 3d ed. Hamden, Conn.: Archon Books, 1962. xvii, 425 p.

An indispensable historical study delineating the modern history, peasant cultures, political systems and experience, and ethnic diversity of the region, with an especially lucid section on international relations, 1918-41. Outstanding analysis of trade-offs between Balkan national aspirations and "Big Power" designs in the interwar period.

151 Summer, B.H. RUSSIA AND THE BALKANS 1870-1880. 1937. Rpt. Hamden, Conn., and London: Archon Books, 1962. xii, 724 p.

Detailed historical study.

152 Ulam, Adam B. EXPANSION AND COEXISTENCE: THE HISTORY OF SOVIET FOREIGN POLICY 1917-1967. New York and Washington, D.C.: Praeger, 1968. vii, 775 p. Paperbound.

A scholarly study of Soviet foreign policy with extensive references to Soviet-East European relations particularly in the post-World War II period. Stronger on analysis of Polish-Soviet relations than on Moscow's interactions with other East European regimes.

153 Wolff, Robert Lee. THE BALKANS IN OUR TIME. Cambridge, Mass.: Harvard University Press, 1956. xxi, 618 p.

Historical Background

An excellent recent history of Albania, Bulgaria, Rumania, and Yugoslavia with emphasis on the period during and immediately following World War II. Author is a professor of history at Harvard University.

Chapter V

EASTERN EUROPE IN THE COLD WAR

See also part II, chapter IV, section B, "Berlin," p. 143.

154　Clay, Lucius D. DECISION IN GERMANY. New York: Doubleday, 1950. xiv, 524 p. Black and white illus.

> A record of General Clay's four years in Germany first as deputy military governor, then as military governor of the American zone. Important memoir material regarding formulation of U.S. policy toward Germany and the role played by U.S.-Soviet relations.

155　Clemens, Diane Shaver. YALTA. London, Oxford, New York: Oxford University Press, 1970. x, 356 p. Paperbound.

> A reconsideration of the Yalta Conference based on a thorough examination of Soviet and Western sources. Among the best of the revisionist historians' analyses of the role of Eastern Europe as a catalyst in the cold war. Written by an associate professor of history at the University of California (Berkeley).

156　Cretzianu, Alexandre. THE LOST OPPORTUNITY. London: Cape, 1957. 188 p.

> Primarily an attack on Allied policy towards Southeastern Europe during World War II. One chapter deals with Russian policy toward Rumania in 1944-45.

157　Daniel, Hawthorne. THE ORDEAL OF CAPTIVE NATIONS. Introduction by Judge Harold R. Medina. New York: Doubleday, 1958. viii, 316 p.

> Typical of the cold war journalistic focus.

158　Davis, Lynn Etheridge. THE COLD WAR BEGINS: SOVIET-AMERICAN CONFLICT OVER EASTERN EUROPE. Princeton, N.J.: Princeton University Press, 1974. x, 427 p.

Focuses on the role of Eastern Europe in U.S.-Soviet postwar confrontation. Argues that the United States was not motivated by desire for economic control and that Washington never contemplated military threats against the Soviet Union over Eastern Europe.

159   Eisenhower, Dwight D. THE WHITE HOUSE YEARS: WAGING PEACE 1956-1961. New York: Doubleday, 1965. xxiii, 741 p. Illus.

Insights into U.S.-East European relations.

160   Feis, Herbert. BETWEEN WAR AND PEACE. Princeton, N.J.: Princeton University Press, 1960. viii, 367 p.

A traditional diplomatic history of the events leading up to, and the issues decided at, the Potsdam conference. Particularly useful regarding Poland and Germany.

161   Fischer, Louis. THE ROAD TO YALTA: SOVIET FOREIGN RELATIONS, 1941-1945. Foreword by George F. Kennan. New York: Harper and Row, 1972. xv, 238 p.

Evaluates Soviet policy toward Eastern Europe in the context of global objectives and postwar Allied diplomacy.

162   Fontaine, Andre. HISTORY OF THE COLD WAR: FROM THE OCTOBER REVOLUTION TO THE KOREAN WAR 1917-1950. Translated by D.D. Paige. New York: Pantheon Books, 1968. ix, 432 p.

A thoughtful analysis of East-West political, diplomatic, and occasional military conflict written by a French journalist. Underlines the author's conviction that "neither scientific socialism nor so-called liberal capitalism" furnishes ready-made solutions. Deals with the early postwar developments in Eastern Europe.

163   Gati, Charles. "From Cold War Origins to Detente: Introduction to the International Politics of Eastern Europe." In his THE INTERNATIONAL POLITICS OF EASTERN EUROPE, pp. 3-13. New York: Praeger, 1976. Paperbound.

164   Gimbel, John. THE AMERICAN OCCUPATION OF GERMANY: POLITICS AND THE MILITARY, 1945-1949. Stanford, Calif.: Stanford University Press, 1968. xiv, 335 p.

165   Hammett, Hugh. "America's New Policy in Eastern Europe and the Origins of the Cold War." SURVEY: A JOURNAL OF EAST AND WEST STUDIES 19 (Autumn 1973): 144-62.

Discusses the link between Franklin Roosevelt's noncommittal policies toward Eastern Europe during World War II, and the development of the cold war, as well as providing an insightful review of the revisionist-traditionalist controversy over the cold war's origins.

166 Hanrieder, Wolfgang. WEST GERMAN FOREIGN POLICY 1949-1963: INTERNATIONAL PRESSURE AND DOMESTIC RESPONSE. Stanford, Calif.: Stanford University Press, 1967. x, 275 p.

A well-documented theoretical study of West German foreign policy focusing on international decisions in relation to domestic political variables. Uses data related to policy of the Federal Republic of Germany towards the Soviet Union, Poland, and East Germany. Most valuable to students of international relations theory.

167 Herring, George C., Jr. AID TO RUSSIA: STRATEGY, DIPLOMACY, THE ORIGINS OF THE COLD WAR. New York and London: Columbia University Press, 1973. xxi, 365 p.

Deals with the relation of lend lease and Soviet policy toward East Europe, with emphasis on the importance of the U.S. domestic political environment.

168 Hiscocks, Richard. THE ADENAUER ERA. New York: J.B. Lippincott, 1966. ix, 312 p.

Primarily an analysis of West Germany during the Konrad Adenauer years. Relevant chapter dealing with the limitations of Adenauer's foreign policy, especially toward the Soviet Union and East Germany.

169 Kase, Francis J. PEOPLE'S DEMOCRACY. Leyden, The Netherlands: A.W. Sijthoff, 1968. 223 p.

A critical analysis of Soviet efforts to provide a theoretical explanation of the Communist regimes in Eastern Europe. Relates the theory of a people's democracy to Soviet policy and gives a philosophical justification for the Communist political systems in Eastern Europe.

170 Kovrig, Bennett. THE MYTH OF LIBERATION. Baltimore, Md.: Johns Hopkins Press, 1973. xi, 360 p.

The role of East Central Europe in U.S. diplomacy and politics since 1941. A good insight into the confused state of U.S. policy toward the region.

171 Kraehe, Enno E. "Eastern Europe and World Affairs." In COLLECTIVIZATION OF AGRICULTURE IN EASTERN EUROPE, edited by Irwin T. Sanders,

pp. 7-23. Lexington: University of Kentucky Press, 1958.

172 Kuklick, Bruce. AMERICAN POLICY AND THE DIVISION OF GERMANY: THE CLASH WITH RUSSIA OVER REPARATIONS. Ithaca, N.Y., and London: Cornell University Press, 1972. viii, 286 p.

173 LaFeber, Walter. AMERICA, RUSSIA, AND THE COLD WAR, 1945-1971. 2d ed. New York, London, Sydney, Toronto: John Wiley and Sons, 1972. 339 p. Paperbound.

A comprehensive treatment. Analyzes not only foreign policies of the United States and the Soviet Union, but also domestic sources for these policies. Essential for placing East European international relations in their global context. Among the most solid of the "revisionist" school of postwar historians.

174 Lukacs, John A. A NEW HISTORY OF THE COLD WAR. 3d ed. Garden City, N.J.: Anchor Books, 1966. xii, 426 p.

East Europe treated primarily as an irritant in the context of Soviet-American relations. Less useful than his earlier work.

175 Mackintosh, Malcolm. "Stalin's Policies towards Eastern Europe, 1939-1948: The General Picture." In THE ANATOMY OF COMMUNIST TAKEOVERS, edited by Thomas T. Hammond, pp. 229-43. New Haven, Conn., and London: Yale University Press, 1975. Paperbound.

176 Maddox, Robert James. THE NEW LEFT AND THE ORIGINS OF THE COLD WAR. Princeton, N.J.: Princeton University Press, 1973. ix, 169 p. Paperbound.

An attack on the "revisionist" school of thinking that Washington's policy both actively and passively contributed to the cold war. Of necessity, involves restating the traditional arguments concerning the key role of Soviet-East European-American relations during the immediate postwar years.

177 Mastny, Vojtech. "Spheres of Influence and Soviet War Aims in 1943." In EASTERN EUROPE IN THE 1970'S, edited by Sylva Sinanian et al., pp. 87-210. New York: Praeger, 1972.

A detailed analysis of the Soviet-East European policy during World War II, demonstrating the interaction of Soviet objectives and the Western allies' war aims.

178 Middleton, Drew. THE STRUGGLE FOR GERMANY. New York: Bobbs-Merrill, 1949. 304 p.

A policy-oriented analysis by the NEW YORK TIMES correspondent in Germany of the drama acted out by the West, the Soviets, and the East German Communists in the struggle for control of defeated Germany at the end of World War II. Particularly useful to students of propaganda and diplomacy.

179ˉ Paterson, Thomas G. SOVIET-AMERICAN CONFRONTATION: POSTWAR RECONSTRUCTION AND THE ORIGIN OF THE COLD WAR. Baltimore, Md., and London: Johns Hopkins Press, 1973. xi, 287 p.

A well-documented, comprehensive study of American postwar foreign economic policy. Takes the revisionist approach that the United States used loans and trade to try to force Soviet concessions in Eastern Europe, thereby ironically tightening Moscow's control.

180 _____, ed. THE ORIGINS OF THE COLD WAR. 2d ed. Lexington, Mass.: D.C. Heath, 1974. xx, 274 p.

A useful text for undergraduate courses in that the editor puts forward statements of the participants as well as presenting the key differences between traditional and revisionist historians on the origin of the cold war. Includes sections dealing with East European political-economic conditions.

181 Roberts, Henry L. EASTERN EUROPE: POLITICS, REVOLUTION, AND DIPLOMACY. New York: Knopf, 1970. xii, 324 p.

A collection of essays, dating from 1951, dealing with the politics and diplomacy of Eastern Europe and the USSR.

182 _____. RUSSIA AND AMERICA: DANGERS AND PROSPECTS. Foreword by John J. McCloy. New York: Harper & Brothers, 1956. xxxvi, 251 p.

Classic establishment account. Separate chapters devoted to the problems posed for U.S. policy by a divided Germany and the East European satellites.

183 Roucek, Joseph S[labey]., ed. MOSCOW'S EUROPEAN SATELLITES. Philadelphia: American Academy of Political and Social Science, 1950. viii, 253 p.

184 Schwartz, Harry. EASTERN EUROPE IN THE SOVIET SHADOW. New York: John Day, 1973. 117 p. Paperbound.

A journalistic survey for the general reader of Soviet-East European relations since World War II. Expresses modest optimism about the future of East European nationalism.

185 Seton-Watson, Hugh. THE EAST EUROPEAN REVOLUTION. 3d ed.
New York: Praeger, 1956. xix, 435 p. Illus. Paperbound.

An analysis of Communist takeover in Eastern Europe and its
impact on the population. Stresses the similarities in the region that have affected country-specific policies.

186 Smith, Gaddis. AMERICAN DIPLOMACY DURING THE SECOND WORLD
WAR, 1941-1945. New York: Wiley, 1965. ix, 194 p. Paperbound.

A standard work including chapters on the future of Germany
and Poland.

187 Stern, Geoffrey. "Eastern Europe 1944-1956." In THE SOVIET UNION
AND EASTERN EUROPE: A HANDBOOK, edited by George Schopflin,
pp. 146-53. New York and Washington, D.C.: Praeger, 1970.

A useful summary for nonspecialists. Discusses Soviet influence
on postwar events in Eastern Europe, the process of establishing
Communist party rule, Stalinist control, and the post-Stalin
thaw.

188 Theoharis, Athan G. THE YALTA MYTHS: AN ISSUE IN U.S. POLITICS,
1945-1955. Columbia: University of Missouri Press, 1970. viii, 263 p.

Valuable for putting U.S. postwar policy toward Eastern Europe
into its domestic, partisan context.

189 Toynbee, Arnold, and Toynbee, Veronica M., eds. THE REALIGNMENT
OF EUROPE. London and New York: Oxford University Press, 1955.
xvi, 619 p.

Valuable on the part played by Eastern Europe in widening
postwar differences between the Soviet Union and the Western
allies, and for Soviet-East European relations in the period of
consolidation.

190 Wheeler-Bennett, Sir John, and Nicholls, Anthony. THE SEMBLANCE OF
PEACE: THE POLITICAL SETTLEMENT AFTER THE SECOND WORLD WAR.
New York: St. Martin's Press, 1972. xiv, 878 p. Illus. Documents.

A well-written counter-revisionist volume, stressing that the
cold war was rooted in events taking place before, rather
than after, 1945.

191 Williams, William Appleman. "The Cold War Revisionists." NATION
205 (13 November 1967): 492-95.

192 _____. THE TRAGEDY OF AMERICAN DIPLOMACY. New York: Dell,
1962. x, 309 p. Paperbound.

Probably the most stimulating single work on the cold war and its origins. An economic interpretation of American diplomacy that touches on Eastern Europe almost in passing while providing a new framework for understanding the threat posed by Stalin's "iron curtain" isolationism for American traditional "open door" outlook.

Chapter VI

THE POST-STALIN ERA

A. POLITICAL CHANGE

See also part 1, chapter IX, "The Warsaw Treaty Organization," p. 85.

193 Aspaturian, Vernon V. "Has Eastern Europe Become a Liability to the Soviet Union? (I) Political Ideological Aspects." In THE INTERNATIONAL POLITICS OF EASTERN EUROPE, edited by Charles Gati, pp. 17-35. New York: Praeger, 1976. Paperbound.

194 _____. "Moscow's Options in a Changing World." PROBLEMS OF COMMUNISM 21 (July-August 1972): 1-20.

   A survey of Soviet foreign policy, including Moscow's East European options from the perspective of global priorities.

195 _____. "The USSR and Eastern Europe in Political Perspective." PARAMETERS 4, no. 2 (1974): 1-12.

   An edited version of a lecture given at the U.S. Army War College, 20 August 1974. Discusses the changing nature of Soviet-East European relations from the perspective of U.S. interests. Also deals with U.S. and Soviet identity crises in the era of detente.

196 Bass, Robert, and Bass, Elizabeth. "Eastern Europe." In AFRICA AND THE COMMUNIST WORLD, edited by Zbigniew [K.] Brzezinski, pp. 84-115. Stanford, Calif.: Stanford University Press for the Hoover Institution, 1963.

197 Bauman, Zygmunt. "Twenty Years After: The Crisis of Soviet-Type Systems." PROBLEMS OF COMMUNISM 20 (November-December 1971): 45-53.

   Analysis of succession problem in Eastern Europe drawing heavily on Polish examples. The author is a Polish sociologist who taught at the University of Warsaw until he left the country as a result of rising tensions in 1968. Currently head of the sociology department at the University of Leeds, Great Britain.

198   Bennett, Edward M. POLYCENTRISM: GROWING DISSIDENCE IN THE COMMUNIST BLOC? Seattle: Washington State University Press, 1967. 63 p.

A collection of lectures by authorities in the field, delivered to Washington State University's eleventh annual World Affairs Institute on issues of Communist political diversity, foreign trade, and boundary disputes.

199   Bochenski, J.M. "The Great Split." STUDIES IN SOVIET THOUGHT. (March 1968): 1-15.

Analysis of the philosophical-ideological polycentrism inherent in East European philosophical "revisionism," which author considers a potentially far deeper split than Sino-Soviet differences.

200   Bociurkiw, Bohdan R., and Strong, John W., eds. RELIGION AND ATHEISM IN THE U.S.S.R. AND EASTERN EUROPE. London and Basingstoke, Engl.: Macmillan, 1975. xviii, 412 p.

201   Bromke, Adam. EASTERN EUROPE IN A DEPOLARIZED WORLD. Toronto: Baxter Publishing Co. for the Canadian Institute of International Affairs, 1965. 26 p.

202   Bromke, Adam, and Rakowska-Harmstone, Teresa, eds. THE COMMUNIST STATES IN DISARRAY 1965-1971. Carleton Series in Soviet and East European Studies. Minneapolis: University of Minnesota Press, 1972. vii, 363 p.

A series of essays by leading scholars. Deals with general phenomena of polycentrism, impact of the Sino-Soviet split, and the international relations, as well as domestic developments of individual East European countries. Inevitably somewhat uneven.

203   Brown, J[ames]. F. "Eastern Europe." In INTERNATIONAL COMMUNISM AFTER KHRUSHCHEV, edited by Leopold Labedz, pp. 65-88. Cambridge, Mass.: MIT Press, 1965.

204   _____. "East Europe, The Soviet Grip Loosens." SURVEY: A JOURNAL OF SOVIET AND EAST EUROPEAN STUDIES no. 57 (October 1965): 14-25.

A survey of Soviet policy toward East Europe during the year following the fall of Khrushchev in October 1964. Concludes that although the Soviet Union will remain the dominant factor in the East European situation for the foreseeable future, its power has greatly diminished and is unlikely to be restored.

205 _____. THE NEW EASTERN EUROPE: KHRUSHCHEV ERA. New York: Praeger, 1966. vii, 306 p.

A balanced introduction to East European developments after World War II until the mid-1960s. Country-by-country analyses. Deals with native nationalisms, intra-East European relations, and the Soviet role. Useful biographical sketches.

206 Burks, R.V. "The Communist Polities of Eastern Europe." In LINKAGE POLITICS: ESSAYS ON THE CONVERGENCE OF NATIONAL AND INTERNATIONAL SYSTEMS, edited by James Rosenau, pp. 275-303. New York: Free Press, 1969.

207 _____, ed. THE FUTURE OF COMMUNISM IN EUROPE. Franklin Memorial Lectures Series. Detroit: Wayne State University Press, 1968. 283 p.

A collection of lectures by top scholars in the field. Includes the significance of the Yugoslav model, economic reform, and the role of Eastern Europe in Soviet policy.

208 Byrnes, Robert F[rancis]. "Russia in Eastern Europe: Hegemony Without Security." FOREIGN AFFAIRS 49 (July 1971): 682-97.

Considers the Soviet position in Eastern Europe fundamentally unstable, declining over time, and likely to lead to still further attempts at repression.

209 Campbell, John C. "Soviet Strategy in the Balkans." PROBLEMS OF COMMUNISM 23 (July-August 1974): 1-16.

Touches on Moscow's relations with Rumania, Yugoslavia, Bulgaria, and Albania as well as Soviet dealings with non-Communist Balkan countries. Warns that unless forces making for local independence get help from a favorable world environment, a Balkan "zone of peace" would amount to a pax sovietica.

210 Collier, David S., and Glaser, Kurt [W.]. ELEMENTS OF CHANGE IN EASTERN EUROPE: PROSPECTS FOR FREEDOM. Chicago: Henry Regnery, 1968. xii, 251 p.

Discusses East Europe in terms of the interplay of global political forces, as well as possibilities for democratic evolution.

211   Croan, Melvin. "Moscow and Eastern Europe." PROBLEMS OF COM-
       MUNISM 15 (September–October 1966): 60–64.

       An overview of Khrushchev's foreign policies toward Eastern
       Europe during the 1950s, and an assessment of permanent
       changes in the nature of bloc relations through the mid-1960s,
       but prior to 1968 Czechoslovakia.

212   Cviic, Christopher. "Soviet-East European Relations." In SOVIET STRAT-
       EGY IN EUROPE, edited by Richard B. Pipes, pp. 105–26. New York:
       Crane, Russak, 1976.

213   DeGeorge, Richard T. THE NEW MARXISM. New York: Pegasus, 1968.
       170 p.

       A study of Soviet and East European Marxism since 1956,
       showing the importance of East European Marxist humanism for
       ideological developments within the bloc. Quotes heavily
       from Schaff, Kolakowski, Lukacs. Good background both for
       understanding the role of the intelligentsia in the Czechoslovak
       crisis of 1968 and the nature of "ideological transfer" in intra-
       Communist politics.

214   Denitch, Bogdan [Denis]. "The Domestic Roots of Foreign Policy in East-
       ern Europe." In THE INTERNATIONAL POLITICS OF EASTERN EUROPE,
       edited by Charles Gati, pp. 239–50. New York: Praeger, 1976. Paper-
       bound.

215   Devlin, Kevin. "Interparty Relations: Limits of 'Normalization.'" PROB-
       LEMS OF COMMUNISM 20 (July–August 1971): 22–35.

       An examination of statements made at the twenty-fourth Soviet
       party (CPSU) congress concerning interparty relations.

216   Faber, Bernard Lewis, ed. THE SOCIAL STRUCTURE OF EASTERN EU-
       ROPE: TRANSITION AND PROCESS IN CZECHOSLOVAKIA, HUNGARY,
       POLAND, RUMANIA, AND YUGOSLAVIA. New York: Praeger, 1976.
       xv, 423 p.

       Current readings focused on analysis of social change within
       its ideological framework.

217   Fejto, Francois. A HISTORY OF THE PEOPLE'S DEMOCRACIES: EAST-
       ERN EUROPE SINCE STALIN. Harmondsworth, Engl.: Penguin Books,
       1974. 586 p. Paperbound.

       An updated analysis of de-Stalinization, revival of East Euro-
       pean nationalisms, and country-specific events that paved the
       way for the polycentrism in intra-Communist affairs that con-
       tributed to the Czechoslovak crisis in 1968 and continues de-
       spite the invasion of Czechoslovakia. Written by a Hungarian-

born commentator on Communist affairs now living in Paris.
Originally published in French in 1969.

218 Fischer-Galati, Stephen [Z.], ed. EASTERN EUROPE IN THE SIXTIES.
New York: Praeger, 1963. xiii, 239 p.

An introductory collection of articles generalizing about social
order, agriculture, industry, and international relations. Area
study approach.

219 Gati, Charles, ed. THE INTERNATIONAL POLITICS OF EASTERN EU-
ROPE. New York: Praeger, 1976. xii, 309 p. Paperbound.

A general survey of East European relations both with the West
and other Communist countries. Emphasis on Soviet-East European relations from the end of World War II to the present.

220 Griffith, William E. "European Communism, 1965." In his COMMU-
NISM IN EUROPE, vol. 2, pp. 1-39. Cambridge, Mass.: MIT Press,
1964. Paperbound.

A good account of interbloc relations revealing the decline
of Soviet authority in East European domestic affairs and foreign policy formation.

221 Gross, Feliks. THE SEIZURE OF POLITICAL POWER IN A CENTURY OF
REVOLUTIONS. New York: Philosophical Library, 1958. 398 p.

Uses East Central Europe as a case study of revolutionary takeover. Includes analysis of unrest following Stalin's death,
specifically Berlin in 1953 and the 1956 events in Poland and
Hungary.

222 Gruenwald, Oskar. "Marxist Humanism." ORBIS 18 (Fall 1974): 888-
916.

Deals with recent reinterpretations of Marx by East European
Marxist philosophers. Focuses on Yugoslav Praxis school, concluding that this group's humanist thinking could eventually
bridge the East-West ideological gap.

223 Gyorgy, Andrew. "Communism in Eastern Europe." In THE NEW COM-
MUNISMS, edited by Dan N. Jacobs. New York; Evanston, Ill.; London:
Harper and Row, 1969. pp. 159-83.

Discusses changing problems in East European foreign policies
in the context of the revolution of rising expectations and increasing ideological indifference.

224 _____. "External Forces in Eastern Europe." In THE COMMUNIST

STATES IN DISARRAY 1965–1971, edited by Adam Bromke and Teresa Rakowska-Harmstone, pp. 221–35. Minneapolis: University of Minnesota Press, 1972.

> The cohesive influence of the Warsaw Pact and CMEA is discussed against the polycentric, centrifugal forces of nationalism in the area as a whole, considers Brezhnev Doctrine as a centralizing force since 1968.

225 _____. "Ostpolitik and Eastern Europe." In THE INTERNATIONAL POLITICS OF EASTERN EUROPE, edited by Charles Gati, pp. 154–70. New York: Praeger, 1976. Paperbound.

226 Ionescu, Ghita. THE BREAK-UP OF THE SOVIET EMPIRE IN EASTERN EUROPE. Baltimore, Md.: Penguin, 1965. 168 p. Paperbound.

227 Isenberg, Irwin, ed. FERMENT IN EASTERN EUROPE. New York: H.W. Wilson, 1965. 216 p.

> A brief collection of academic essays and expert journalistic accounts of the changing nature of East European communism in the mid-1960s. Useful insights.

228 Kanet, Roger E. "Modernizing Interaction Within Eastern Europe." In THE POLITICS OF MODERNIZATION IN EASTERN EUROPE: TESTING THE SOVIET MODEL, edited by Charles Gati, pp. 275–303. New York: Praeger, 1974.

229 Kertesz, Stephen D., ed. EAST CENTRAL EUROPE AND THE WORLD: DEVELOPMENTS IN THE POST-STALIN ERA. Notre Dame, Ind.: University of Notre Dame Press, 1962. x, 386 p.

> A discussion of changes in the Communist bloc since Stalin; the process of de-Stalinization; internal developments and foreign relations; and, specifically, the importance of China as a political factor.

230 Korbonski, Andrzej. "External Influences on Eastern Europe." In THE INTERNATIONAL POLITICS OF EASTERN EUROPE, edited by Charles Gati, pp. 253–71. New York: Praeger, 1976.

231 Kuhlman, James [A.]. "A Framework for Viewing Domestic and Foreign Policy Patterns." In THE INTERNATIONAL POLITICS OF EASTERN EUROPE, edited by Charles Gati, pp. 275–91. New York: Praeger, 1976. Paperbound.

232 Laquer, Walter, and Labedz, Leopold, eds. POLYCENTRISM: THE NEW FACTOR IN INTERNATIONAL COMMUNISM. New York: Praeger, 1962. 259 p.

A collection of previously published articles. Country-by-country approach.

233 Lendvai, Paul. ANTI-SEMITISM WITHOUT JEWS. New York: Double-day. 1971. vi, 398 p.

Compares anti-Semitism in Poland and Czechoslovakia, where Jews were less than 1 percent of the population, with the developments in Rumania and Hungary, where numbers were larger and persecution less. Treats exacerbation of the situation since 1968, including international implications.

234 Leonhard, Wolfgang. THREE FACES OF MARXISM: THE POLITICAL CONCEPTS OF SOVIET IDEOLOGY; MAOISM; AND HUMANIST MARX-ISM. New York: Holt, Rinehart and Winston, 1974. xiv, 497 p.

Most relevant for section dealing with East European Marxists, in which the author frequently quotes from key figures in the contemporary debates.

235 Lesage, Michel. LES REGIMES POLITIQUES DE L'URSS ET DE L'EUROPE DE L'EST. Paris: Presses universitaires, 1971. 365 p. Illus.

A discussion of the extent to which the East European states have applied the Soviet model to their own particular needs, and the variations of Soviet-type institutions functioning outside the USSR.

236 London, Kurt, ed. EASTERN EUROPE IN TRANSITION. Baltimore, Md.: Johns Hopkins Press, 1966. xx, 364 p. Paperbound.

A collection of essays by leading scholars in the field. Emphasis on growing nationalism and polycentrism in Eastern Europe. Case studies dealing with East Germany, Poland, and Rumania, as well as an analysis of national minorities under communism.

237 Lowenthal, Richard. WORLD COMMUNISM: THE DISINTEGRATION OF A SECULAR FAITH. New York: Oxford University Press, 1964. xxii, 296 p.

A collection of earlier essays. Useful regarding importance of Soviet-Yugoslav rapprochement as a decentralizing force in the international Communist movement.

238 McNeal, Robert, ed. INTERNATIONAL RELATIONS AMONG COM-MUNISTS. Englewood Cliffs, N.J.: Prentice-Hall, 1967. x, 181 p.

A concise summary. Includes both documents and political analysis.

239 Mensonides, Louis J., and Kuhlman, James A., eds. THE FUTURE OF
INTER-BLOC RELATIONS IN EUROPE. New York; Washington, D.C.;
London: Praeger, 1974. xiv, 217 p.

> A wide-ranging collection of essays including analysis of system
> change, aggregate statistical comparison of each bloc, and a
> variety of political, military, and economic issues. Poten-
> tially controversial methodology, but undoubtedly valuable to
> students of integration in theory and practice.

240 Morton, Henry W. THE SOVIET UNION AND EASTERN EUROPE. New
York: Macmillan, 1971. 152 p. Paperbound.

241 Nagy, Laszlo. DEMOCRATIES POPULAIRES: DU BLOC SOVIETIQUE
AU COMMUNISM DES PATRIES. Paris: B. Arthaud, 1968. 376 p.
Paperbound. Black and white illus.

242 Neuberg, Paul. THE HERO'S CHILDREN: THE POSTWAR GENERATION
IN EASTERN EUROPE. New York: William Morrow, 1973. 384 p.

> An interesting, readable account of the youth culture in East-
> ern Europe. Discusses attitudes toward family, society, dissent,
> work, school, and recreation. Important insight into the ex-
> tent to which the Iron Curtain has been penetrated and the
> appeal of Western culture for these young people. Useful for
> those attempting to understand Soviet-East European reluctance
> to agree to "the free flow of ideas" as a part of an all-Euro-
> pean security agreement.

243 Porro, J.D. CONTROLLED PLURALISM: IS HUNGARY THE FUTURE OF
EAST EUROPE? Santa Monica, Calif.: RAND Memorandum P-5386,
February 1975. 18 p.

> Speculates on the development of East European pluralism under
> the umbrella of the party's "leading role."

244 Potichnyj, Peter J., and Shapiro, Jane P., eds. CHANGE AND ADAP-
TATION IN SOVIET AND EAST EUROPEAN POLITICS. New York:
Praeger, 1976. xii, 236 p.

245 _____. FROM COLD WAR TO DETENTE. New York: Praeger, 1976.
xii, 223 p.

246 Ripka, Hubert. EASTERN EUROPE IN THE POST-WAR WORLD. Introduction by Hugh Seton-Watson. New York: Praeger, 1961. xv, 266 p.

> The problems of Eastern Europe as seen after the 1956 upheavals
> in Poland and Hungary. A posthumous study by one of the fore-
> most Czech journalists in the late 1930s, minister of foreign

trade in 1945 and a professor of political history in Prague until he went into exile following the 1948 Communist coup.

247   Schopflin, George, ed. THE SOVIET UNION AND EASTERN EUROPE: A HANDBOOK. New York and Washington, D.C.: Praeger, 1970. xii, 614 p.

A comprehensive survey, uneven but useful, particularly on the implications of rising East European nationalism for the region's international relations.

248   Shub, Anatole. AN EMPIRE LOSES HOPE. THE GHOST OF STALIN. New York: Norton, 1970. xvi, 474 p. Illus.

The personal pessimistic reports of an American journalist in the 1960s on the internal evolution and trends in Eastern Europe and the Soviet Union.

249   Simon, Gerhard. "The Catholic Church and the Communist State in the Soviet Union and Eastern Europe." In RELIGION AND ATHEISM IN THE U.S.S.R. AND EASTERN EUROPE, edited by Bohdan R. Bociurkiw and John W. Strong, pp. 190–221. London and Basingstoke, Engl.: Macmillan, 1975.

250   Staar, Richard F. "Polycentrism in Eastern Europe." In ASPECTS OF MODERN COMMUNISM, edited by Richard F. Staar, pp. 117–41. Columbia: University of South Carolina Press, 1968.

A summary of the author's largely negative views on the limits of diversity within Eastern Europe as spelled out in his longer works.

251   _____ . "What Next in East European Intrabloc Relations." EAST EUROPE, nos. 11–12 (November–December 1969): 19–28.

Summary of recent developments, Warsaw Pact, CMEA, Sino-Soviet dispute, and the intervention in Czechoslovakia. Concludes that the answer to the question posed by the title depends primarily on still unclear preferences of the Soviet leadership.

252   _____ , ed. ASPECTS OF MODERN COMMUNISM. Columbia: University of South Carolina Press, 1968. xxiv, 416 p.

A collection of edited papers and the remarks of discussants at a closed conference on the Communist world. Part 3 devoted to analysis of Eastern Europe as a region with separate papers on both the Warsaw Pact and CMEA.

253 Steele, Jonathan, ed. EASTERN EUROPE SINCE STALIN. New York: Crane, Russak, 1974. 215 p.

A sensitively compiled collection of statements by both East European dissidents and officials. Captures much of the flavor of de-Stalinization, East European rebellions in 1956, and subsequent attempts at reforms throughout the 1960s. Covers both the Czechoslovak experiment with liberalization in 1968 and "the consumer revolution" of the early 1970s.

254 Stojanovic, Svetozar. BETWEEN IDEALS AND REALITY: A CRITIQUE OF SOCIALISM AND ITS FUTURE. Translated by Gerson S. Sher. New York: Oxford University Press, 1973. xvii, 222 p. Paperbound.

A philosophical analysis by a Yugoslav Marxist and member of the Praxis group. Important for students interested in the role played by philosophers in the interaction of ideology and politics throughout Eastern Europe.

255 Terry, Sarah Meiklejohn. "External Influences on Political Change in Eastern Europe: A Framework for Analysis." In POLITICAL DEVELOPMENT IN EASTERN EUROPE, edited by Jan F. Triska and Paul [M.] Cocks, pp. 277-314. New York: Praeger, 1977.

256 Toma, Peter A., ed. THE CHANGING FACE OF COMMUNISM IN EASTERN EUROPE. Tucson: University of Arizona Press, 1970. xv, 413 p. Paperbound.

Emphasis on changes in the USSR and the West and the impact of these developments on East Europe. Two final chapters deal explicitly with foreign relations.

257 Triska, Jan F., and Johnson, Paul M. "Political Development and Political Change." In COMPARATIVE SOCIALIST SYSTEMS: ESSAYS ON POLITICS AND ECONOMICS, edited by Carmelo Mesa-Lago and Carl Beck, pp. 249-85. Pittsburgh, Pa.: University of Pittsburgh Center for International Studies, 1975.

257a Triska, Jan F., and Cocks, Paul [M.], eds. POLITICAL DEVELOPMENT IN EASTERN EUROPE. New York: Praeger, 1977. xxiv, 374 p. Paperbound.

A collection of conference papers including analysis of coalition politics, prospects for integration, and external pressures for political change in Eastern Europe.

258 Wolfe, Thomas W. SOVIET POWER AND EUROPE, 1945-1970. Baltimore, Md.: Johns Hopkins Press, 1970. x, 534 p. Paperbound.

Primarily an analysis of Soviet foreign policy with emphasis
on strategic considerations. Relevant chapters include discussion of the Soviet relation with East Europe, 1966-68, and
an analysis of the impact of the invasion of Czechoslovakia
on Moscow's European policy. A serious work by one of the
leading scholars in the field.

259 Zinner, Paul E. "Scope and Limits of Polycentrism in Eastern Europe."
In POLYCENTRISM: GROWING DISSIDENCE IN THE COMMUNIST
BLOC?, edited by Edward M. Bennett, pp. 24-41. Seattle: Washington
State University Press, 1967.

A thoughtful analysis of both the mixed responses and barriers
to accepting the apparent option for increased freedom of maneuver vis-à-vis Moscow in the Eastern Europe of the 1960s.

B. ECONOMIC DEVELOPMENT

See also part I, chapter VIII, "Council for Mutual Economic Assistance," p. 69.

259a Berend, Ivan T., and Ranki, Gyorgy. ECONOMIC DEVELOPMENT IN
EAST-CENTRAL EUROPE IN THE 19TH AND 20TH CENTURIES. New
York: Columbia University Press, 1974. xiii, 402 p. Illus.

See no. 125.

260 Bornstein, Morris, ed. PLAN AND MARKET: ECONOMIC REFORM IN
EASTERN EUROPE. New Haven, Conn., and London: Yale University
Press, 1973. viii, 416 p.

A solid study by top economists in the field linking domestic
economic development to regional political implications.

261 Bryson, Phillip J. "Investment Planning and Economic Control in East
European Centralism." EAST EUROPEAN QUARTERLY XI 1 (Spring 1977):
109-25.

Section on investment control and international economic integration.

262 Csikos-Nagy, Bela. SOCIALIST ECONOMIC POLICY. London: Long-
man, 1973. 238 p.

263 Dellin, L.A.D., ed. REFORMS IN SOVIET AND EASTERN EUROPEAN
ECONOMIES. Lexington, Mass.; Toronto; London: D.C. Heath, 1972.
vii, 175 p.

A country-by-country approach to reform.

264 Drachkovitch, Milorad M. UNITED STATES AID TO YUGOSLAVIA AND
     POLAND: ANALYSIS OF A CONTROVERSY. Washington, D.C.: Ameri-
     can Enterprise Institute for Policy Research, 1963. v, 124 p.

         Evaluates U.S. aid in terms of its impact on internal democ-
         ratization of Communist regimes.

265 Fallenbuchl, Zbigniew M., ed. ECONOMIC DEVELOPMENT IN THE
     SOVIET UNION AND EASTERN EUROPE, 2 vols. New York: Praeger,
     1975. v, 360 p.

266 Garmarnikow, Michael. ECONOMIC REFORMS IN EASTERN EUROPE.
     Detroit: Wayne State University Press, 1968. 204 p.

         A well-written comparative analysis of the economic aspects
         of East European reforms. The first of its kind on a bloc
         scale.

267 _____. "Industrial Cooperation: East Looks West." PROBLEMS OF
     COMMUNISM 20 (May–June 1971): 41–48.

         A brief examination of trends in "economic cooperation" be-
         tween East European industrial enterprises and Western firms,
         with emphasis on joint production contracts, and technological
         information trading.

268 Grossman, Gregory. "Economic Reforms: Interplay of Economics and Poli-
     tics." In THE FUTURE OF COMMUNISM IN EUROPE, edited by R.V.
     Burks, pp. 103–40. Detroit: Wayne State University Press, 1968.

269 _____, ed. ESSAYS IN SOCIALISM AND PLANNING IN HONOR OF
     CARL LANDAURER. Englewood Cliffs, N.J.: Prentice-Hall, 1970.
     211 p.

270 Hohmann, Hans–Hermann, et al., eds. THE NEW ECONOMIC SYSTEMS
     OF EASTERN EUROPE. Berkeley and Los Angeles: University of Cali-
     fornia Press, 1975. xxiv, 585 p.

         A cross–system comparison of East European economies dealing
         with pricing, planning, finance, agriculture, and foreign trade.
         A useful reference, dull reading. Includes Yugoslav and
         Albanian data.

271 Hunter, William D.G. CURRENT PROBLEMS OF SOCIALIST ECONOMIES.
     Hamilton, Ontario: McMaster University and Canada Council, 1971. vi,
     228 p. Paperbound.

272 Ingram, David. THE COMMUNIST ECONOMIC CHALLENGE. New

York: Praeger, 1965. 158 p.

> Includes a chapter on the East European countries, information
> on CMEA integration, and economic contacts with the non-
> Communist world. Broad, somewhat superficial coverage.

273 Kaser, Michael. "Eastern Europe's Economies in 1976-1980." THE
WORLD TODAY 32 (September 1976): 327-38.

> Brief country-by-country survey.

274 Korbel, Josef. DETENTE IN EUROPE; REAL OR IMAGINARY? Princeton,
N.J.: Princeton University Press, 1972. viii, 302 p. Paperbound.

> Chapter 3 deals with the economic implications of detente,
> intra-European trade, CMEA, and East-West industrial coopera-
> tion.

275 Lauter, Geza P[eter]., and Dickie, Paul M. MULTINATIONAL CORPORA-
TIONS AND EAST EUROPEAN SOCIALIST ECONOMIES. New York:
Praeger, 1975. xii, 137 p.

> Emphasis on impact of multinational corporations on East-West
> potential economic collaboration. Argues that traditional form
> of "joint ventures" is on the way out.

276 Marer, Paul. "Has Eastern Europe Become a Liability to the Soviet Union?
(III) The Economic Aspect." In THE INTERNATIONAL POLITICS OF
EASTERN EUROPE, edited by Charles Gati, pp. 59-79. New York:
Praeger, 1976. Paperbound.

277 _____. "Soviet Economic Policy in Eastern Europe." In REORIENTA-
TION AND COMMERCIAL RELATIONS OF THE ECONOMIES OF EAST-
ERN EUROPE, U.S. Congress. Joint Economic Committee, pp. 135-63.
Washington, D.C.: Government Printing Office, 1974.

> A thorough historical survey of Soviet-East European economic
> relations with important political insights. Discusses capital
> transfers, terms of trade, price determination within CMEA and
> commodity composition.

278 Marer, Paul, and Neuberger, Egon. "Commercial Relations Between the
United States and Eastern Europe: Options and Prospects." In REORIENTA-
TION AND COMMERCIAL RELATIONS OF THE ECONOMIES OF EASTERN
EUROPE, U.S. Congress. Joint Economic Committee, pp. 556-98. Wash-
ington, D.C.: Government Printing Office, 1974.

> A detailed evaluation by two leading economists in the field
> that treats political as well as economic issues influencing U.S.-
> East European trade. Useful insight into the problem of whether

or not to grant Most Favored Nation status to East European nations.

279 Markovich, Stephen C. "American Foreign Aid and Yugoslav Internal Policies." EAST EUROPEAN QUARTERLY 9 (Summer 1975): 184-95.

280 Mendershausen, H. THE EUROPEAN COMMUNITY AND THE SOVIET BLOC. Santa Monica, Calif.: RAND Memorandum P-2577-2, November 1962. 24 p.

281 Nagorski, Zygmunt, Jr. THE PSYCHOLOGY OF EAST-WEST TRADE: ILLUSIONS AND OPPORTUNITIES. Foreword by Jean Francois Revel. New York: Mason and Lipscomb, 1974.

Emphasis on trade, detente, and change. Specific attention to economic reforms in Hungary and Poland.

282 Neuberger, Egon. TRADE WITH COMMUNIST COUNTRIES--YES OR NO? Santa Monica, Calif.: RAND Memorandum P-2912, May 1964. 15 p.

Argues against oversimplifying the problems in favor of specific criteria for deciding the fundamental question of whether to use trade policy for noneconomic purposes.

283 Nichols, Patrick J. "Western Investment in Eastern Europe: The Yugoslav Example." In REORIENTATION AND COMMERCIAL RELATIONS OF THE ECONOMIES OF EASTERN EUROPE, U.S. Congress. Joint Economic Committee, pp. 725-43. Washington, D.C.: Government Printing Office, 1974.

A close look at the legal framework, negotiating contracts, industrial and regional impact, and motivation of Western investment in Yugoslavia from the perspective of possible lessons to be learned about investing in other East European countries. In the end the author underlines that the problems, in fact, are very different.

284 Portes, Richard. "East Europe's Debt to the West: Interdependence is a Two-Way Street." FOREIGN AFFAIRS 55 (July 1977): 751-82.

285 Pounds, Bonnie M., and Levine, Mona F. "Legislative, Industrial, and Negotiating Aspects of United States-East European Trade and Economic Relations." In REORIENTATION AND COMMERCIAL RELATIONS OF THE ECONOMIES OF EASTERN EUROPE, U.S. Congress. Joint Economic Committee, pp. 531-55. Washington, D.C.: Government Printing Office, 1974.

A technical, policy-oriented paper outlining the historical background, institutional mechanisms for normalization of trade, and major negotiating issues.

286 Ryans, John K., Jr.; Negandhi, A.N.; and Baker, James C., eds. CHINA, THE U.S.S.R. AND EASTERN EUROPE: A U.S. TRADE PERSPECTIVE. Kent, Ohio: Kent State University Press, 1964. x, 196 p.

287 Selucky, Radoslav. ECONOMIC REFORMS IN EASTERN EUROPE. New York: Praeger, 1972. x, 179 p.

Written by one of the Czech economists intimately associated with the Prague Spring of 1968. Focus on the inevitable connection between political and economic reform and the implications for both East and West.

288 Snell, Edwin M. "Eastern Europe's Trade and Payments With the Industrialized West." In REORIENTATION AND COMMERCIAL RELATIONS OF THE ECONOMIES OF EASTERN EUROPE, U.S. Congress. Joint Economic Committee, pp. 682-724. Washington, D.C.: Government Printing Office, 1974.

An examination of Eastern Europe's fast growing trade with the West and the region's even faster-growing payment deficits. Emphasis that the long-term future of trade depends both on political decisions about public financing and continued peaceful coexistence.

289 Spulber, Nicolas. "East-West Trade and the Paradoxes of the Strategic Embargo." In INTERNATIONAL TRADE AND CENTRAL PLANNING, edited by Alan A. Brown and Egon Neuberger, pp. 104-26. Berkeley and Los Angeles: University of California Press, 1968.

290 _____. SOCIALIST MANAGEMENT AND PLANNING: TOPICS IN COMPARATIVE SOCIALIST ECONOMICS. Bloomington: Indiana University Press, 1971. xviii, 235 p.

A collection of earlier essays covering the basic groundwork of reforms, agriculture, foreign trade, growth rates, and convergence.

291 _____. THE STATE AND ECONOMIC DEVELOPMENT IN EASTERN EUROPE. New York: Random House, 1966. 179 p.

292 Starr, Robert, ed. EAST-WEST BUSINESS TRANSACTIONS. New York: Praeger, 1974. xv, 577 p.

Practical guide for businessmen concerned with the ground rules of East-West trade.

293 U.S. Congress. Joint Economic Committee. ECONOMIC DEVELOPMENTS IN COUNTRIES OF EASTERN EUROPE, 91st Congress, 2d sess. Washington, D.C.: Government Printing Office, 1970. viii, 634 p. Paperbound.

A compendium of papers written by leading scholars in the field particularly useful to economists or political scientists studying the economic component of Soviet-East European relations.

294 _____. REORIENTATION AND COMMERCIAL RELATIONS OF THE ECONOMIES OF EASTERN EUROPE, 93d Congress, 2d sess. Washington, D.C.: Government Printing Office, 1974. v, 771 p. Paperbound.

A compendium of papers submitted to the Joint Economic Committee of the Congress, covering policy formation, planning, performance, resource allocation and commercial relations of East European states. Detailed, analytical pieces written by top scholars in the field. Extremely valuable for students of either the economics or politics of East European foreign trade.

295 Uren, Philip E., ed. EAST-WEST TRADE. Introduction by Hon. Michell W. Sharp. Toronto: Canadian Institute of International Affairs, 1966. 181 p.

296 Velebit, Vladimir. "The Future of East-West Trade." JOURNAL OF INTERNATIONAL AFFAIRS 22, no. 1 (1968): 79-88.

A Yugoslav viewpoint written by a former undersecretary of state for foreign affairs. At the time of this article, the author was executive secretary of the UN Economic Commission for Europe.

297 Volgyes, Ivan, ed. ENVIRONMENTAL DETERIORATION IN THE SOVIET UNION AND EASTERN EUROPE. New York: Praeger, 1975. xiii, 168 p.

298 Wasowski, Stanislaw, ed. EAST-WEST TRADE AND THE TECHNOLOGY GAP: A POLITICAL AND ECONOMIC APPRAISAL. New York: Praeger, 1970. 214 p.

Detailed essays dealing with the level of East European technology and its importance for trade, economic reform, and East-West cooperation.

299 Wilczynski, Jozef. THE ECONOMICS AND POLITICS OF EAST-WEST TRADE. New York: Praeger, 1969. 416 p.

A comprehensive if uneven study.

300 _____. THE ECONOMICS OF SOCIALISM: PRINCIPLES GOVERNING THE OPERATION OF CENTRALLY PLANNED ECONOMIES IN THE USSR AND EASTERN EUROPE. London: Allen and Unwin, 1970. 233 p. Paperbound.

301 _____. THE MULTINATIONALS AND EAST-WEST RELATIONS: TO-
WARDS TRANSIDEOLOGICAL COLLABORATION. Boulder, Colo.: Westview Press, 1976. 235 p.

302 _____. SOCIALIST ECONOMIC DEVELOPMENT AND REFORMS: FROM
EXTENSIVE TO INTENSIVE GROWTH UNDER CENTRAL PLANNING IN THE
USSR, EASTERN EUROPE AND YUGOSLAVIA. New York: Praeger,
1972. xvii, 350 p.

   See no. 486a.

303 Wiles, P[eter].J.D., ed. THE PREDICTION OF COMMUNIST ECONOM-
IC PERFORMANCE. London: Cambridge University Press, 1971. x,
390 p.

   A comparative analysis of planning, industry, and ownership
   in European socialist countries. Primarily concerned with for-
   casting economic development on a country-by-country basis.

304 Zwass, Adam. MONETARY COOPERATION BETWEEN EAST AND WEST.
Introduction by George Garvy. White Plains, N.Y.: International Arts
and Sciences Press, 1975. xvii, 265 p.

C. EAST-WEST RELATIONS

See also part I, chapter VI, section B, "Economic Development," p. 47, and
chapter VIII, "Council for Mutual Economic Assistance," p. 69.

305 THE ATLANTIC COMMUNITY AND EASTERN EUROPE: PERSPECTIVES
AND POLICY. Paris: Atlantic Institute, 1967. 104 p.

   Papers selected from an Atlantic Institute conference on Eastern Europe in Rome, October 1966. Emphasis on issues of
   importance to East-West relations.

306 Atlantic Council of the United States. EAST-WEST TRADE: MANAGING
ENCOUNTER AND ACCOMMODATION. Boulder, Colo.: Westview Press,
1977. xix, 194 p.

307 Birnbaum, Immanuel. "Germany's Eastern Policy, Yesterday and Tomorrow."
In THE POLITICS OF POSTWAR GERMANY, edited by Walter Stahl,
pp. 447-57. New York: Praeger, 1963.

308 Birnbaum, Karl E. "Human Rights and East-West Relations." FOREIGN
AFFAIRS 55 (July 1977): 783-99.

   Deals with impact on East Germany, Czechoslovakia, and
   Poland.

309   Bromke, Adam, and Uren, Philip E., eds. THE COMMUNIST STATES
       AND THE WEST. New York and London: Praeger and Pall Mall Press,
       1967. x, 242 p.

       Evaluates the impact of the Sino-Soviet split and growing
       polycentrism in the Communist world on East-West relations.

310   Byrnes, Robert F[rancis]. THE UNITED STATES AND EASTERN EUROPE.
       Englewood Cliffs, N.J.: Prentice-Hall, 1967. ix, 176 p. Paperbound.

       Policy-oriented survey by experts in the field. Deals with
       modernization and political development in the context of
       Soviet-East European relations.

311   Campbell, John C. AMERICAN POLICY TOWARDS COMMUNIST EAST-
       ERN EUROPE: THE CHOICES AHEAD. Minneapolis: University of Min-
       nesota Press, 1965. xi, 136 p.

       A policy-oriented study by a serious scholar of U.S.-East
       European relations. Includes historical background, survey of
       recent trends, economic factors, and separate chapters on
       Yugoslavia and Poland.

312   _____. "European Security: Prospects and Possibilities for East
       Europe." EAST EUROPE 19 (November 1970): 2-8.

       Favors institutionalizing the European security conference as an
       ongoing mechanism for facilitating multilateral contacts and
       interlocking interests between East and West. Concludes that
       if East and West Europe wish to carry on a dialogue, it is
       hard to see what the United States has to lose.

313   Collier, David S., and Glaser, Kurt W. WESTERN POLICY AND EAST-
       ERN EUROPE. Chicago: Henry Regnery, 1966. ix, 245 p.

       A collection of scholarly essays on East European domestic and
       international affairs. Part 2 devoted to the impact of the
       German problem on East European policy. Also useful for
       students of East-West cultural and economic contacts.

314   Croan, Melvin. "Party Politics and the Wall." SURVEY: A JOURNAL
       OF SOVIET AND EAST EUROPEAN STUDIES, no. 61 (October 1966):
       38-46.

       Considers the Berlin Wall to have initiated a new era in West
       German politics. Focus on the problems caused for Bonn by
       increasing East German consolidation.

315   Dalma, Alfons. "The Risk of Detente Policy to Central Europe." In
       CHANGING EAST-WEST RELATIONS AND THE UNITY OF THE WEST,

edited by Arnold Wolfers, pp. 93-125. Baltimore, Md.: Johns Hopkins Press, 1964. Paperbound.

> Primarily concerned about the danger to West Germany inherent in detente. Based on the increasingly shaky assumption that Soviet control of Eastern Europe can weather detente, while Western strategic stability can not.

316 Dean, Robert W. WEST GERMAN TRADE WITH THE EAST: THE POLITICAL DIMENSION. New York: Praeger, 1974. xvi, 269 p.

> Emphasis on the politics of trade between East and West Germany with reference to other East European trading patterns. Good general treatment of the political role of trade in an era of detente.

317 Dulles, Eleanor Lansing. ONE GERMANY OR TWO? THE STRUGGLE AT THE HEART OF EUROPE. Stanford, Calif.: Stanford University Press for the Hoover Institution, 1970. xiv, 315 p.

> A survey of West German foreign policy toward the USSR and East Europe that includes chapters on Berlin and East Germany. Considers that eventual German reunification is essential for world peace. Stress on implications for U.S. policy.

318 Gati, Charles. "East Central Europe: Touchstone for Detente." JOURNAL OF INTERNATIONAL AFFAIRS 17, no. 2 (1974): 158-74.

> Views Soviet unwillingness to allow the principles of "non-interference" and "free access" to be applied in East Central Europe as a roadblock in the path of further detente.

319 _____. "Through Diplomacy or 'Westernization': A Critique of American Approaches to Eastern Europe." In POLITICAL DEVELOPMENT IN EASTERN EUROPE, edited by Jan F. Triska and Paul [M.] Cocks, pp. 315-33. New York: Praeger, 1977.

320 Goodman, Elliot. "NATO and German Reunification." SURVEY: A JOURNAL OF SOVIET AND EAST EUROPEAN STUDIES no. 76 (Summer 1970): 30-40.

321 Gorgey, Laszlo. BONN'S EASTERN POLICY 1964-1971: EVOLUTION AND LIMITATIONS. Hamden, Conn.: Archon Books, 1972. ix, 191 p.

> Forsees a series of setbacks for West Germany's future Eastern policy in the context of detente between East and West.

322 Griffith, William E. "The German Problem and American Policy." SURVEY: A JOURNAL OF SOVIET AND EAST EUROPEAN STUDIES, no. 61

(October 1966): 105-17.

> Primarily focused on U.S.-West German relations including a discussion of the importance of intra-German relations for other policies of the Federal Republic of Germany.

323 Handlery, George. "Propaganda and Information: The Case of U.S. Broadcasts to Eastern Europe." EAST EUROPEAN QUARTERLY 8 (January 1975): 391-412.

> Historian's analysis of Radio Free Europe broadcasts concludes that materials disseminated are primarily informational and balanced.

324 Hassner, Pierre. "Polycentrism, West and East: East European Implications of the Western Debates." In EASTERN EUROPE IN TRANSITION, edited by Kurt London, pp. 325-54. Baltimore, Md.: Johns Hopkins Press, 1966. Paperbound.

> Discusses the Western debate about the merits of detente and efforts at "bridge-building" to Eastern Europe in terms of the policy implications for Eastern Europe and the salient question of who should have contacts with whom in the new era.

325 Heneghan, Thomas E. "Human Rights Protest in Eastern Europe." THE WORLD TODAY 33 (March 1977): 90-100.

> Relates domestic protests to the Belgrade conference scheduled to review the 1975 Helsinki agreement in June 1977.

326 Kaiser, Karl. GERMAN FOREIGN POLICY IN TRANSITION: BONN BETWEEN EAST AND WEST. Oxford: Oxford University Press, 1968. x, 153 p. Paperbound.

> An informed West German scholar's discussion of the prospects and problems of intra-German relations developing under the umbrella of detente.

327 Kanet, Roger [E.]. "East-West Trade and the Limits of Western Influence." In THE INTERNATIONAL POLITICS OF EASTERN EUROPE, edited by Charles Gati, pp. 192-211. New York: Praeger, 1976. Paperbound.

328 Keesing's Research Report. GERMANY AND EASTERN EUROPE SINCE 1945. FROM POTSDAM AGREEMENT TO CHANCELLOR BRANDT'S 'OSTPOLITIK.' New York: Charles Scribner's Sons, 1973. xi, 322 p. Paperbound.

> Detailed factual survey. Valuable reference to scholars.

329 Kohl, Wilfred, and Taubman, William. "American Policy Towards Europe:

The Next Phase." ORBIS 17 (Spring 1973): 51-74.

> Argues for increasing trade between the United States and Eastern Europe as the first step in developing a coherent American policy toward East Europe.

330 Korbonski, Andrzej. "The United States and East Europe." CURRENT HISTORY 65 (May 1973): 193-97.

> Brief summary indicating the reasons for Washington's virtual nonpolicy toward Eastern Europe in the administrations from Eisenhower to Johnson in the context of the new American initiatives taken toward the region during the Nixon years.

331 Kotyk, Vaclav. "Problems of East-West Relations." JOURNAL OF IN-TERNATIONAL AFFAIRS 22, no. 1 (1968): 48-58.

> Statement by a former member of the Institute of International Politics and Economics in Prague. Although the institute was dissolved and Kotyk, personally, in disgrace after the 1968 intervention, he can be considered a careful, informed spokesman of the Czechoslovak position for that time.

332 Kovrig, Bennett. "The United States: 'Peaceful Engagement' Revisited." In THE INTERNATIONAL POLITICS OF EASTERN EUROPE, edited by Charles Gati, pp. 131-51. New York: Praeger, 1976. Paperbound.

333 Larrabee, F. Stephen. "Balkan Security." ADELPHI PAPERS 135 (1977): 44 p.

334 Legvold, Robert. "European Security Conference. SURVEY: A JOURNAL OF SOVIET AND EAST EUROPEAN STUDIES, no. 76 (Summer 1970): 41-52.

335 Lukaszewski, Jerzy. "The U.S., the West, and the Future of Eastern Europe." JOURNAL OF INTERNATIONAL AFFAIRS 22, no. 1 (1968): 16-25.

> Urges clear definition of U.S. policy in support of integration of Eastern Europe which the author somewhat unrealistically equates with an independent East Europe.

336 Mehnert, Klaus. "Westerly Winds Over Eastern Europe." In EASTERN EUROPE IN TRANSITION, edited by Kurt London, pp. 310-23. Baltimore, Md.: Johns Hopkins Press, 1966. Paperbound.

337 Mensonides, Louis J. "European Realpolitics II: Bonn's Ostpolitik." In THE FUTURE OF INTER-BLOC RELATIONS IN EUROPE, edited by Louis

J. Mensonides and James A. Kuhlman, pp. 162–80. New York; Washington, D.C.; London: Praeger, 1974.

Surveys from the postwar era to the 1970s. Considers the real beneficiary of Brandt's "Ostpolitik" to have been East Germany.

338 Merkl, Peter H. GERMAN POLICIES; WEST AND EAST: ON THE THRESHOLD OF A NEW EUROPEAN ERA. Santa Barbara, Calif.: ABC-Clio Press, 1974. ix, 232 p. Paperbound.

Summary of the foreign policies of East and West Germany taking into account the common past of this divided nation and the impact of opposing political systems since 1945.

339 "Normalization of Relations Between the Federal Republic of Germany and Eastern Europe." In EASTERN EUROPE IN THE 1970'S, edited by Sylva Sinanian et al., pp. 228–41. New York: Praeger, 1972.

A roundtable discussion of experts from West Germany, Poland, France, and the United States with emphasis on acceptance of the reality of the East German state, although the participants disagree to the extent to which this development is or is not optimistic for the security of Europe.

340 Planck, Charles R. THE CHANGING STATUS OF GERMAN REUNIFICA-TION IN WESTERN DIPLOMACY, 1955–1966. Baltimore, Md.: Johns Hopkins Press, 1967. 65 p. Paperbound.

A brief summary useful for understanding East German foreign policy.

341 Remington, Robin Alison. "Moscow, Washington, and Eastern Europe." In THE SOVIET EMPIRE: EXPANSION AND DETENTE, edited by William E. Griffith, pp. 345–82. Lexington, Mass.: Lexington Books, D.C. Heath, 1976.

342 Schroeder, Gerhard. DECISION FOR EUROPE. London: Thames and Hudson, 1964. 248 p.

Excerpts from Schroeder's speeches from the late 1940s until the early 1960s when he speaks not as a member of the Bundestag but as the Federal Republic of Germany foreign minister. Gives insight into West German policy toward both East Germany and the USSR.

343 Schutz, Wilhelm Wolfgang. RETHINKING GERMAN POLICY: NEW AP-PROACHES TO REUNIFICATION. Translated by Paul Stevenson. New York; Washington, D.C.; London: Praeger, 1967. 154 p.

A West German plea for realistic but continued pressure toward reunification of Germany. Serious implications for intra-German relations if taken seriously and a good example of the reasons for East German fears about the Federal Republic of Germany intentions.

344 Simon, Jeffrey. RULING COMMUNIST PARTIES AND DETENTE: A DOCUMENTARY HISTORY. Washington, D.C.: American Enterprise Institute for Public Policy, 1975. 314 p. Paperbound.

Directed toward undergraduates and informed general readers. Excerpts from a key of documents to party congresses; grouped according to substantive world views.

345 Skilling, H. Gordon. "Eastern Europe and the West." In THE COMMUNIST STATES AND THE WEST, edited by Adam Bromke and Philip E. Uren, pp. 35-53. New York and London: Praeger and Pall Mall Press, 1967.

346 Stehle, Hansjakob. "The Federal Republic and Eastern Europe." SURVEY: A JOURNAL OF SOVIET AND EAST EUROPEAN STUDIES, no. 61 (October 1966): 70-79.

A general summary of the mosaic of policies involved in Bonn's emerging "Ostpolitik."

347 Urban, G.R., ed. SCALING THE WALL: TALKING TO EASTERN EUROPE. Detroit: Wayne State University Press, 1964. 303 p.

A collection of broadcasts and background reports originally commissioned by Radio Free Europe and directed to managerial and intellectural elites in Eastern Europe. Insight into use of Radio Free Europe as an instrument of U.S. policy toward the region.

348 Vali, Ferenc A. THE QUEST FOR A UNITED GERMANY. Baltimore, Md.: Johns Hopkins Press, 1967. xii, 318 p.

A detailed scholarly study of the problem of German reunification from the perspective of the political actors most intimately involved: West Germany, East Germany, and the USSR. Includes a chapter on Berlin, as well as dealing with Poland, the Oder-Neisse border, and reunification.

349 Von Brentano, Heinrich. GERMANY AND EUROPE: REFLECTIONS ON GERMAN FOREIGN POLICY. Translated by Edward FitzGerald. New York: Praeger, 1962. 223 p. Paperbound.

Sections on West German policy toward East Europe and the problem of reunification.

350   Whetten, Lawrence L. GERMANY'S OSTPOLITIK: RELATIONS BETWEEN THE FEDERAL REPUBLIC OF GERMANY AND THE WARSAW PACT COUNTRIES. London: Oxford University Press, 1971. x, 244 p. Paperbound.

See no. 559a.

351   Windsor, Philip. GERMAN REUNIFICATION. London: Elek Books, 1969. 140 p.

A concise analysis of attitudes toward German reunification by key political actors in both East and West Germany within the larger East-West context.

D. CHINA AND EASTERN EUROPE

See also part II, chapter I, "Albania," p. 101, and part II, chapter VII, "Rumania," p. 177.

352   Bromke, Adam, ed. THE COMMUNIST STATES AT THE CROSSROADS: BETWEEN MOSCOW AND PEKING. Introduction by Philip E. Mosely. New York; Washington, D.C.; London: Praeger, 1965. viii, 270 p.

A collection of scholarly essays focused on the impact of the Sino-Soviet dispute upon intra-Communist relations. Combines general analysis and a country-by-country approach.

353   Dallin, Alexander, ed. DIVERSITY IN INTERNATIONAL COMMUNISM: A DOCUMENTARY RECORD, 1961-1963. New York: Columbia University Press, 1963. xliv, 867 p. Paperbound.

One hundred and twenty documents dealing with issues that have divided the international Communist movement since the Soviet twenty-second party congress in October 1961. Contains Albanian-Sino-Soviet polemics as well as East European commentary. Impressive list of documents. Unfortunately, often excerpts rather than complete texts.

354   Dziewanowski, M. Kamil. "Peking and Eastern Europe." SURVEY: A JOURNAL OF SOVIET AND EAST EUROPEAN STUDIES, no. 77 (Autumn 1970): 59-74.

Sketches the development of Chinese influence on Eastern Europe throughout the 1950s and 1960s.

355   Kux, Ernst. "Eastern Europe's Relations with Asian Communist Countries." In EASTERN EUROPE IN TRANSITION, edited by Kurt London, pp. 277-306. Baltimore, Md.: Johns Hopkins Press, 1966. Paperbound.

Primary focus on China and the Sino-Soviet split. Does deal with North Korean and North Vietnamese contacts with Eastern Europe.

356   Levesque, Jacques. LE CONFLICT SINO-SOVIETIQUE ET L'EUROPE DE
      L'EST. Montreal, Canada: Les Presses de l'Université de Montreal, 1970.
      xx, 387 p. Paperbound.

      The effects of the Sino-Soviet dispute on Soviet relations with
      Eastern Europe, focusing on Poland from 1956-59 and Rumania
      from 1960-68; the importance of nationalism and factional and
      personal struggles in Poland and Rumania affecting Warsaw and
      Bucharest's attitudes toward the Sino-Soviet dispute.

357   Mitchell, R. Judson. "The Revised 'Two Camps Doctrine' in Soviet Foreign
      Policy." ORBIS 6 (Spring 1972): 21-35.

      Reviews impact of economic decline, Czechoslovak and Ru-
      manian challenges to Moscow's authority and Chinese aliena-
      tion on Soviet foreign policy.

358   Ray, Hemen. "China's Initiatives in Eastern Europe." CURRENT SCENE:
      DEVELOPMENTS IN MAINLAND CHINA 7 (1 December 1969): 1-17.

359   Remington, Robin Alison. "China's Emerging Role in East Central Europe."
      In THE INTERNATIONAL POLITICS OF EASTERN EUROPE, edited by
      Charles Gati, pp. 82-99. New York: Praeger, 1976. Paperbound.

360   Stern, Carola [pseud.]. "Relations Between the DDR and the Chinese
      People's Republic, 1949-65." In COMMUNISM IN EUROPE, vol. 2,
      edited by William E. Griffith, pp. 97-156. Cambridge, Mass.: MIT
      Press, 1964. Paperbound.

      Focuses on East German-Chinese relations. Includes German
      imitation of Chinese methods of socializing the economy during
      the mid-1950s, diplomatic exchanges and relations during this
      period.

361   Uren, Philip E. "Economic Relations Among the Communist States."
      In THE COMMUNIST STATES AT THE CROSSROADS: BETWEEN MOSCOW
      AND PEKING, edited by Adam Bromke, pp. 199-218. New York; Wash-
      ington, D.C.; London: Praeger, 1965.

      General survey of the impact of the Sino-Soviet split on
      intrabloc economic relations. Emphasis on Rumanian positions
      within CMEA.

Chapter VII

NATIONALISM AS AN ALTERNATIVE

See also part II, chapter VIII, "Yugoslavia," p. 185, particularly regarding the Croatian crisis of 1971.

362   Barany, George. "Magyar Jew or Jewish Magyar (The Question of Jewish Assimilation in Hungary)." CANADIAN AMERICAN SLAVIC STUDIES 8 (Spring 1974): 1-44.

362a Bertsch, Gary K. NATION-BUILDING IN YUGOSLAVIA: A STUDY OF POLITICAL INTEGRATION AND ATTITUDINAL CONSENSUS. Beverly Hills, Calif.: Sage Publications, 1971. 48 p.

      Particularly useful for students of the multiethnic component as a factor in the integration process.

363   _____. VALUE CHANGE AND POLITICAL COMMUNITY: THE MULTI-NATIONAL CZECHOSLOVAK, SOVIET, AND YUGOSLAV CASES. Beverly Hills, Calif.: Sage Publications, 1974. 60 p.

363a Brock, Peter. THE SLOVAK NATIONAL AWAKENING: AN ESSAY IN THE INTELLECTUAL HISTORY OF EAST CENTRAL EUROPE. Toronto and Buffalo, N.Y.: University of Toronto Press, 1976. x, 104 p.

364   Brown, J[ames]. F. "Nationalism in Eastern Europe." In THE SOVIET UNION AND EASTERN EUROPE: A HANDBOOK, edited by George Schopflin, pp. 233-41. New York and Washington, D.C.: Praeger, 1970.

      A country-by-country survey of the influence of rising nationalism on domestic developments throughout Eastern Europe and Soviet-East European international relations.

365   Dean, Robert W. NATIONALISM AND POLITICAL CHANGE IN EASTERN EUROPE: THE SLOVAK QUESTION AND THE CZECHOSLOVAK REFORM MOVEMENT. Denver: University of Denver, 1973. 67 p.

Extensively documented. A brief but important monograph for students of multinational federalism as well as those concerned with the manifestation of East European nationalism. Author is a senior analyst for Czechoslovak and Polish Affairs at Radio Free Europe.

366 Demaitre, Edmund. "The Great Debate on National Communism." STUDIES IN COMPARATIVE COMMUNISM 5 (Summer-Autumn 1972): 234-57.

An analysis of the ideological debates between Moscow and various East European Communists on the relations between socialism, patriotism, nationalism, and internationalism. Dismisses the common assumption that Titoism may be considered a model for national communism.

367 Ezergailis, Andres. "'Monolithic' vs. 'Crumbling' Communism." PROBLEMS OF COMMUNISM 19 (January-February 1970): 1-27.

A policy-oriented analysis of the current polycentric forces within the international Communist movement. Relevant to East European intra-Communist politics. Part one of a two-part symposium entitled "International Communism: Myths, Perceptions, Policy."

368 Gyorgy, Andrew. "Competitive Patterns of Nationalism in Eastern Europe." CANADIAN SLAVONIC PAPERS 10 (Winter 1968): 557-80.

Distinguishes between deep-seated patriotic sentiments and more simplistic anti-Sovietism stemming from postwar subjection to Soviet policy dictates. Does not view anti-Sovietism as nationalism. Also discusses relationship of traditional nationalism to recurring East European international problems, such as the Macedonian question and policy toward West Germany.

369 Halasz, Nicolas. IN THE SHADOW OF RUSSIA: EASTERN EUROPE IN THE POSTWAR WORLD. New York: Ronald Press, 1959. viii, 390 p.

A background country-by-country historical analysis that moves to collective treatment in dealing with Eastern Europe during the cold war years. Considers both East European nationalism and communism as sinister forces, seeing in communism no safeguard against potentially tyrannical nationalism.

370 Hammond, Thomas T. "Nationalism and National Minorities in Eastern Europe." JOURNAL OF INTERNATIONAL AFFAIRS 20, no. 1 (1966): 9-31.

371 Janos, Andrew C. "Ethnicity, Communism and Political Change in Eastern Europe." WORLD POLITICS 23 (April 1971): 493-521.

Analytical review article.

372 _____. "Nationalism and Communism in Hungary." EAST EUROPEAN QUARTERLY 5 (March 1971): 74-103.

Traces the changing nature of Soviet and Hungarian Communist Party policy toward Hungarian nationalism from 1920 to the present.

373 Jelavich, Charles. TSARIST RUSSIA AND BALKAN NATIONALISM: RUSSIAN INFLUENCE IN THE INTERNAL AFFAIRS OF BULGARIA AND SERBIA 1876-1886. Berkeley and Los Angeles: University of California Press, 1958. x, 304 p.

Excellent historical background to the contemporary relations of these Balkan countries with the Soviet Union. Written by a leading scholar of East European history.

374 Karcz, Jerzy F. "Reflections on the Economics of Nationalism and Communism in Eastern Europe." EAST EUROPEAN QUARTERLY 5 (June 1971): 232-59.

Highly theoretical. Attempt to interpret Soviet foreign policy toward the East European states in terms of macroeconomic theory. Should be evaluated in a historical, political, and cultural context.

375 King, Robert R. MINORITIES UNDER COMMUNISM: NATIONALITIES AS A SOURCE OF TENSION AMONG BALKAN COMMUNIST STATES. Cambridge, Mass.: Harvard University Press, 1973. vii, 326 p.

One of the few studies dealing with the impact of national minorities on relations among Communist states. Deals with this problem in Southeast Europe from 1945 until the 1970s. His book is unique contribution to a little-explored area.

376 Klein, George. "The Role of Ethnic Politics in the Czechoslovak Crisis of 1968 and the Yugoslav Crisis of 1971." STUDIES IN COMPARATIVE COMMUNISM 8 (Winter 1975): 339-69.

A detailed, insightful comparison of the ethnic component of Communist crisis and crisis management.

377 Lendvai, Paul. EAGLES IN COBWEBS: NATIONALISM AND COMMUNISM IN THE BALKANS. London: Macdonald, 1969. ix, 396 p.

A well-written, country-by-country survey of Balkan communism. Particularly good on the interaction of domestic and

international developments. Postscript on the impact of the
intervention in Czechoslovakia in 1968.

378 Lengyel, Emil. NATIONALISM--THE LAST STAGE OF COMMUNISM.
New York: Funk & Wagnalls, 1969. xiv, 369 p.

A popularly written study of the ongoing conflict of native
nationalism and Communist ideology within Eastern Europe.
A good survey for the general reader.

379 Montias, J[ohn]. M[ichael]. "Economic Nationalism in Eastern Europe."
JOURNAL OF INTERNATIONAL AFFAIRS 20, no. 1 (1966): 45-71.

380 Nanay, Julia. TRANSYLVANIA: THE HUNGARIAN MINORITY IN
RUMANIA. Astor, Fla.: Danubia Press, 1976. 85 p.

381 Palmer, Stephen E., Jr., and King, Robert R. YUGOSLAV COMMUNISM
AND THE MACEDONIAN QUESTION. Hamden, Conn.: Shoe String Press,
1971. vii, 247 p. Maps.

A detailed history and analysis of the Macedonian question
from the interwar period, during World War II, and under
Yugoslav communism. Important for students of nationalism;
also valuable regarding Yugoslav-Bulgarian relations. Chapter
2 deals directly with the Macedonian issue's impact on Yugoslav
foreign policy.

382 Seton-Watson, Hugh. NATIONALISM AND COMMUNISM: ESSAYS,
1946-1963. New York: Praeger, 1964. x, 253 p.

Primarily focused on the question of revolutionary leadership.
Concerned with elite recruitment, social conditions, and personal motives that compel men and women to rebel. Part 2
articles written during the author's journeys to Eastern Europe
during the period of Communist seizure of power.

383 _____. THE "SICK HEART" OF MODERN EUROPE: THE PROBLEM OF
THE DANUBIAN LANDS. Seattle and London: University of Washington
Press, 1975. xi, 75 p.

Three lectures delivered at the University of Washington in the
fall of 1973. A thoughtful discussion of the rise and fall of
empires in the heart of Europe, concluding with the reestablishment of Russian hegemony by the Soviet Union in the post-
World War II period. Emphasis on continuation of latent, ex-
plosive nationalisms exacerbated by Soviet repression of national identities.

384 Shoup, Paul. "Communism, Nationalism and the Growth of the Communist Community of Nations After World War II." AMERICAN POLITICAL SCIENCE REVIEW 56 (December 1962): 886-98.

> An analysis of the impact of nationalism on Communist political systems that accurately predicts the direction taken not only in the 1960s but in the 1970s as well. Points to the paradox of competing modes of socialism encouraging identification of "national" institutions with universally desired ends.

385 _____. "The National Question and the Political Systems of Eastern Europe." In EASTERN EUROPE IN THE 1970'S, edited by Sylva Sinanian et al., pp. 121-70. New York: Praeger, 1972.

> Discusses the impact of nationality problems on the political systems of Eastern Europe. Good background for understanding intra-East European relations.

386 Skilling, H. Gordon. COMMUNISM, NATIONAL AND INTERNATIONAL: EASTERN EUROPE AFTER STALIN. Toronto: University of Toronto Press, 1964. ix, 168 p. Paperbound.

> Impressionistic, but insightful early statement by a recognized scholar about the pluralistic and nationalistic nature of the bloc countries with summaries of domestic politics and international relations of the states in nontechnical language.

387 Steiner, Eugen. THE SLOVAK DILEMMA. New York and London: Cambridge University Press, 1973. ix, 229 p.

> A study of the Slovaks as a nation, the interwar period, early manifestations of Slovak nationalism under communism, the purges of the 1950s, and the fate of Slovak Communists under Novotny. Concludes with a detailed analysis of the role played by Slovak nationalism in the Czechoslovak experiment with reform communism during 1968.

388 Sugar, Peter F., and Lederer, Ivo J., eds. NATIONALISM IN EASTERN EUROPE. Seattle: University of Washington Press, 1969. vii, 465 p. Paperbound.

> A collection of scholarly essays by experts in the field on the history and development of East European nationalism, the chief ideological challenge faced by the postwar Communist regimes in the region. Extremely useful for historical detail, but somewhat confusing to readers without background in the area. Best for graduate courses.

Chapter VIII
COUNCIL FOR MUTUAL
ECONOMIC ASSISTANCE (CMEA)

See also part I, chapter VI, section B, "Economic Development," p. 47.

389 Adams, Arthur E. "The Soviet Agricultural Model in Eastern Europe."
EAST EUROPEAN QUARTERLY 8 (January 1974): 462-77.

Useful introduction to impact of Soviet methods on post-World
War II agricultural development in Eastern Europe.

390 Adams, Arthur E., and Adams, Jan S. MEN VERSUS SYSTEMS. New
York: Free Press, 1971. vlii, 327 p.

Based on travel and interviews in 1957. Emphasizes the sociological impact of socialization of agriculture, evolution,
and the implementation of agricultural policies.

391 Agostin, Istvan. LE MARCHE COMMUN COMMUNISTE: PRINCIPES ET
PRATIQUE DU COMECON. Geneva: Droz, 1965. xii, 353 p. Illus.

Includes comparison of East and West integration attempts.

392 Alton, Thad Paul, et al. CZECHOSLOVAKIA'S NATIONAL INCOME
AND PRODUCTION 1947-1948 AND 1955-1956. Columbia University
East Central European Studies Series. New York and London: Columbia
University Press, 1962. xiv, 255 p.

See no. 624a.

393 _____. "Economic Growth and Resource Allocation in Eastern Europe."
In REORIENTATION AND COMMERCIAL RELATIONS OF THE ECONO-
MIES OF EASTERN EUROPE, U.S. Congress. Joint Economic Committee,
pp. 251-98. Washington, D.C.: Government Printing Office, 1974.

A detailed study of changes in the structure of East European
economic activity, rates of growth, labor and capital productivity. Important for understanding CMEA resource base.
Primarily useful to economists and political scientists.

394 Amacher, Ryan C. YUGOSLAVIA'S FOREIGN TRADE: A STUDY OF STATE TRADE DISCRIMINATION. New York: Praeger, 1972. xii, 185 p.

A detailed, quantitative analysis of Yugoslav foreign trade with the Council for Mutual Economic Assistance and the West.

395 Ausch, Sandor D. "International Division of Labor and the Present Form of Economic Mechanism in CMEA Countries." In REFORM OF THE ECONOMIC MECHANISM IN HUNGARY, edited by Istvan Friss, pp. 223-46. Budapest: Akademiai Kiado, 1971.

A Hungarian analysis of intrabloc cooperation in light of New Economic Mechanism (NEM).

396 _____. THEORY AND PRACTICE OF CMEA COOPERATION. Budapest: Akademiai Kiado, 1972. 279 p.

Written by a Hungarian economist who was a counsellor of the Council for Mutual Economic Assistance in Moscow both in 1949 and 1962-64. Examines forms, methods, and content of economic cooperation with emphasis on the techniques used by member countries for controlling their planned economies.

397 Bergson, Abram. "Development Under Two Systems: Comparative Productivity Growth Since 1950." WORLD POLITICS 24 (July 1971): 579-617.

Discusses USSR and East European postwar recovery. Deals with growth of investments, productivity, and sources of growth in the bloc. Considers that the Soviet model of economic development works but has been overrated. The author is a professor of economics at Harvard University.

398 Bird, Richard M. "COMECON and Economic Integration in the Soviet bloc." THE QUARTERLY REVIEW OF ECONOMICS AND BUSINESS 4 (Winter 1964): 37-49.

Discusses historical development, organization of foreign trade, problems and prospects. Concludes that the key steps for fuller economic integration of European Soviet-type economies have barely begun.

399 Bohtho, Andrea. FOREIGN TRADE CRITERIA IN SOCIALIST ECONOMIES. London: Cambridge University Press, 1971. viii, 176 p.

Interesting hypotheses but deals with events only until the mid-1960s.

400 Brainard, Lawrence J. "Policy Cycles in Socialist Economies: Examples from Czechoslovak Agriculture." In REORIENTATION AND COMMERCIAL RELATIONS OF THE ECONOMIES OF EASTERN EUROPE, U.S. Congress. Joint Economic Committee, pp. 214-28. Washington, D.C.:

Government Printing Office, 1974.

Section on the problems of socialist agriculture 1961-67 and post-1967 developments indicate greater weight should be placed on economic consideration. Potentially important for future Council for Mutual Economic Assistance integration patterns.

401 Brown, Alan A., and Marer, Paul. "Foreign Trade and East European Reforms." In PLAN AND MARKET: ECONOMIC REFORM IN EASTERN EUROPE, edited by Morris Bornstein, pp. 153-206. New Haven, Conn., and London: Yale University Press, 1973.

402 Brown, Alan A., et at. PRICE ADJUSTMENT MODELS FOR SOCIALIST ECONOMIC THEORY AND AN EMPIRICAL TECHNIQUE. Bloomington: Indiana University Development Research Center, 1973. 52 p.

403 Brzezinski, Zbigniew K. "The Soviet Alliance System." In THE SOVIET BLOC: UNITY AND CONFLICT, pp. 456-84. Cambridge, Mass.: Harvard University Press, 1971.

403a Burks, R.V. "The Political Hazards of Economic Reform." In REORIENTATION AND COMMERCIAL RELATIONS OF THE ECONOMIES OF EASTERN EUROPE, U.S. Congress. Joint Economic Committee, pp. 51-78. Washington, D.C.: Government Printing Office, 1974.

A detailed analysis of the implication of reforms in specific economic sectors including price reform, enterprise autonomy, agriculture, tourism, and industrial cooperation.

404 Byrson, Phillip J., and Klinkmuller, Erich. "European Integration: Constraints and Prospects." SURVEY: A JOURNAL OF EAST AND WEST STUDIES 21 (Winter-Spring 1975): 101-27.

Analyzes the obstacles to economic integration and planning from an economist's perspective. Seems to perceive specific national economic systems as "obstacles" rather than legitimate responses to historical, demographic, and political conditions.

405 Clark, Cal. "Foreign Trade as an Indicator of Political Integration in the Soviet Bloc." INTERNATIONAL STUDIES QUARTERLY 15 (September 1971): 259-95.

406 _____. "The Study of East European Integration: A 'Political' Perspective." EAST CENTRAL EUROPE II, part 2 (1975): 132-45.

407 Crawford, J.T., and Haberstoh, John. "Survey of Economic Policy Issues

in Eastern Europe: Technology, Trade and the Consumer." In REORIEN-
TATION AND COMMERCIAL RELATIONS OF THE ECONOMIES OF EAST-
ERN EUROPE, U.S. Congress. Joint Economic Committee, pp. 32-50.
Washington, D.C.: Government Printing Office, 1974.

> Covers core problems of increased dependence on the West,
> continued reliance on the Council for Mutual Economic Assis-
> tance bloc and progress toward integration, the energy crisis,
> consumer demands, and difficult planning options ahead.

408 Csikos-Nagy, Bela. "Price Planning: Content and Pattern of the Price
Plan." SOVIET STUDIES 27 (July 1975): 443-59.

> A technical discussion of the Council for Mutual Economic
> Assistance pricing policies showing the indirect fashion in
> which world market inflation penetrates East bloc economies.

409 Czeitler, Sandor. "Regulations of Foreign Trade." In REFORM OF THE
ECONOMIC MECHANISM IN HUNGARY: DEVELOPMENT 1968-1971,
edited by Otto Gado, pp. 109-30. Budapest: Akademiai Kiado, 1972.

> A discussion by the Hungarian deputy minister of foreign trade.

410 Datar, Asha L. INDIA'S ECONOMIC RELATIONS WITH THE U.S.S.R.
AND EASTERN EUROPE 1953-54 AND 1969-70. London and New York:
Cambridge University Press, 1972. xiv, 278 p.

> Evaluation of the contribution of Soviet bloc countries to
> Indian economic development. Not limited to terms of "how
> much" aid, this study also analyzes these interactions in terms
> of their effectiveness and impact. Recommended for specialists
> in the field.

411 Dewar, Margaret. SOVIET TRADE WITH EASTERN EUROPE: 1945-1949.
London and New York: Royal Institute of International Affairs, 1951.
vii, 123 p.

> Early postwar patterns in Soviet-East European trade showing
> the extent to which the USSR replaced Germany as both a
> market for and supplier of East Europe. Separate chapters on
> Bulgaria, Czechoslovakia, Hungary, Poland, Rumania, and
> Yugoslavia.

412 Dobrin, Bogoslav. BULGARIAN ECONOMIC DEVELOPMENT SINCE
WORLD WAR II. New York: Praeger, 1973. xv, 185 p.

> See no. 611a.

413 Elias, Andrew, and Searing, M.E. "A Quantitative Assessment of U.S.

Constraints on Trade with Eastern Europe and the U.S.S.R." In REORIEN-
TATION AND COMMERCIAL RELATIONS OF THE ECONOMIES OF EAST-
ERN EUROPE, U.S. Congress. Joint Economic Committee, pp. 599-661.
Washington, D.C.: Government Printing Office, 1974.

> An invaluable reference for specialists concerned with exactly
> what U.S. political restraints on trade with Communist coun-
> tries in Europe cost the American economy in dollar terms.

414 Fallenbuchl, Zbigniew M. "East European Integration: Comecon." In
REORIENTATION AND COMMERCIAL RELATIONS OF THE ECONOMIES
OF EASTERN EUROPE, U.S. Congress. Joint Economic Committee,
pp. 79-135. Washington, D.C.: Government Printing Office, 1974.

> A two-part study divided into historical analysis of COMECON
> and the actual mechanisms of integration, such as coordination
> of plans, collaboration in production, scientific and technical
> collaboration, and the importance of market forces.

415 Freedman, Robert O. ECONOMIC WARFARE IN THE COMMUNIST BLOC:
A STUDY OF SOVIET ECONOMIC PRESSURE AGAINST YUGOSLAVIA,
ALBANIA, AND COMMUNIST CHINA. New York: Praeger, 1970.
xvi, 192 p.

> Useful for understanding the economic component of power
> politics and why such tactics so frequently fail to have po-
> litical payoffs.

416 Garmarnikow, Michael. "Balance Sheet of Economic Reforms." In RE-
ORIENTATION AND COMMERCIAL RELATIONS OF THE ECONOMIES
OF EASTERN EUROPE, U.S. Congress. Joint Economic Committee,
pp. 164-213. Washington, D.C.: Government Printing Office, 1974.

> A country-by-country survey of economic reforms prior to 1968,
> during the Prague Spring, and after 1968. Underlines the on-
> going need within these economies for economic reorganization
> that, despite setbacks, no longer can be reversed. Extensive
> use of East European sources.

417 _____. "The Future of COMECON." EAST EUROPE 11 (June 1962):
3-10.

418 _____. "Industrial Cooperation: East Looks West." PROBLEMS OF
COMMUNISM 20 (May-June 1971): 41-48.

419 Gehlen, Michael. "The Integrative Process in East Europe." JOURNAL
OF POLITICS 30 (February 1968): 91-98.

420 Ginsburgs, George. "The Constitutional Foundations of the 'Socialist

Commonwealth': Some Theoretical and Organizational Principles." In THE YEARBOOK OF WORLD AFFAIRS 1973, edited by George W. Keeton and Georg Schwarzenberger, pp. 173-211. London: Stevens & Sons, 1973.

> An analysis of the key conceptual principles of the intergovernmental and nonmilitary organizations among socialist states. Includes historical survey as well as information on CMEA membership, statutes, associate membership, and withdrawal procedures.

421 Granick, David. "The Pattern of Foreign Trade in Eastern Europe and Its Relations to Economic Development." QUARTERLY JOURNAL OF ECONOMICS 68 (1954): 377-400.

422 _____. "Variations in Management of the Industrial Enterprise in Socialist Eastern Europe." In REORIENTATION AND COMMERCIAL RELATIONS OF THE ECONOMIES OF EASTERN EUROPE, U.S. Congress. Joint Economic Committee, pp. 229-47. Washington D.C.: Government Printing Office, 1974.

> Analysis of two centralized economies, Rumania and the German Democratic Republic, and two market economies, Hungary and Yugoslavia. Demonstrates wide managerial differences. Useful to students of comparative politics, particularly those interested in experiments with workers' participation.

423 Gregory, Paul R. "Some Indirect Estimates of Capital Stocks and Factor Productivity." SOVIET STUDIES 27 (January 1975): 71-85.

> A technical article useful to economists dealing with comparative economic data.

424 Gross, Herman. "Economic Integration of Eastern Europe." In ASPECTS OF MODERN COMMUNISM, edited by Richard F. Staar, pp. 143-73. Columbia: University of South Carolina Press, 1968.

> A largely negative analysis of prospects for integration and economic development within the bloc.

425 Grossman, Gregory, ed. MONEY AND PLAN: FINANCIAL ASPECTS OF EAST EUROPEAN ECONOMIC REFORMS. Berkeley and Los Angeles: University of California Press, 1968. 188 p.

> An impressive collection.

426 Haas, Ernst B., and Schmitter, Philippe C. "Economics and Differential Patterns of Political Integration: Projections about Unity in Latin America." INTERNATIONAL ORGANIZATION 18 (Autumn 1964): 705-36.

> Includes CMEA among seven integration schemes tested, con-

cluding that the chances for automatic politicization were
"possible-doubtful." One of the first systematic attempts to
deal with Communist economic integration in a broader theoretical framework.

427 Hewett, Edward A. FOREIGN TRADE PRICES IN THE COUNCIL FOR
MUTUAL ECONOMIC ASSISTANCE. New York: Cambridge University
Press, 1974. xii, 196 p.

A technical study of price structures useful in understanding
the broader question of CMEA integration.

428 _____. "Price and Resource Allocation in Intra-CMEA Trade." Paper
prepared for a conference on The Consistency and Efficiency of the Socialist Price System, University of Toronto, 8-9 March 1974.

429 Hoffman, George W. REGIONAL DEVELOPMENT STRATEGY IN SOUTH-
EAST EUROPE. New York: Praeger, 1972. xx, 322 p.

A comparative analysis of the changing economic activities in
Albania, Bulgaria, Greece, Rumania, and Yugoslavia, explained from the point of view of the decision making in development strategy; the results and regional implications of the
strategies of economic development in Socialist and non-Socialist
countries.

430 Holzman, Franklyn D. FOREIGN TRADE UNDER CENTRAL PLANNING.
Cambridge, Mass.: Harvard University Press, 1974. xiii, 436 p.

431 _____. INTERNATIONAL TRADE UNDER COMMUNISM: POLITICS
AND ECONOMICS. New York: Basic Books, 1976. xvi, 239 p.

Includes chapter on intrabloc economic relations.

431a Jamgotch, Nish, Jr. SOVIET-EAST EUROPEAN DIALOGUE: INTERNA-
TIONAL RELATIONS OF A NEW TYPE? Stanford, Calif.: Hoover Institution on War, Revolution, and Peace, 1968. 165 p.

Chapter devoted to the role of East European international
organizations includes a brief survey of the origin and development of CMEA. Uses primarily Soviet sources and appears to evaluate the Council from Moscow's perspective.

432 Jaster, R.S. "CMEA's Influence on Soviet Politics in Eastern Europe."
WORLD POLITICS 14 (April 1962): 505-18.

Discusses CMEA's changed role in interbloc relations since
Stalin's death. Views emphasis on increased scope and importance of such organizational activity as indicating fragmenta-

tion of authority within the international Communist movement.

433 Joyner, Christopher C. "The Energy Situation in Eastern Europe: Problems and Prospects." EAST EUROPEAN QUARTERLY 4 (Winter 1976): 495-516.

Survey Soviet energy trade policy with Eastern Europe, pricing and role of CMEA.

434 Kaser, Michael. COMECON. London: Oxford University Press, 1965. 203 p.

The first substantial study of East bloc integration. Still a classic in the field.

435 _____. COMECON: INTEGRATION PROBLEMS OF PLANNED ECONOMIES. 2d ed. London: Oxford University Press, 1967. vi, 215 p. Illus.

A basic scholarly study on this institution. History, prospects, and problems.

436 _____. "East European Development Aid: Comparative Record and Prospects." THE WORLD TODAY 26 (November 1970): 467-78.

One of the few analyses dealing with East European interactions with developing countries separate from Soviet policy.

437 _____. "East-West Trade--Comecon's Commerce." PROBLEMS OF COMMUNISM (July-August 1973): 1-15.

438 _____. "Trends in Industrial Management in Eastern Europe." THE WORLD TODAY 25 (June 1969): 237-46.

438a Kaser, Michael, and Zielinski, Janusz [G.]. PLANNING IN EASTERN EUROPE. London: Bodley Head, 1970. 184 p.

A study of industrial management and attempted decentralization within Eastern Europe.

439 Kidron, Michael. PAKISTAN'S TRADE WITH EASTERN BLOC COUNTRIES. New York: Praeger, 1972. xv, 130 p.

440 Kiss, Tibor. INTERNATIONAL DIVISION OF LABOUR IN OPEN ECONOMIES: WITH SPECIAL REGARD TO CMEA. Budapest: Akademiai Kiado, 1971. 322 p.

Special attention to relation of intrabloc cooperation and economic growth, foreign trade, and CMEA integration processes from the Hungarian view. Author former member of the Hungarian National Planning Office and secretary of the government's Permanent Economic Committee.

441 Kohler, Heinz. ECONOMIC INTEGRATION IN THE SOVIET BLOC: WITH AN EAST GERMAN CASE STUDY. New York: Praeger, 1965. xxi, 402 p.

A detailed, scholarly study with some problems of organization. Based on the author's dissertation.

442 Korbonski, Andrzej. "The Agricultural Problem in East Central Europe." JOURNAL OF INTERNATIONAL AFFAIRS 20, no. 1 (1966): 72-88.

443 _____. "COMECON." INTERNATIONAL CONCILIATION, no. 549 (September 1964): entire issue.

A survey of institutional structures, policies, and national attitudes within the council. Also deals with attitudes toward the EEC. Pessimistic about rapid integration in view of commitment to autarky and heavy industry on the part of member states. Expectation that sovereignty will be protected by voluntary bilateral agreements.

444 _____. "Theory and Practice of Regional Integration: The Case of COMECON." In REGIONAL INTEGRATION THEORY AND PRACTICE, edited by L.N. Lindberg and S.A. Schingold, pp. 338-73. Cambridge, Mass.: Harvard University Press, 1971.

Primarily useful to scholars of integration theory. Deals with coordination of planning, product specialization, and trade policies within the context of regional and international environments.

445 Korda, B., and Moravcik, I. "The Energy Problem in Eastern Europe and the Soviet Union." CANADIAN SLAVONIC PAPERS 18 (March 1976): 1-14.

446 Kramer, John M. "The Energy Gap in Eastern Europe." SURVEY, A JOURNAL OF EAST & WEST STUDIES 21 (Winter-Spring 1975): 65-78.

Discussion of the tensions within CMEA inherent in sharply rising costs and Eastern Europe's dependence on the Soviet Union to meet regional energy needs.

447 Lampe, John R., and Jackson, Marvin. "An Appraisal of Recent Balkan Economic Historiography." EAST EUROPEAN QUARTERLY 9 (Summer 1975): 197-240.

An excellent appraisal and bibliographic essay on economics as a discipline in Eastern Europe.

448 Laski, Kazimierz. THE RATE OF GROWTH AND THE RATE OF INTEREST IN SOCIALIST ECONOMY. Vienna and New York: Springer-Verlag, 1972. 238 p. Paperbound.

449 Laulan, Yves, ed. BANKING, MONEY, AND CREDIT IN EASTERN EUROPE--COLLOQUIUM. Brussels: NATO Information Service, 1973. 166 p. Paperbound.

Papers from a meeting of specialists 24-26 January 1973.

450 Lavigne, Marie. LE COMECON. LE PROGRAMME DU COMECON ET L'INTEGRATION SOCIALISTE. Paris: Editions Cajas, 1973. 292 p.

A general survey. Somewhat lacking in analytical method.

451 Lee, J. Richard. "Petroleum Supply Problems in Eastern Europe." In REORIENTATION AND COMMERCIAL RELATIONS OF THE ECONOMIES OF EASTERN EUROPE, U.S. Congress. Joint Economic Committee, pp. 406-20. Washington, D.C.: Government Printing Office, 1974.

A brief, excellent summary of what will be one of the key problems exacerbating relations among CMEA countries, particularly Soviet-East European relations, in the near future.

452 Machowski, Heinrich. "Toward a Socialist Economic Integration of Eastern Europe." In EASTERN EUROPE IN THE 1970'S, edited by Sylva Sinanian et al., pp. 189-200. New York: Praeger, 1972.

Somewhat cautiously concludes that progress toward economic integration among Socialist countries will depend on the desire (or lack of it) for political unity. Author is a staff member of the Deutsches Institut fur Wirtschaftsforschung in Berlin, Federal Republic of Germany.

453 Marczewski, J. CRISIS IN SOCIALIST PLANNING: EASTERN EUROPE AND THE USSR. Translated by Noel Lindsay. New York: Praeger, 1974. xvii, 247 p.

A country-by-country survey of planning and economic reforms in Eastern Europe as well as information on foreign trade within the bloc. Yugoslavia included.

454 _____. "The Role of Prices in a Planned Economy." SOVIET STUDIES 23 (July 1971): 109-19.

A readable, theoretical article.

455   Marer, Paul. POSTWAR PRICING AND PRICE PATTERNS IN SOCIALIST
FOREIGN TRADE, 1946-1971. Bloomington: International Development
Research Center, Indiana University, 1972. iv, 102 p. Paperbound.

Deals with both intra-CMEA and East-West Trade.

456   _____ . "Prospects for Integration in Eastern Europe." In POLITICAL
DEVELOPMENT IN EASTERN EUROPE, edited by Jan F. Triska and Paul [M.]
Cocks, pp. 256-74. New York: Praeger, 1977.

457   _____ . SOVIET AND EAST EUROPEAN FOREIGN TRADE, 1946-1969.
STATISTICAL COMPENDIUM AND GUIDE. Computer programs by Gary
J. Eubands. Bloomington: Indiana University Press, 1972. xviii, 408 p.

A valuable reference for East European trade data. Essential
for comparative economic analysis including European Communist states. Covers Yugoslav and Albanian data as well as
CMEA member states.

458   Matusek, Ivan. "Eastern Europe: The Political Context." In REORIEN-
TATION AND COMMERCIAL RELATIONS OF THE ECONOMIES OF EAST-
ERN EUROPE, U.S. Congress. Joint Economic Committee, pp. 17-31.
Washington, D.C.: Government Printing Office, 1974.

A current survey of the political situation in Eastern Europe
and its implications for that area's economic relations both
within the bloc and with the West.

459   Mellor, Roy E.H. COMECON: CHALLENGE TO THE WEST. New York:
Van Nostrand Reinhold, 1971. vii, 152 p. Paperbound.

460   Mieczkowski, Bogdan. PERSONAL AND SOCIAL CONSUMPTION IN
EASTERN EUROPE: POLAND, CZECHOSLOVAKIA, HUNGARY, AND
EAST GERMANY. New York: Praeger, 1975. xxiv, 342 p.

A study of consumption as an index of success of Socialist
economies. Includes comparative data from Rumania, Bulgaria,
and Yugoslavia.

460a Mitchell, R. Judson. "A Theoretical Approach to the Study of Communist
International Organizations." In COMMUNIST PARTY-STATES: COM-
PARATIVE AND INTERNATIONAL STUDIES, edited by Jan F. Triska,
pp. 81-105. Indianapolis, Ind.: Bobbs-Merrill, 1969.

461   Montias, J[ohn].M[ichael]. "Background and Origin of the Rumanian
Dispute with Comecon." SOVIET STUDIES 16 (October 1964): 125-51.

462   _____ . "Economic Nationalism in Eastern Europe: Forty Years of Con-

tinuity and Change." In EASTERN EUROPE IN TRANSITION, edited by Kurt London, pp. 173–203. Baltimore, Md.: Johns Hopkins Press, 1966. Paperbound.

463 _____. "Obstacles to the Economic Integration of Eastern Europe." STUDIES IN COMPARATIVE COMMUNISM 2 (July–October 1969): 38–60.

464 _____. "The Structure of Comecon Trade and the Prospects for East-West Exchanges." In REORIENTATION AND COMMERCIAL RELATIONS OF THE ECONOMIES OF EASTERN EUROPE, U.S. Congress. Joint Economic Committee, pp. 662–81. Washington, D.C.: Government Printing Office, 1974.

> Includes analysis of Soviet trade statistics, commodity composition of intra-CMEA trade, and some hypotheses on direction of CMEA trade in manufacturing. A useful reinterpretation for policy makers and scholars.

465 Neuberger, Egon. "International Division of Labor in CMEA: Limited Regret Strategy." AMERICAN ECONOMIC REVIEW 54 (May 1964): 506–15.

> Examines slow progress of economic integration within CMEA. First published as a RAND memorandum.

466 _____. SOVIET BLOC ECONOMIC INTEGRATION: SOME SUGGESTED EXPLANATIONS FOR SLOW PROGRESS. Santa Monica, Calif.: RAND Memorandum RM-3629-PR, July 1963. vii, 24 p.

> A preliminary study stressing those features of Soviet bloc history, political, social, and economic relations that have acted as barriers to successful integration.

467 Osborne, R.H. EAST-CENTRAL EUROPE: AN INTRODUCTORY GEOGRAPHY. New York and Washington, D.C.: Praeger, 1967. 384 p. Paperbound.

> Useful reference regarding resource base as a factor in international options.

468 Pinder, John. "The Community and Comecon: What Could Negotiations Achieve?" THE WORLD TODAY 33 (May 1977): 176–85.

469 Podolski, T.M. SOCIALIST BANKING AND MONETARY CONTROL: THE EXPERIENCE OF POLAND. London: Cambridge University Press, 1973. xii, 392 p.

> A topical study for specialists representing a solid contribution to a key aspect of centrally planned economies.

470 Pryor, Frederic L. "Barriers to Market Socialism in Eastern Europe in the Mid 1960's." STUDIES IN COMPARATIVE COMMUNISM 3 (April 1970): 31-64.

   A detailed analysis demonstrating that despite industrial reforms in most of the East European countries throughout the 1960s, the major structural and functional prerequisites for an effective socialist market system have yet to be created.

471 _____. THE COMMUNIST FOREIGN TRADE SYSTEM. Cambridge, Mass.: MIT Press, 1963. 206 p.

   A technical, thorough economists' analysis of intrabloc economic planning and organizational structures and policies. Problems of planning, trade contracts, pricing systems, and trade patterns within and without are emphasized.

472 Ranson, C.F.G. "The Future of EEC-COMECON Relations." THE WORLD TODAY 27 (October 1971): 438-48.

473 Ray, George F. "Reforms in Eastern Europe." THE WORLD TODAY 27 (December 1971): 530-40.

474 Sanders, Irwin T., ed. COLLECTIVIZATION OF AGRICULTURE IN EASTERN EUROPE. Lexington: University of Kentucky Press, 1958. x, 214 p.

   Combines area analysis with a country-specific approach. Valuable appendixes.

475 Schaefer, Henry Wilcox. COMECON AND THE POLITICS OF INTEGRATION. New York: Praeger, 1972. xiv, 200 p.

   The development of the integration program of COMECON since 1968, approached chronologically from the political point of view. A survey of intrabloc relations based on the official sources.

476 Shulman, Marshall D. "The Communist States and Western Integration." INTERNATIONAL ORGANIZATION 17 (Summer 1963): 649-62.

   Sees increased economic integration within the Soviet sphere of influence as a reaction to developments within the European Common Market. Conversely, considers the central political consequence to be a potentially expanded autonomy for East European member states.

477 Singleton, F[red].[B.]. "Finland, COMECON, and the EEC." THE WORLD TODAY 30 (February 1974): 64-72.

478   Spigler, Iancu. ECONOMIC REFORM IN RUMANIAN INDUSTRY. New
York: Oxford University Press, 1973. xxi, 176 p.

See no. 1048a.

479   Spulber, Nicolas. THE ECONOMIES OF COMMUNIST EASTERN EUROPE.
Cambridge, Mass., and New York: MIT Press and Wiley, 1957. xxviii,
525 p.

A basic economic text underlining Soviet postwar penetration
of East European economies both domestically and in terms of
foreign trade.

480   Staar, Richard F. "Economic Integration, the CMEA." In his THE COM-
MUNIST REGIMES IN EASTERN EUROPE, pp. 239-60. Stanford, Calif.:
Hoover Institution, 1977.

481   Vajda, Imre, and Simai, Mihaly, eds. FOREIGN TRADE IN A PLANNED
ECONOMY. Cambridge, Engl.: At the University Press, 1971. xii,
221 p. Illus.

A popular overview of foreign trade by CMEA countries with
particular reference to Hungary. Somewhat dated.

482   van Bradant, Jozef M.P. ESSAYS ON PLANNING; TRADE AND INTE-
GRATION IN EASTERN EUROPE. Rotterdam: Rotterdam University Press,
1974. ix, 310 p. Paperbound.

A series of essays on the myths and realities of Socialist integration. Focus on problem of prices and the difficulties of
reconciling national plans with central directions.

483   Vasilev, Dimitur. "The International Socialist Division of Labor and Its
Role in the Increased Profitability of Bulgarian Foreign Trade." EASTERN
EUROPEAN ECONOMICS 8 (Fall 1969): 90-99.

Favorable Bulgarian account of CMEA policy.

484   Welsh, William A. "Economic Change and East European Regional Integration." In THE FUTURE OF INTER-BLOC RELATIONS IN EUROPE,
edited by Louis J. Mensonides and James A. Kuhlman, pp. 105-20.
New York; Washington, D.C.; London: Praeger, 1974.

Uses content analysis and factor analysis to aid in predicting
integrative versus counter-integrative tendencies.

485   Wilczynski, Jozef. "Cybernetics, Automation and the Transition to Communism." In COMPARATIVE SOCIALIST SYSTEMS: ESSAYS ON POLITICS
AND ECONOMICS, edited by Carmelo Mesa-Lago and Carl Beck,
pp. 397-420. Pittsburgh, Pa.: University of Pittsburgh Center for International

Studies, 1975.

> Useful regarding cooperation in the development of computer technology and production.

486 _____. PROFIT, RISK, AND INCENTIVES UNDER SOCIALIST ECONOMIC PLANNING. London: Macmillan, 1973. viii, 232 p.

> An extensive treatment, valuable for specialists.

486a _____. SOCIALIST ECONOMIC DEVELOPMENT AND REFORMS: FROM EXTENSIVE TO INTENSIVE GROWTH UNDER CENTRAL PLANNING IN THE USSR, EASTERN EUROPE AND YUGOSLAVIA. New York: Praeger, 1972. xvii, 350 p.

> Considerable attention to the role of CMEA in East European economic development. Subsection dealing with intra-CMEA technological cooperation. Particularly useful to students involved in comparative economic analysis.

487 Wiles, P[eter].J.D. COMMUNIST INTERNATIONAL ECONOMICS. New York: Praeger, 1968. xvi, 566 p.

> An original, provocative study. Points to difficulties that must arise in intra-CMEA trade in the absence of supranational planning.

488 _____. "Foreign Trade in Eastern Europe: A Summary Appraisal." In INTERNATIONAL TRADE AND CENTRAL PLANNING, edited by Alan A. Brown and Egon Neuberger, pp. 166-73. Berkeley and Los Angeles: University of California Press, 1968.

489 Wszelaki, Jan. COMMUNIST ECONOMIC STRATEGY: THE ROLE OF EAST-CENTRAL EUROPE. Foreword by Henry G. Aubrey. Washington, D.C.: National Planning Association, 1959. xii, 132 p.

> An analysis of East Central European capabilities within the network of Soviet foreign relations, in which East European resources are viewed as an extention of Soviet options. Until 1945, author a member of the Polish Foreign Service.

490 Zauberman, Alfred. INDUSTRIAL DEVELOPMENT IN CZECHOSLOVAKIA, EAST GERMANY, AND POLAND, 1937-1956. Oxford: Oxford University Press, 1958. 70 p.

> A summary comparison of the three industrial countries in Eastern Europe.

491 _____. INDUSTRIAL PROGRESS IN POLAND, CZECHOSLOVAKIA, AND EAST GERMANY 1937-1962. London, New York, Toronto: Oxford Uni-

versity Press, 1964. xiv, 338 p.

Comparative economic analysis showing differences between prewar period and postwar Communist consolidation. Chapter 7 deals with foreign economic relations, including trade, pricing, and mechanism of integration within the Eastern bloc.

492 Zsoldos, Laszlo. THE ECONOMIC INTEGRATION OF HUNGARY INTO THE SOVIET BLOC. Columbus: Ohio University Press, 1963. xvii, 149 p.

An academic study covering a decade of Hungary's foreign trade relations with the Soviet bloc and the West. Also deals with the impact of trade policies and decisions on domestic developments.

Chapter IX

THE WARSAW TREATY ORGANIZATION (WTO)

493 Alton, Thad Paul, et al. "Military Expenditures in Eastern Europe: Some Alternate Estimates." In REORIENTATION AND COMMERCIAL RELATIONS OF THE ECONOMIES OF EASTERN EUROPE, U.S. Congress. Joint Economic Committee, pp. 299-327. Washington, D.C.: Government Printing Office, 1974.

> A valuable, although not totally successful, attempt to make the military expenditures throughout Eastern Europe meaningful for comparative purposes. A useful reference.

494 Bender, Peter. EAST EUROPE IN SEARCH OF SECURITY. Baltimore, Md.: Johns Hopkins Press, 1972. x, 144 p. Paperbound.

> Translated from the German, a survey of the security policies with regard to Europe of the Warsaw Pact countries, with emphasis on the special circumstances of each country which affects its attitudes toward security. A brief analysis of the meaning of security for each of the countries concerned. Followed by a country-by-country breakdown of the security from the East European point of view, considering the historical background, dangers, basic principles of the policy and the prospects; focusing on the lack of unity in security policies in Eastern Europe.

495 _____. "Inside the Warsaw Pact." SURVEY: A JOURNAL OF SOVIET AND EAST EUROPEAN STUDIES, nos. 74-75 (Winter-Spring 1970): 253-68.

> A country-by-country summary of the security problems uppermost on the mind of Warsaw Pact member states. Emphasis on differently perceived military-political needs.

496 Birnbaum, Karl E. "The Member States of the Warsaw Treaty Organization (WTO) and the Conference on Security and Cooperation in Europe (CSCE): Current Preoccupations and Expectations." COOPERATION AND CONFLICT: NORDIC JOURNAL OF INTERNATIONAL POLITICS, no. 1 (1974): 29-34.

Deals with Soviet-Rumanian differences that surfaced during
the course of multilateral negotiations in 1973. Concludes
that the impact of the European Security Conference on intra-
alliance relations is likely to be marginal and long-term.

497 Bromke, Adam. "The CSCE and Eastern Europe." THE WORLD TODAY
29 (May 1973): 196-205.

Discusses the different attitudes toward security in East and
West. Considers likely effect of relaxation of tension to be
moving Eastern Europe closer to the West, despite continued
Soviet reluctance to give up the region as a sphere of influence.

498 Brown, J[ames]. F. "Detente and Soviet Policy in Eastern Europe."
SURVEY: A JOURNAL OF EAST & WEST STUDIES 20 (Spring-Summer
1974): 46-58.

A general analysis with special attention to the implications
of detente for Soviet policy towards Rumania and Hungary.

499 Brown, Kent N. "Coalition Politics and Soviet Influence in Eastern Europe." In POLITICAL DEVELOPMENT IN EASTERN EUROPE, edited by
Jan F. Triska and Paul [M.] Cocks, pp. 241-55. New York: Praeger,
1977.

500 Brzezinski, Zbigniew K. "The Soviet Alliance System." In THE SOVIET
BLOC: UNITY AND CONFLICT, pp. 456-84. Cambridge, Mass.: Harvard University Press, 1971.

500a Caldwell, Lawrence T. "CSCE, MFR, and Eastern Europe." In THE
INTERNATIONAL POLITICS OF EASTERN EUROPE, edited by Charles
Gati, pp. 173-88. New York: Praeger, 1976.

501 _____. "The Warsaw Pact: Directions of Change." PROBLEMS OF
COMMUNISM 24 (September-October 1975): 1-19.

Analysis of impact of the 1969 reforms and current organizational arrangements within the Warsaw Pact. Touches briefly
on the East European perspective.

502 Clemens, Walter C., Jr. "The Changing Warsaw Pact." EAST EUROPE
17 (June 1968): 7-12.

Sees West German initiatives, Rumanian attempts at alliance
reform, and Czechoslovak policy under Dubcek having potentially weakened the Warsaw Treaty Organization. Considers
the pact increasingly viewed by Moscow as an instrument for
maintaining political solidarity.

503 _____. "The European Alliance Systems: Exploitation or Mutual Aid?"
In THE INTERNATIONAL POLITICS OF EASTERN EUROPE, edited by
Charles Gati, pp. 217-36. New York: Praeger, 1976. Paperbound.

504 _____. "The Future of the Warsaw Pact." ORBIS 11 (Winter 1968):
996-1033.

Discusses the interplay of endogenous and exogenous forces
influencing future developments within the East bloc alliance.
Gives primary weight to East European domestic stability,
Soviet reaction to pressures for expanding decision-making
power within the pact, and latent vs. active nationalism as
a defining factor in Soviet-East European relations. Emphasis
on implications for U.S. policy.

505 _____. "NATO and the Warsaw Pact: Comparisons and Contrasts."
PARAMETERS 4, no. 2 (1974): 13-22.

Breaks down and evaluates the Soviet perception of the differences between the Warsaw Pact and NATO as put forward by
Marshal Ivan I. Yakubovsky, commander-in-chief of the Joint
Armed Forces of the Warsaw Treaty Organization, in Russian
sources after the April 1974 meeting of the political consulta-
tive committee of the Warsaw Pact.

506 Cohen, S.T., and Lyons, W.C. "A Comparison of U.S.-Allied and
Soviet Tactical Nuclear Forces Capabilities and Policies." ORBIS 19
(Spring 1975): 72-92.

A review of current nuclear tactical capabilities.

507 Dinerstein, Herbert S. "The Future of Ideology in Alliance Systems."
JOURNAL OF INTERNATIONAL AFFAIRS 25, no. 2 (1971): 238-65.

508 Donaldson, Robert H. "An Analysis of the Warsaw Pact Conference Proposal." In THE FUTURE OF INTER-BLOC RELATIONS, edited by Louis
J. Mensonides and James A. Kuhlman, pp. 66-101. New York; Washington, D.C.; London: Praeger, 1974.

A historical analysis of the Warsaw Pact's campaign for a European Security Conference. Good background survey for students and scholars who were interested as the Helsinki European
Security Conference drew near, but who had not been following the zig-zag progress toward such a meeting since it was
first suggested in 1954.

509 Dzirkals, Lilita, and Johnson, A. Ross, eds. SOVIET AND EAST EURO-
PEAN FORECASTS OF EUROPEAN SECURITY: PAPERS FROM THE 1972
VARNA CONFERENCE. Santa Monica, Calif.: RAND Memorandum

R-1272-PR, June 1973. v, 51 p.

A useful collection of public Warsaw Pact and Yugoslav views on present and future military, political, and economic aspects of European security. Presents both an analysis of the current European situation and a ten-year forecast.

510 Erickson, John. "The Military Potential of the Warsaw Pact Countries." In THE SOVIET UNION AND EASTERN EUROPE: A HANDBOOK, edited by George Schopflin, pp. 178-90. New York and Washington, D.C.: Praeger, 1970.

Discusses post-Khrushchev policies, Soviet offensive and defensive strategic forces, Warsaw Pact organization, and the development of military and political integration within the alliance. Author is professor of politics (defence studies) at the University of Edinburgh.

511 _____. "Soviet Military Posture and Policy in Europe." In SOVIET STRATEGY IN EUROPE, edited by Richard [B.] Pipes, pp. 162-209. New York: Crane, Russak, 1976.

512 Ermarth, Fritz. INTERNATIONALISM, SECURITY, AND LEGITIMACY: THE CHALLENGE TO SOVIET INTERESTS IN EAST EUROPE, 1964-1968. Santa Monica, Calif.: RAND Memorandum RM-5909-PR, 1969. 162 p.

See no. 677a.

513 Forster, Thomas M. THE EAST GERMAN ARMY: A PATTERN OF A COMMUNIST MILITARY ESTABLISHMENT. Introduction by Brigadier W.K.F. Thompson. Translated by Anthony Buzek. London: Allen and Unwin, 1967. 255 p. Black and white illus.

See no. 773a.

514 Fowler, Col. Delbert M. "How Many Divisions? A NATO-Warsaw Pact Assessment." MILITARY REVIEW 52 (November 1972): 76-88.

Written on the assumption that numbers are a key factor in deterring aggression by Warsaw Pact troops in Europe. Discusses manpower needed to retain a relative balance of forces.

514a Franck, Thomas M., and Weisband, Edward. WORD POLITICS: VERBAL STRATEGY AMONG THE SUPERPOWERS. New York: Oxford University Press, 1972. xiii, 176 p. Paperbound.

A well-written, thoughtful analysis of the justifications for superpower intervention into the internal affairs of its "client states" using crises taken from both East and West experience.

515 Garder, M. "Der Warschauer Pakt im System der sowjetischen Aussen-

politik." EUROPA ARCHIV (December 1966): 895-904.

516 Garthoff, Raymond L. SOVIET MILITARY POLICY: A HISTORICAL ANALYSIS. New York and Washington, D.C.: Praeger, 1966. viii, 276 p.

> Subsection on Soviet military relations with Eastern Europe on a country-by-country basis, 1945-65, briefly describes the Warsaw Pact. Emphasis on origin, organization, military maneuvers. Based on the assumption that East European armies would be incorporated into Soviet forces in time of war.

517 Haigh, Patricia. "Reflections on the Warsaw Pact." THE WORLD TODAY 24 (April 1968): 166-72.

> Sees the Eastern alliance as a compromise between principles of bilateralism and federalism that has potential value as a genuine multilateral coalition acting as a forum for discussion and coordination of regional problems.

518 Herspring, Dale R. EAST GERMAN CIVIL-MILITARY RELATIONS: THE IMPACT OF TECHNOLOGY, 1949-1972. Foreword by Peter C. Ludz. New York: Praeger, 1973. xxxvii, 216 p.

> See no. 779.

519 Hinaman, Robert T., and Kling, Nancy M. "Military Spending in Eastern Europe." In ECONOMIC DEVELOPMENTS IN COUNTRIES OF EASTERN EUROPE, U.S. Congress. Joint Economic Committee, pp. 338-47. Washington, D.C.: Government Printing Office, 1970.

> A general view of the size, structure, and funding of the defense establishments of six presently active East European members of the Warsaw Pact. Good background for understanding the size and trends of East European military programs.

520 Hinterhoff, Eugene. "The Warsaw Pact." MILITARY REVIEW 42 (June 1962): 89-94.

> Brief discussion of the 1961 Warsaw Pact maneuvers in the context of speculation on the reliability of East European forces to the Soviet Union in the event of war in Europe. Deals with nature, organization, and control function of the alliance. Originally published in West Germany in WEHR UND WIRTSCHAFT, December 1961.

521 Holloway, David. "The Warsaw Pact in the Era of Negotiation." MILITARY REVIEW 53 (July 1973): 49-55.

> An academic analysis of the changing nature of the Warsaw

Pact toward an alliance that on foreign policy issues functions as much more than a transmission belt indicating Soviet wishes to its East European subordinates. Cites East German and Rumanian examples. Also deals with the importance of the 1969 reorganization of the alliance.

522 Jacobsen, C.G. SOVIET STRATEGY-SOVIET FOREIGN POLICY: MILITARY CONSIDERATIONS AFFECTING SOVIET POLICY MAKING. Glasgow: Robert MacLebose, 1972. 236 p.

An academic analysis of Soviet strategic debates and their implications for Russian foreign policy. Concluding chapter deals with the Warsaw Pact and potential integration of East European forces into the Soviet command structure.

522a Jain, Jagdish, comp. DOCUMENTARY STUDY OF THE WARSAW PACT. New York: Asia Publishing House, 1973. xxi, 413 p.

523 Jamgotch, Nish, Jr. SOVIET-EAST EUROPEAN DIALOGUE: INTERNATIONAL RELATIONS OF A NEW TYPE? Stanford, Calif.: Hoover Institution Press, 1968. 165 p.

Chapter devoted to the role of East European international organizations includes a subsection on the Warsaw Treaty Organization as an instrument of Soviet policy.

524 Johnson, A. Ross. "Has Eastern Europe Become a Liability to the Soviet Union? (II) The Military Aspect." In THE INTERNATIONAL POLITICS OF EASTERN EUROPE, edited by Charles Gati, pp. 37-57. New York: Praeger, 1976. Paperbound.

Interesting analysis of domestic-foreign policy linkages and their implications for East European military establishments.

525 _____. THE WARSAW PACT 'EUROPEAN SECURITY' CAMPAIGN. Santa Monica, Calif.: RAND Memorandum R-565-PR, November 1970. 88 p.

An analysis of the political and military implications for NATO of the Soviet bloc's proposal for a European Security Conference. Examines the Warsaw Pact's specific proposals and interpretations related to the security of Europe. Emphasis on the new elements in the post-March 1969 "campaign" for the conference.

526 Kaiser, Karl. "USA and European Security." SURVEY: A JOURNAL OF EAST & WEST STUDIES 19 (Spring 1973): 11-39.

Analyzes the types of threats possibly posed by the Warsaw Pact, the nature and impact of U.S. military force, West

European defense efforts, and the changing U.S. role in West European support.

527 King, Robert R., and Dean, Robert W., eds. EAST EUROPEAN PERSPEC-TIVES ON EUROPEAN SECURITY AND COOPERATION. New York: Praeger, 1974. xxi, 254 p.

Essays by Radio Free Europe analysts.

528 Kinter, William R. "The Warsaw Pact and Western Security." In AS-PECTS OF MODERN COMMUNISM, edited by Richard F. Staar, pp. 173-92. Columbia: University of South Carolina Press, 1968.

Concerned with the role of the Warsaw Pact in Soviet policy, military potential of the alliance, and its relation to NATO. Suspects Rumanian "independent policy" of being a Trojan horse to deceive the West. Strong cold war analysis.

529 Kinter, William R., and Klaiber, Wolfgang. EASTERN EUROPE AND EUROPEAN SECURITY. Foreword by William E. Griffith. New York: Dunellen, 1971. xix, 303 p. Paperbound.

Comparative approach toward the changing relations between the Soviet Union and East Europe. Also discusses West German Ostpolitik in the security context.

530 Kinter, William R., and Scott, Harriet Fast, eds. THE NUCLEAR REVO-LUTION IN SOVIET MILITARY AFFAIRS. Norman: University of Okla-homa Press, 1967. xiii, 420 p.

A collection of key articles and speeches by high-ranking Soviet military officials dealing with the impact of nuclear weapons on strategic thinking in the Kremlin. Scattered ref-erences to the Warsaw Pact are a better indication of Soviet preferences than political reality. Valuable reference for scholars unable to use Russian sources in the original.

531 Kiraly, Bela. "Why the Soviets Need the Warsaw Pact." EAST EUROPE 18 (April 1969): 8-17.

A survey of Soviet goals vis-à-vis the Warsaw Pact since its origin in 1955. Points to the shift in the pact's original ob-jective of gaining a counterpart to NATO to the alliance's current value in Europe should the Sino-Soviet dispute tie down Soviet forces on the Eastern front. Emphasis on control function with respect to Moscow's East European buffer states.

532 Klaiber, Wolfgang. "Security Priorities in Eastern Europe." PROBLEMS OF COMMUNISM 19 (May-June 1970): 32-44.

Discusses the gains to East European countries from the Warsaw
Pact's all-European security policy. Emphasis on Rumania,
Hungary, Poland, and East Germany.

533 Kolkowicz, Roman. "The Warsaw Pact: Entangling Alliance." SURVEY:
A JOURNAL OF SOVIET AND EAST EUROPEAN STUDIES 70-71 (Winter-
Spring 1969): 86-101.

An analysis of the increasing importance of the Warsaw Pact
in Soviet policy within the Communist bloc. Emphasis on the
alliance as an institutional instrument serving Soviet national
interests.

534 _____, ed. "The Warsaw Pact." Report on a Conference on the Warsaw
Treaty Organization held at the Institute for Defense Analyses, 17-19 May
1967. IDA Research Paper P-496. Arlington, Va.: Institute for Defense
Analyses, 1969. 190 p. Multilith.

A collection of scholarly papers. Deals with the WTO as an
instrument of Soviet policy; structure, organization, and problems of integration within the alliance; relationship of the
WTO to the future of Europe.

535 Korbonski, Andrzej. "The Warsaw Pact." INTERNATIONAL CONCILIA-
TION, no. 573 (May 1969): 73 p.

A survey of the origins, institutional framework, military activity, and political purposes of the Warsaw Pact. Sees ero-
sion in Soviet control of the alliance but remains dubious
about any transformation of the alliance into "a truly free
association."

536 Laux, Jeanne Kirk. "Intra-Alliance Politics and European Detente: The
Case of Poland and Rumania." STUDIES IN COMPARATIVE COMMU-
NISM 8 (Spring-Summer 1975): 98-122.

537 Legvold, Robert. "The Problem of European Security." PROBLEMS OF
COMMUNISM 23 (January-February 1974): 13-33.

An analysis of Soviet conceptions of security that includes
emphasis on the importance of Eastern Europe for Moscow's
security considerations. Discusses Soviet goals for the Warsaw
Pact, also vis-à-vis the multilateral negotiating forums of the
1975 European Security Conference and ongoing discussions of
force reductions (MBFR).

538 Mackintosh, Malcolm. "The Evolution of the Warsaw Pact." ADELPHI
PAPERS 58 (1969). 25 p.

A concise summary of the origins, structure, and development
of the Warsaw Pact. Brief discussion of the pact during the

Czechoslovak crisis of 1968, and the implications for future intra-alliance developments. Useful appendixes.

539 _____. "The Warsaw Pact Today." SURVIVAL 16 (May-June 1974): 122-26.

Concise summary of post-1969 reforms. Considers creation of the Military Council an improvement from the East European perspective despite continued Soviet dominance within the alliance.

540 Pool, Ithiel de Sola, et al. SATELLITE GENERALS: A STUDY OF MILITARY ELITES IN THE SOVIET SPHERE. Stanford, Calif.: Stanford University Press, 1955. vi, 165 p.

Survey of careers of generals in Czechoslovakian, Polish, Rumanian, Hungarian, and Chinese armies. Interesting for evidence of the extent to which East European command structures were integrated into the Soviet system before creation of the Warsaw Pact in 1955.

541 Povolny, Mojmir. "The Soviet Union and the European Security Conference." ORBIS 18 (Spring 1974): 201-30.

A review of Soviet efforts to promote a European Security Conference from a somewhat dated perspective on Soviet motives.

542 Rattinger, Hans. "Armaments, Detente, and Bureaucracy: The Case of the Arms Race in Europe." JOURNAL OF CONFLICT RESOLUTION 19 (December 1975): 571-94.

Explores extent to which defense spending of NATO and WTO European member states can be characterized as an action-reaction process.

543 Reitz, Col. James T. "The Satellite Armies." MILITARY REVIEW 45 (October 1965): 28-35.

Emphasis on Sovietization, standardization, and modernization of East European forces within the Warsaw Pact. Viewed as essentially a conventional adjunct to Soviet armed forces. Author formerly served as chief of the army section, Soviet Bloc Research, Defense Intelligence Agency.

544 Remington, Robin Alison. "The Changing Soviet Perception of the Warsaw Pact." Cambridge, Mass.: MIT Center for International Studies, November 1967. 157 p. Multilith.

A study of the changing role of the Warsaw Pact in Soviet policy toward Eastern Europe. Concludes that the evolution is away from use of that organization as a mechanism for control and in the direction of an institutional forum for conflict resolution among the member states.

545 _____. "Czechoslovakia: Multilateral Intervention." In COMPARATIVE DEFENSE POLICY, edited by Frank B. Horton III et al., pp. 511-23. Baltimore, Md., and London: Johns Hopkins Press, 1974.

A survey of the Warsaw Pact's role in the "allied socialist" intervention into the internal affairs of Czechoslovakia in August 1968. Based on the assumption that action on the part of members of an alliance does not imply automatic institutional sanction in either East or West.

546 _____. THE WARSAW PACT: CASE STUDIES IN COMMUNIST CONFLICT RESOLUTION. Cambridge, Mass.: MIT Press, 1971. xix, 268 p. Paperbound.

An analysis of how the Communist regional defense organization responded to conflict among its member states using data involving intra-alliance crises from 1956 to the 1970s. Emphasis on increased sophistication of East European organizational maneuvering and its interaction with the changing perception of the need for uniformity in Moscow. Useful to student of international organization, international relations, and comparative politics.

547 _____. "The Warsaw Pact: Communist Coalition Politics in Action." In THE YEARBOOK OF WORLD AFFAIRS 1973, edited by George W. Keeton and Georg Schwarzenberger, pp. 153-73. London: Stevens & Sons, 1973.

Current summary of the politics of intra-Communist conflict as manifested within the Warsaw Pact. Emphasis on the changing nature of the alliance and its role in European politics.

548 Robinson, William F. "Czechoslovakia and its Allies: Part I January-June 1968." STUDIES IN COMPARATIVE COMMUNISM 1 (July-October 1968): 141-70.

549 Shirk, Col. Paul R. "The Warsaw Treaty Organization." MILITARY REVIEW 49 (May 1969): 28-37.

Emphasis that the Warsaw Pact faces a period of uncertainty, even crisis, due to the professionalization of East European armies to such an extent that they will potentially demand a greater decision-making role within the alliance. Speculates that the intervention in Czechoslovakia will retard such a development, making still more difficult equal relations within the pact.

550 Staar, Richard F. "The East European Alliance." UNITED STATES NA-
VAL INSTITUTE PROCEEDINGS, no. 9 (September 1964): 26-39.

551 _____. "Military Constraints in East-West Relations." In THE FUTURE
OF INTER-BLOC RELATIONS IN EUROPE, edited by Louis J. Mensonides
and James A. Kuhlman, pp. 49-65. New York; Washington, D.C.;
London: Praeger, 1974.

   Discusses problems inherent in Mutual Balanced Force Reduction
   (MBFR) negotiations between NATO and Warsaw Pact states.
   Emphasis on need for reciprocity, including foreign as well as
   national troops, and verification. Not optimistic about perspectives.

552 _____. "Military Integration: The Warsaw Treaty Organization." In
his THE COMMUNIST REGIMES IN EASTERN EUROPE. pp. 213-38.
Stanford, Calif.: Hoover Institution on War, Revolution, and Peace,
1977. Paperbound.

553 _____. "The Warsaw Treaty Organization." In ALLIANCES: LATENT
WAR COMMUNITIES IN THE CONTEMPORARY WORLD, edited by Francis
A. Beer, pp. 158-84. New York: Holt, Rinehart and Winston, 1970.

   A traditional analysis, focusing on the history and military
   aspects of the Warsaw Treaty Organization. Emphasis on
   Soviet control of that institution.

554 Starr, Harvey. "A Collective Goods Analysis of the Warsaw Pact After
Czechoslovakia." INTERNATIONAL ORGANIZATION 28 (Summer 1974):
521-32.

   Analysis of the Warsaw Pact using contemporary political science models to determine extent to which national interests of
   member states are realized. Unfortunately, based on the in-
   correct assumption that the 1968 invasion of Czechoslovakia
   was a Warsaw Pact operation. Useful for methodology not
   substance.

555 Turbiville, Graham H. "Warsaw Pact Exercise Shield-72." MILITARY
REVIEW 53 (July 1973): 17-24.

   A detailed discussion of the Warsaw Pact September 1972 maneuvers, dealing with the objectives, tactics, equipment, and
   importance of these military exercises.

556 Tykocinski, Wadysaw. "Poland's Plans for the 'Northern Tier.'" EAST
EUROPE 15 (November 1966): 9-16.

   A former chief of the Polish Mission in West Berlin discusses
   Polish "triangle policy" within Soviet bloc, a plan that en-
   visioned tripartite cooperation amounting to a loose federation

between Poland, East Germany, and Czechoslovakia. Spells out implications of this attitude for Polish-West German relations. Author defected in May 1965.

557 Ulam, Adam B. "The Destiny of Eastern Europe." PROBLEMS OF COM-MUNISM 23 (January-February 1974): 1-12.

Deals with impact of detente on East Europe, on both a regional and country-specific basis. Pessimistic about convergence or lessening of authoritarian controls.

558 von Krannhals, Hanns. "Command Integration Within the Warsaw Pact." MILITARY REVIEW 41 (May 1961): 40-52.

A country-by-country analysis of the problems initially faced by the Soviets in their attempts to integrate East European forces into a unified command. Warsaw Pact is considered to have been the culmination rather than the beginning of the integration process. Originally published in West Germany in WEHRWISSENSCHAFFTLICHE RUNDSCHAU, January 1961.

559 Washburn, John N. "The Current Legal Status of Warsaw Pact Membership." INTERNATIONAL LAWYER 5 (January 1971): 129-34.

Discusses the legal effect of Albanian denunciation and withdrawal from the Warsaw Pact following intervention of the "fraternal" forces of "allied socialist countries" in Czechoslovakia in 1968. Political rather than legal judgment.

559a Whetten, Lawrence L. GERMANY'S OSTPOLITIK: RELATIONS BETWEEN THE FEDERAL REPUBLIC OF GERMANY AND THE WARSAW PACT COUNTRIES. London: Oxford University Press, 1971. x, 244 p. Paperbound.

A concise, reliable analysis of West German relations with East Europe. Useful regarding European security and the Warsaw Pact.

560 _____. "Recent Changes in East European Approaches to European Security." THE WORLD TODAY 26 (July 1970): 277-88.

A brief historical survey followed by a discussion of the differences in attitude toward European security among East European countries. Advocates progress on a bilateral basis.

561 Windsor, Philip. GERMANY AND THE MANAGEMENT OF DETENTE. London: Chatto and Windus for the Institute for Strategic Studies, 1971. 207 p.

See chapter 5 for a good analysis of the economic and political impact of detente in Eastern Europe.

562 _____. "Security Seen From the East." In THE SOVIET UNION AND EASTERN EUROPE: A HANDBOOK, edited by George Schopflin, pp. 167-77. New York and Washington, D.C.: Praeger, 1970.

Emphasis on the role played by relations with Germany on East European perceptions of European security. Puts the Soviet-East European-German triangular international relations into sharp relief.

563 Wolfe, Thomas W. ROLE OF THE WARSAW PACT IN SOVIET POLICY. Santa Monica, Calif.: RAND Memorandum P-4973, March 1973. 19 p.

Explores prospects for major change in Soviet policy toward the alliance.

564 _____. SOVIET ATTITUDES TOWARD MBFR AND THE USSR'S MILITARY PRESENCE IN EUROPE. Santa Monica, Calif.: RAND Memorandum P-4819, April 1972. 17 p.

Does not consider significant changes in Soviet attitudes likely. Useful regarding arms control aspects of the European Security Conference and mutual force reduction (MBFR) negotiations.

565 _____. "Soviet Military Capabilities and Intentions in Europe." In SOVIET STRATEGY IN EUROPE, edited by Richard [B.] Pipes, pp. 129-67. New York: Crane, Russak, 1976.

566 _____. THE SOVIET UNION'S STRATEGIC AND MILITARY STAKES IN THE GDR. Santa Monica, Calif.: RAND Memorandum P-4549, January 1971. 19 p.

Considers the trade-offs involved in Moscow's desired detente from the perspective of Soviet-East German military relations.

567 _____. "The Warsaw Pact in Evolution." THE WORLD TODAY 22 (May 1966): 191-98.

Analysis of the change in the character and potential of the Warsaw Pact. Considers military upgrading has paralleled Soviet emphasis on garrison and control function of their troops in Eastern Europe.

568 Zimmerman, William. "Hierarchical Regional Systems and the Politics of System Boundaries." INTERNATIONAL ORGANIZATION 26 (Winter 1972): 18-36.

A theoretical analysis comparing the Organization of American States and the Warsaw Pact in order to achieve a better understanding of when a member state's attitudes toward system boundaries are determined by international variables, and when they are explained by domestic structures. Provocative and useful to students of international relations and regional politics.

Part II

COUNTRY-SPECIFIC SOURCES

Chapter I

ALBANIA

569 Brown, J[ames].F. "Albania, Mirror of Conflict." SURVEY: A JOUR-
NAL OF SOVIET AND EAST EUROPEAN STUDIES, no. 40 (January 1962):
24-41.

A good early discussion of Tirana's break with Moscow and
turn toward Peking.

570 Costa, Nicolas J. "Invasion--Action and Reaction Albania, As a Case
Study." EAST EUROPEAN QUARTERLY 10 (Spring 1976): 53-63.

Analysis of the 1939 Italian invasion of Albania.

571 Dallin, Alexander. "The Albanian Crisis." In his DIVERSITY IN INTER-
NATIONAL COMMUNISM: A DOCUMENTARY RECORD, 1961-1963,
pp. 85-200. New York: Columbia University Press, 1963. Paperbound.

Documents dealing with the early stage of the Soviet-Albanian
split in 1961-62. Includes a number of "verbal notes" concerning the withdrawal of ambassadors and other embassy staff
members as well as Tirana's protest at being excluded from
Warsaw Treaty Organization meetings.

572 Djilas, Milovan. CONVERSATIONS WITH STALIN. New York: Harcourt, Brace, 1962. 211 p. Paperbound.

Insightful regarding Albanian-Yugoslav relations during the
civil war. See also no. 1209.

572a Freedman, Robert O. ECONOMIC WARFARE IN THE COMMUNIST BLOC:
A STUDY OF SOVIET ECONOMIC PRESSURE AGAINST YUGOSLAVIA,
ALBANIA, AND COMMUNIST CHINA. New York: Praeger, 1970.
xvi, 192 p.

See no. 415.

573 Gilberg, Trond. "Yugoslavia, Albania, and Eastern Europe." In THE INTERNATIONAL POLITICS OF EASTERN EUROPE, edited by Charles Gati, pp. 103-23. New York: Praeger, 1976. Paperbound.

574 Griffith, William E. ALBANIA AND THE SINO-SOVIET RIFT. Cambridge, Mass.: MIT Press, 1963. xv, 407 p. Paperbound.

> The fundamental documentary dealing with the Soviet-Albanian split.

575 Hamm, Harry. ALBANIA--CHINA'S BEACHHEAD IN EUROPE. Translated by Victor Andersen. New York: Praeger, 1963. x, 176 p.

> A journalistic analysis of the history, factors, and progression of the Soviet-Albanian dispute. Emphasis on growing Chinese influence in Tirana. Written by a West German reporter, one of the few Western journalists allowed to visit Albania.

576 Lendvai, Paul. "Albania: A Traditional Fuse to the Balkan Powder Keg." In his EAGLES IN COBWEBS: NATIONALISM AND COMMUNISM IN THE BALKANS, pp. 173-206. London: Macdonald, 1969.

> Discussion of Albanian evolution from Tirana's postwar position as a Yugoslav satellite to the country's alliance with China that precipitated the Soviet-Albanian split in the early 1960s.

577 Logoreci, Anton. "Albania: The Anabaptists of European Communism." PROBLEMS OF COMMUNISM 16 (May-June 1967): 22-28.

> Brief overview of the Albanian-Soviet split, Chinese support of Tirana, and Albanian internal politics through 1965.

578 Marmullaku, Ramadan. ALBANIA AND THE ALBANIANS. Translated from the Serbo-Croatian by Margot and Bosko Milosavljevic. Hamden, Conn.: Archon Books, 1975. x, 178 p.

> Deals with Albanian relations with the West, the Balkans, and the Socialist camp. Part 3 devoted to the Albanians in Yugoslavia. Largely based on Yugoslav sources. Author a Yugoslav official of Albanian ethnic origin.

579 Meier, Viktor. "The Political Dynamics of the Balkans in 1974." In THE WORLD AND THE GREAT-POWER TRIANGLE, edited by William E. Griffith, pp. 34-84. Cambridge, Mass., and London: MIT Press, 1975.

> See no. 1117c.

580 Pano, Nicholas C. "The Albanian Cultural Revolution." PROBLEMS OF COMMUNISM 23 (July-August 1974): 44-57.

> Emphasis on foreign policy inputs into the Albanian domestic

political upheaval somewhat misleadingly referred to by Tirana
as a "cultural revolution" despite its substantial differences
from the Chinese model.

581 _____. THE PEOPLE'S REPUBLIC OF ALBANIA. Foreword by Jan F.
Triska. Integration and Community Building in the Communist States of
East Europe Series. Baltimore, Md.: Johns Hopkins Press, 1968. xvi,
183 p. Paperbound.

Details of Albania's stormy relations with both Yugoslavia and
the Soviet Union, the turn toward alliance with China, and
subsequent policy within the international Communist movement.

582 Peters, Stephen. "Ingredients of Communist Takeover in Albania." In
THE ANATOMY OF COMMUNIST TAKEOVERS, edited by Thomas T.
Hammond, pp. 273-92. New Haven, Conn., and London: Yale Uni-
versity Press, 1975. Paperbound.

583 Prifti, Peter R. "Albania." In THE COMMUNIST STATES IN DISARRAY
1965-1971, edited by Adam Bromke and Teresa Rakowska-Harmstone,
pp. 198-220. Minneapolis: University of Minnesota Press, 1972.

Discusses how the fostering of national sentiment has abetted
the rejection of Soviet influence, and the almost total ideological and diplomatic turn toward China. Focused on the
internal reforms of the 1960s, the impact of the Czechoslovak
invasion, and the hesitant reestablishment of Yugoslav-Albanian
relations.

584 _____. "Albania After Khrushchev." SURVEY: A JOURNAL OF EAST
AND WEST STUDIES, no. 77 (Autumn 1970): 109-27.

Discusses Albanian foreign policy and domestic policies as influenced by relevant cultural-historical elements during the
mid-1960s, with attention to the cultural revolution, Soviet-
Albanian enmities, and Chinese relations.

585 _____. "Albania and the Baltic Republics: Mini-Nations in a Modern
World." In PROBLEMS OF MININATIONS BALTIC PERSPECTIVES, edited
by Arvids Ziedonis, Jr. et al., pp. 49-55. San Jose, Calif.: Association for the Advancement of Baltic Studies, 1973.

An analysis of Albanian foreign policy from the perspective of
viewing the disadvantages inherent to tiny Communist nations
who maneuver in an international system dominated by superpowers intent on retaining their "client states."

586 _____. "Albania and the Sino-Soviet Conflict." STUDIES IN COM-
PARATIVE COMMUNISM 6 (Autumn 1973): 241-66.

An analysis of contemporary Albanian relations with both China and the Soviet Union in the context of vital national and ideological interests at the core of Tirana's foreign policy. Followed by twelve key Albanian documents dating from 1962 to 1973.

587 _____. "Albanian Realignment? A Potential By-Product of Soviet Invasion of Czechoslovakia." Cambridge, Mass.: MIT Center for International Studies, October 1968. 11p. Multilith.

Monograph on impact of Soviet invasion of Czechoslovakia on Albanian foreign policy toward Yugoslavia and other Balkan countries.

588 _____. "Albania's 'Cultural Revolution.'" Cambridge, Mass.: MIT Center for International Studies, September 1968. 19 p. Multilith.

An analysis of the impact of the Chinese cultural revolution on Albanian domestic policy. Emphasis on differences as well as similarities in the process of domestic upheaval labelled a "cultural revolution" by both Peking and Tirana.

589 _____. "Albania's Expanding Horizons." PROBLEMS OF COMMUNISM 21 (January-February 1972): 30-39.

Continuation of earlier research on the role of Albania in Sino-Soviet polemics. Insight into the potential impact of U.S.-Chinese "normalization of relations" on Albanian foreign policy options.

590 _____. "Albania Towards an Atheist Society." In RELIGION AND ATHEISM IN THE U.S.S.R. AND EASTERN EUROPE, edited by Bohdan R. Bociurkiw and John W. Strong, pp. 388-405. London and Basingstoke, Engl.: Macmillan, 1975.

A discussion of the conflict of religion and official ideology in the most dogmatic of Communist nations on this subject. Albania became the first atheist state in the world with the banning of religion in 1967, a move yet to be even seriously considered by either the Soviets or Tirana's current ostensible model within the Communist world, China.

591 _____. "Armed Forces and Society in Albania." In POLITICAL-MILITARY SYSTEMS: COMPARATIVE PERSPECTIVES, edited by Catherine McArdle Kelleher, pp. 191-99. Beverly Hills, Calif., and London: Sage Publications, 1974.

Treats party-army relations in Albania, showing the early influence of the Yugoslav Communists on the Albanian civil war. Also describes reorientation of Albanian foreign and military policy with the Tito-Stalin break in 1948, followed by the turn to China for military aid in the 1960s.

592 _____. "The Communist Seizure of Power in Albania." Cambridge, Mass.: MIT Center for International Studies, August 1974. 47 p. Mimeograph.

Detailed recounting of the method of Communist takeover in Albania. Shows the close contacts of the Albanian party leadership with Yugoslav Communists as well as lack of Soviet participation in the process.

593 _____. "The Development of Culture in Socialist Albania." Cambridge, Mass.: MIT Center for International Studies, September 1974. 55 p. Multilith.

Interesting insight into cultural policy as a manifestation of Albanian nationalism.

594 _____. "Kosovo In Fement." Cambridge, Mass.: MIT Center for International Studies, 1969. 37 p. Multilith.

Interesting for insight into the influence of Tirana on manifestations of Yugoslav-Albanian nationalism within the Kosovo. Also useful to those students of the impact of domestic nationalisms on Yugoslavia's international relations with its Balkan neighbors.

595 _____. "The Politics of Language: The Albanian Minority in Yugoslavia." BALKANISTICA: OCCASIONAL PAPERS IN SOUTHEAST EUROPEAN STUDIES 2 (1975): 7-18.

A study of Albanian nationalism among Yugoslav-Albanians. Important for impact of these developments on cultural and political relations between these often warring Balkan neighbors.

596 _____. SOCIALIST ALBANIA SINCE 1944: DOMESTIC AND FOREIGN DEVELOPMENTS. Cambridge, Mass.: MIT Press, 1978 forthcoming.

597 Singleton, F[red].B. "Albania and her Neighbors: The End of Isolation." THE WORLD TODAY 31 (September 1975): 383-90.

598 Skendi, Stavro. THE ALBANIAN NATIONAL AWAKENING 1878-1912. Princeton, N.J.: Princeton University Press, 1967. xiii, 498 p.

Scholarly history of the rise of Albanian nationalism in the context of Austro-Hungarian rivalry with Italy for influence in the area and intra-Balkan politics. Written under the auspices of the American Council for Learned Societies and the Social Science Research Council.

599 _____, ed. ALBANIA. Foreword by Robert F[rancis]. Byrnes. New York: Praeger, 1956. xiv, 388 p.

> Detailed mass of data on the development of communism in Albania. Written during the honeymoon of Soviet-Albanian relations in the 1950s, thus providing interesting background for the subsequent split.

600 Tretiak, Daniel. "The Founding of the Sino-Albanian Entente." CHINA QUARTERLY 10 (April-June 1962): 123-43.

600a Washburn, John N. "The Current Legal Status of Warsaw Pact Membership." INTERNATIONAL LAWYER 5 (January 1971): 129-34.

> Discusses Albanian formal withdrawal from the pact in 1968.

601 Weiner, Robert. "Albanian and Romanian Deviance in the U.N." EAST EUROPEAN QUARTERLY 7 (Spring 1973): 65-83.

> Examines voting records and in the context of specific substantive conflicts with the USSR.

602 Wolff, Robert Lee. "Political Life in the Balkan Satellites Since 1948: Albania." In his THE BALKANS IN OUR TIME, pp. 489-96. Cambridge, Mass.: Harvard University Press, 1956.

> Earlier historical treatment also useful.

Chapter II
BULGARIA

603   Barros, James. THE LEAGUE OF NATIONS AND THE GREAT POWERS: THE GREEK-BULGARIAN INCIDENT OF 1925. Oxford: Clarendon Press, 1970. xiv, 143 p.

604   Black, Cyril E. THE ESTABLISHMENT OF CONSTITUTIONAL GOVERN-MENT IN BULGARIA. Princeton, N.J.: Princeton University Press, 1943. x, 323 p.

> A significant political history of the constitutional movement in Bulgaria in the 1870s and 1880s. Good background.

605   Brown, J[ames]. F. BULGARIA UNDER COMMUNIST RULE. London; Washington, D.C.; New York: Praeger, 1970. ix, 339 p.

> Solid analysis. Valuable appendixes. Largely based on Radio Free Europe archives in Munich.

606   _____. "Romania and Bulgaria." In THE COMMUNIST STATES AT THE CROSSROADS: BETWEEN MOSCOW AND PEKING, edited by Adam Bromke, pp. 106-25. New York; Washington, D.C.; London: Praeger, 1965.

607   Carter, F.W. "Bulgarian Economic Ties with Her Immediate Neighbors and Prospects for Future Development." EAST EUROPEAN QUARTERLY 4 (June 1970): 209-25.

> Outlines the growth of interbloc trade, focusing on Bulgaria's growing trade with Yugoslavia, Rumania, and Greece. Sees closer ties as inevitable.

608   Chary, Frederick B. THE BULGARIAN JEWS AND THE FINAL SOLUTION, 1940-1944. Pittsburgh, Pa.: University of Pittsburgh Press, 1972. xiv, 246 p.

> A scholarly treatment of the fate of Bulgarian Jews in Hitler's

Europe with implications for Bulgaria's international relations at the time.

609 Costello, Michael. "Bulgaria." In THE COMMUNIST STATES IN DIS-
ARRAY 1965-1971, edited by Adam Bromke and Teresa Rakowska-Harmstone,
pp. 135-37. Minneapolis: University of Minnesota Press, 1972.

Discusses the near integration of Soviet and Bulgarian economies, and the hesitant development of autonomous direction
in foreign policy matters from 1965 until the "retreat" in the
late 1960s.

610 Dellin, L.A.D. "Bulgarian Economic Reform--Advance and Retreat."
PROBLEMS OF COMMUNISM 19 (September-October 1970): 45-52.

611 _____, ed. BULGARIA. East Central Europe Under the Communists
Series. New York: Praeger, 1957. xvii, 457 p.

Traces history of the Bulgarian Communist party from the takeover through 1956-57.

611a Dobrin, Bogoslav. BULGARIAN ECONOMIC DEVELOPMENT SINCE
WORLD WAR II. New York: Praeger, 1973. xv, 185 p.

Examination of causes and the pattern of Bulgarian economic
development from 1948-68. Emphasis on Bulgaria's overwhelming dependence on the Soviet Union. Chapter 5 deals with
foreign trade and CMEA.

612 Horner, John E. "The Ordeal of Nikola Petkov and Consolidation of
Communist Power Rule in Bulgaria." SURVEY: A JOURNAL OF EAST
& WEST STUDIES 20 (Winter 1974): 75-83.

612a Jelavich, Charles, and Jelavich, Barbara. THE BALKANS. Englewood
Cliffs, N.J.: Prentice-Hall, 1965. xi, 148 p.

Good summary of Bulgarian post-World War II international
relations. See also no. 138.

613 Larrabee, F. Stephen. "Bulgaria's Politics of Conformity." PROBLEMS
OF COMMUNISM 21 (July-August 1972): 42-52.

Points to cracks in Bulgarian-Soviet harmony, both regarding
West Germany and the ever-rankling Macedonian question.

614 Lendvai, Paul. "Bulgaria: Humble Vassal or Faithful Ally?" In his
EAGLES IN COBWEBS: NATIONALISM AND COMMUNISM IN THE
BALKANS, pp. 206-62. London: Macdonald, 1969.

An analysis of Bulgarian subservience to Moscow. Insight into potential Bulgarian military discontent with the situation, particularly during the abortive coup attempt in 1965.

615   Miller, Marshall Lee. BULGARIA DURING THE SECOND WORLD WAR. Stanford, Calif.: Stanford University Press, 1975. xii, 290 p.

A scholarly study dealing with the diplomatic maneuvers that brought Bulgaria into war on the Axis side and the country's subsequent attempts to maintain at least a partially independent policy.

616   Oren, Nissan. BULGARIAN COMMUNISM: THE ROAD TO POWER, 1934-1944. New York: Columbia University Press, 1972. xii, 288 p.

A study of Bulgarian politics and the rise of the Communist party in the decade before it came to power. Includes analysis of the Bulgarian party's relationship to the Comintern.

617   _____. REVOLUTION ADMINISTERED: AGRARIANISM AND COMMUNISM IN BULGARIA. Baltimore, Md.: Johns Hopkins Press, 1973. xv, 204 p. Paperbound.

Survey of Bulgarian domestic and foreign policy. Treats the policy-making process as a clash between the agrarianism of a peasant population and revolutionary Communist demands for urbanization. Deals with specific conditions and regional conflicts contributing to Bulgaria's dependence on the Soviet Union.

618   _____. "A Revolution Administered: The Sovietization of Bulgaria." In THE ANATOMY OF COMMUNIST TAKEOVERS, edited by Thomas T. Hammond, pp. 321-38. New Haven, Conn., and London: Yale University Press, 1975. Paperbound.

619   Robbins, Keith. "British Diplomacy and Bulgaria." THE SLAVONIC AND EAST EUROPEAN REVIEW 42 (October 1971): 560-85.

England's futile efforts to prevent Bulgaria from joining the Central Powers.

620   Rothschild, Joseph. THE COMMUNIST PARTY OF BULGARIA: ORIGINS AND DEVELOPMENT 1883-1936. New York: Columbia University Press, 1959. vii, 354 p.

A scholarly study of the political dynamics that contributed to the rise of Bulgarian communism. Includes material on Russian-Bulgarian relations, Bulgaria's Balkan policy, and the Bulgarian party's relations with the Comintern. Particularly useful as background for understanding the party's subsequent attitude toward the Macedonian question.

621   Shoup, Paul. COMMUNISM AND THE YUGOSLAV NATIONAL QUES-
      TION. New York: Columbia University Press, 1968. 308 p.

      See for relations of Yugoslav-Bulgarian parties on the issue of
      Macedonia. See also no. 1154a.

622   Stillman, Edmund O. "The Collectivization of Bulgarian Agriculture."
      In COLLECTIVIZATION OF AGRICULTURE IN EASTERN EUROPE, edited
      by Irwin T. Sanders, pp. 67-102. Lexington: University of Kentucky
      Press, 1958.

623   Vasilev, Dimitur. "The International Socialist Division of Labor and Its
      Role in the Increased Profitability of Bulgaria's Foreign Trade." EASTERN
      EUROPEAN ECONOMICS 8 (Fall 1969): 90-99.

      Bulgarian analysis of the impact of CMEA policy on Bulgarian
      trade.

624   Zakariev, Iv., et al. "The Bulgarian Economy." EASTERN EUROPEAN
      ECONOMICS 3 (Fall 1964): 3-68.

Chapter III

CZECHOSLOVAKIA

624a Alton, Thad Paul, et al. CZECHOSLOVAKIA'S NATIONAL INCOME
AND PRODUCTION 1947-1948 AND 1955-1956. Columbia University
East Central European Studies Series. New York and London: Columbia
University Press, 1962. xiv, 255 p.

> Part of a larger study of the structure and growth of Soviet-
> type economies by the Research Project on National Income
> in East Central Europe. A useful reference for economists.
> Includes data dealing with the foreign sector of the economy.

625 Benes, Eduard. MEMOIRS OF DR. EDUARD BENES: FROM MUNICH
TO NEW WAR AND VICTORY. Translated by Godfrey Lias. London:
Allen and Unwin, 1954. xi, 436 p.

> Most important for President Benes's reflections on wartime
> diplomacy with both East and West.

626 Bittman, Ladislav. THE DECEPTION GAME: CZECHOSLOVAK INTELLI-
GENCE IN SOVIET POLITICAL WARFARE. Syracuse, N.Y.: Syracuse
University Research Corporation, 1972. xxv, 246 p. Black and white
illus.

> Includes information on extent of integration of Soviet-East
> European intelligence efforts. Author worked in Czechoslovak
> intelligence from 1954 until 1968 when he refused to collabo-
> rate with the Soviet invasion and left the country.

627 Bradley, J.F.N. CZECHOSLOVAKIA. Edinburgh: Edinburgh University
Press, 1971. xii, 212 p.

> A survey of Czechoslovak history until 1968, focused on the
> central problem for Czech and Slovak leaders of how to survive
> their country's unfortunate geographical location and protect
> themselves from their neighbors. Emphasis on the Czechoslovak
> attempts to seek refuge in Central European groupings.

627a Brock, Peter. THE SLOVAK NATIONAL AWAKENING: AN ESSAY IN THE INTELLECTUAL HISTORY OF EAST CENTRAL EUROPE. Toronto and Buffalo, N.Y.: University of Toronto Press, 1976. x, 104 p.

628 Bruegel, Johann Wolfgang. CZECHOSLOVAKIA BEFORE MUNICH: THE GERMAN MINORITY PROBLEM AND BRITISH APPEASEMENT POLICY. New York: Cambridge University Press, 1973. xiv, 334 p.

   A scholarly analysis based on primary sources. Shorter than the 1967 German version, but includes new archival material.

629 Campbell, F. Gregory. CONFRONTATION IN CENTRAL EUROPE: WEIMAR GERMANY AND CZECHOSLOVAKIA. Chicago: University of Chicago Press, 1975. xvi, 383 p.

   A useful bibliographical essay based on intensive research of diplomatic records.

630 Elias, Zdenek, and Netik, Jaromir. "Czechoslovakia: Toward a Socialist State." In COMMUNISM IN EUROPE, vol. 2, edited by William E. Griffith, pp. 232-35. Cambridge, Mass.: MIT Press, 1966.

   Emphasizes Czech dependence on Soviets in foreign policies. Trade agreements and cooperation with Chinese during 1957–59, and then progressive isolation from China as a by-product of the Sino-Soviet dispute.

631 Gadourek, Ivan. THE POLITICAL CONTROL OF CZECHOSLOVAKIA: A STUDY IN SOCIAL CONTROL OF A SOVIET SATELLITE STATE. Leiden, Netherlands: Stenfert Kroese, 1953. xvi, 285 p.

   Based on refugee reports, materials smuggled out by resistance groups, and the personal experience of the author.

632 Heyman, Frederick G. POLAND AND CZECHOSLOVAKIA. Englewood Cliffs, N.J.: Prentice-Hall, 1966. viii, 181 p.

   A concise history of Polish-Czechoslovak relations from the Middle Ages until the eve of World War II when, in the author's view, bankrupt foreign policy contributed to the eventual Nazi occupation.

633 Howard, Harry Nicholas. "The Little Entente and the Balkan Entente." In CZECHOSLOVAKIA, edited by Robert J. Kerner, pp. 368-85. Berkeley and Los Angeles: University of California Press, 1940.

634 Kaplan, Morton A. THE COMMUNIST COUP IN CZECHOSLOVAKIA. Princeton, N.J.: Princeton University Center for International Studies, 1960. 40 p.

A monograph on the mechanics of coup d'etat in Czechoslovakia.
Interesting for comparative perspective.

635 Kennan, George F. FROM PRAGUE AFTER MUNICH: DIPLOMATIC
PAPERS, 1938-1940. Princeton, N.J.: Princeton University Press, 1968.
xxviii, 266 p. Black and white illus. Paperbound.

Poignant background in view of the parallel to the intervention in 1968 and the extent to which Czechoslovakia has been
subject to unfortunate international pressures since that country's
creation at the end of World War I.

636 Kerner, Robert J., ed. CZECHOSLOVAKIA. Berkeley and Los Angeles:
University of California Press, 1940. xxi, 504 p.

A classic in the field.

637 Koralka, J. "The Czech Question in International Relations at the Beginning of the 20th Century." THE SLAVONIC AND EAST EUROPEAN
REVIEW 48 (April 1970): 284-360.

Brief historical and theoretical sketch of the big power dominance of Czechoslovakia prior to World War I, illustrating
wider phenomena of the area in international relations of the
time.

638 Korbel, Josef. THE COMMUNIST SUBVERSION OF CZECHOSLOVAKIA
1938-1948: THE FAILURE OF COEXISTENCE. Princeton, N.J.: Princeton University Press, 1958. xii, 258 p. Paperbound.

A personalized story of Communist maneuvering prior to the
coup in 1948 and subsequent consolidation of power. Shows
the role of international politics in narrowing postwar Czechoslovakia's domestic options. Written by a former Czechoslovak
career diplomat.

639 _____. TWENTIETH CENTURY CZECHOSLOVAKIA: THE MEANINGS
OF ITS HISTORY. New York: Columbia University Press, 1977. xii,
346 p.

640 Korbonski, Andrzej. "Bureaucracy and Interest Groups in Communist
Societies: The Case of Czechoslovakia." STUDIES IN COMPARATIVE
COMMUNISM 4 (January 1971): 57-79.

641 Krefci, Jaroslav. SOCIAL CHANGE AND STRATIFICATION IN POST-
WAR CZECHOSLOVAKIA. New York: Columbia University Press, 1972.
xvi, 207 p.

A sociological study of Czechoslovak society relating postwar
social stratification to ethnic and institutional considerations.

Valuable for scholars regarding the interplay of societal forces that culminated in 1968, or for comparative elite analysis.

642 Liptak, Julius. "The Position of Slovakia in the Foreign Trade of the CSSR." EASTERN EUROPEAN ECONOMIC 9 (Fall 1970): 42–61.

643 Luza, Radomir. THE TRANSFER OF THE SUDETEN GERMANS: A STUDY OF CZECH-GERMAN RELATIONS, 1933–1962. New York: New York University Press, 1964. xxiv, 365 p.

644 Mamatey, Victory S., and Luza, Radomir, eds. A HISTORY OF THE CZECHOSLOVAK REPUBLIC, 1918–1948. Princeton, N.J.: Princeton University Press, 1973. xi, 534 p. Paperbound.

A political history. Probably the best survey of its kind in English.

645 Masaryk, Tomas G. THE MEANING OF CZECH HISTORY. Edited with introduction by Rene Wellek. Translated by Peter Kussi. Chapel Hill: University of North Carolina Press, 1974. xxiii, 169 p.

A valuable discussion, weaving philosophy and history into a political program by the long-revered president of the interwar Czechoslovak republic.

646 Mastny, Vojtech. THE CZECHS UNDER NAZI RULE: THE FAILURE OF NATIONAL RESISTENCE 1939–1942. New York: Columbia University Press, 1971. xiii, 274 p.

647 Michal, Jan M. CENTRAL PLANNING IN CZECHOSLOVAKIA: ORGAN-IZATION FOR GROWTH IN A MATURE ECONOMY. Stanford, Calif.: Stanford University Press, 1960. xiii, 274 p.

Chapter on foreign trade useful for economic component of Czechoslovak international relations. Extensive tables. Based primarily on Czechoslovak sources.

648 _____. "Czechoslovakia's Foreign Trade." SLAVIC REVIEW, no. 2 (1968): 212–29.

649 Mikus, Joseph A. SLOVAKIA: A POLITICAL HISTORY: 1918–1950. Translated from the French by Kathy Day Wyatt and Joseph A. Mikus. Foreword to the English edition by Roman Smal-Stocki. Milwaukee, Wis.: Marquette University Press, 1963. xxxiii, 392 p.

A study, first published in Paris in 1955, of Slovakia's unsuccessful attempt to survive by balancing first between Hungarian and Czech patronage, and subsequently on the tightrope between

German and Soviet imperialism. Excellent background for understanding the rise of Slovak nationalism in Communist Czechoslovakia.

650 Miller, Herbert Adolphus. "What Woodrow Wilson and America Meant to Czechoslovakia." In CZECHOSLOVAKIA, edited by Robert J. Kerner, pp. 71-87. Berkeley and Los Angeles: University of California Press, 1940.

651 Roucek, Joseph S[labey]. "Czechoslovakia and Her Minorities." In CZECHOSLOVAKIA, edited by Robert J. Kerner, pp. 171-92. Berkeley and Los Angeles: University of California Press, 1940.

652 Schmidt, Dana Adams. ANATOMY OF A SATELLITE. Boston: Little, Brown, 1952. ix, 512 p.

One of the classic journalistic accounts of Communist consolidation of power in Czechoslovakia. Written by the NEW YORK TIMES correspondent in Prague in 1949.

653 Seton-Watson, Robert William. A HISTORY OF THE CZECHS AND SLOVAKS. London: Hutchinson, 1943. 413 p.

A detailed academic history of Czech and Slovak political fortunes from the origin of the Bohemian state in the late eighth century until the aftermath of the Munich agreement in 1938. Important reference for background to subsequent international relations of postwar Czechoslovakia.

654 Sharp, Samuel L. "The Czechs and the Slovaks: New Aspects of an Old Problem." AMERICAN PERSPECTIVE 1 (October 1947): 311-22.

655 Sik, Ota. ECONOMIC PLANNING AND MANAGEMENT IN CZECHOSLOVAKIA. Prague: Orbis, 1966. 29 p.

Concise summary of the "new system" of planning and management by a leading architect of the Czechoslovak economic reforms in 1968. Author was, at that time, director of the Institute of Economics of the Czechoslovak Academy of Sciences.

656 Skilling, H. Gordon. "Czechoslovakia." In THE COMMUNIST STATES AT THE CROSSROADS: BETWEEN MOSCOW AND PEKING, edited by Adam Bromke, pp. 87-105. New York; Washington, D.C.; London: Praeger, 1965.

657 Sterling, Claire. THE MASARYK CASE. New York and London: Harper and Row, 1968. xvii, 366 p. Black and white illus.

A biographical, political analysis of the implications of Foreign Minister Jan Masaryk's death in March 1948 for Czechoslovakia. Timely insight in view of the role played by the Masaryk case in the crisis of 1968.

658　Stolnik, Marian Mark. THE ROLE OF AMERICAN SLOVAKS IN CREATION OF CZECHOSLOVAKIA, 1914-1918. Cleveland and Rome: Slovak Institute, 1968. 82 p.

Originally a master's thesis at the University of Ottawa. Useful to historians unable to work with primary Czech and Slovak materials.

659　Suda, Zdenek. THE CZECHOSLOVAK SOCIALIST REPUBLIC. Integration and Community Building in Eastern Europe Series. Baltimore, Md.: Johns Hopkins Press, 1969. viii, 180 p. Paperbound.

Focuses on the 1960s. Historical background for a general reader to the crisis of 1968.

660　Taborsky, Edward. COMMUNISM IN CZECHOSLOVAKIA 1948-1960. Princeton, N.J.: Princeton University Press, 1961. xii, 628 p.

A detailed account by the secretary of Czechoslovak President Eduard Benes during World War II, who became minister to Sweden after the war, and is now a professor at the University of Texas. Emphasis on major trends of development and operational patterns. Based on the assumption that the "writings and pronouncements of Czechoslovak Communists merely repeat Soviet-made and Soviet-interpreted precepts."

661　_____. "Czechoslovakia: The Return to 'Normalcy.'" PROBLEMS OF COMMUNISM 19 (November-December 1970): 31-41.

661a　Teichova, Alice. AN ECONOMIC BACKGROUND TO MUNICH: INTERNATIONAL BUSINESS AND CZECHOSLOVAKIA 1918-1938. New York: Cambridge University Press, 1974. xix, 422 p.

Carefully researched and well-written. A useful reference for scholars with insight into operation of international cartels in foreign policy.

662　Thomson, S. Harrison. CZECHOSLOVAKIA IN EUROPEAN HISTORY. Hamden, Conn.: Archon Books, 1965. x, 485 p.

663　Tigrid, Pavel. "The Prague Coup of 1948: The Elegant Takeover." In THE ANATOMY OF COMMUNIST TAKEOVERS, edited by Thomas T. Hammond, pp. 399-432. New Haven, Conn., and London: Yale University Press, 1975. Paperbound.

664   Ulc, Otto.   "Class Struggle and Social Justice: The Case of Czechoslo-
       vakia." AMERICAN POLITICAL SCIENCE REVIEW   61 (September 1967):
       727-43.

       See for impact of Soviet legal theory on Czechoslovak court
       system.

665   Ullmann, Walter.   "Some Aspects of American-Czechoslovak Relations,
       1945-1947." EAST EUROPEAN QUARTERLY 10 (Spring 1976): 65-76.

666   Vondracek, Felix John.   "Diplomatic Origins and Foreign Policy." In
       CZECHOSLOVAKIA, edited by Robert J. Kerner, pp. 349-67. Berkeley
       and Los Angeles: University of California Press, 1940.

667   Zauberman, Alfred.   INDUSTRIAL PROGRESS IN POLAND, CZECHO-
       SLOVAKIA, AND EAST GERMANY 1937-1962. Oxford: Oxford Univer-
       sity Press, 1964. xiv, 338 p.

       See no. 491.

668   Zeman, Zbynek [A.B.].   THE MASARYKS: THE MAKING OF CZECHOSLO-
       VAKIA. New York: Barnes & Noble, 1976. 230 p.

668a   Zinner, Paul E.   COMMUNIST STRATEGY AND TACTICS IN CZECHO-
       SLOVAKIA, 1918-1948. New York: Praeger, 1963. 264 p.

       Essential background to the 1948 coup. Not a history of the
       party but a case study of the takeover useful to students of
       revolution irrespective of the ideology of the revolutionary
       elite.

A. PRAGUE SPRING AND INVASION, 1968

669   Bernasek, Miroslav.   "The Czechoslovak Economic Recession 1962-1965."
       SOVIET STUDIES 20 (April 1969): 444-61.

       Considers the recession to have resulted from incorrect appli-
       cation of the Soviet system of management.

670   Brada, Josef C.   "The Czechoslovak Economic Recession 1962-1965: Com-
       ment." SOVIET STUDIES 22 (January 1971): 402-5.

       Reply to Bernasek article contending that domestic factors were
       more important to the recession in Czechoslovakia than a flawed
       Soviet model.

671   Burks, R.V.   "The Decline of Communism in Czechoslovakia." STUDIES
       IN COMPARATIVE COMMUNISM 2 (January 1969): 21-49.

A general survey of the domestic situation that led to Czechoslovak reform communism in 1968, linked to Czechoslovakia's
international situation during the 1940s and 1950s. Concludes
with a brief discussion of the conflict of interests that led to
invasion as an at least temporary solution.

672   Conquest, Robert. "Czechoslovakia: The Soviet Outlook." STUDIES IN
COMPARATIVE COMMUNISM 1 (July-October 1968): 7-16.

An analysis of Soviet hopes and fears concerning the political
changes in Czechoslovakia dating from Brezhnev's visit to
Prague in December 1967. Discusses the motivations behind
the intervention. Primarily an ideological interpretation.

673   "Czechoslovakia: The Brief Spring of 1968." PROBLEMS OF COMMU-
NISM 17 (November-December 1968): entire issue.

The entire issue is devoted to examination of the causes, developments, consequences, and implications of the Soviet 1968
invasion of Czechoslovakia.

674   Czerwinski, E.J., and Piekalkiewicz, Jaroslaw [A.], eds. THE SOVIET
INVASION OF CZECHOSLOVAKIA: ITS EFFECTS ON EASTERN EU-
ROPE. New York: Praeger, 1972. x, 214 p.

A collection showing in detail the impact of the Czechoslovak
crisis on Soviet foreign policy toward East European states as
well as other repercussions for the area.

675   Dean, Robert W. NATIONALISM AND POLITICAL CHANGE IN EASTERN
EUROPE: THE SLOVAK QUESTION AND THE CZECHOSLOVAK REFORM
MOVEMENT. Denver: University of Denver, 1973. 67 p.

676   Devlin, Kevin. "The New Crisis in European Communism." PROBLEMS
OF COMMUNISM 17 (November-December 1968): 57-68.

Sophisticated analysis of the impact of intervention in Czechoslovakia on European Communist parties.

677   Ello, Paul, comp. CZECHOSLOVAKIA'S BLUEPRINT FOR "FREEDOM".
Washington, D.C.: Acropolis Books, 1968. x, 304 p. Paperbound.

A hastily compiled collection of Dubcek's speeches and official Czechoslovak documents leading to the breakdown in com-
munication between Czechoslovakia and the "allied socialist
states" that invaded in August 1968. Brought out within a
month of that invasion.

677a   Ermarth, Fritz. INTERNATIONALISM, SECURITY, AND LEGITIMACY:

THE CHALLENGE TO SOVIET INTERESTS IN EAST EUROPE, 1964-1968.
Santa Monica, Calif.: RAND Memorandum RM-5909-PR, March 1969.
162 p.

One of the best analyses of Soviet policy toward Eastern Europe leading up to and during the Czechoslovak crisis of 1968.

678 Feiwel, George R. NEW ECONOMIC PATTERNS FOR CZECHOSLOVAKIA: IMPACT OF GROWTH, PLANNING AND MARKET. New York: Praeger, 1968. xxiv, 589 p.

A detailed, technical study. Special attention to causes of stagnation in the economy after 1967.

678a Franck, Thomas M., and Weisband, Edward. WORD POLITICS: VERBAL STRATEGY AMONG THE SUPERPOWERS. New York: Oxford University Press, 1972. xiii, 176 p. Paperbound.

Includes a specific comparison of the justifications of intervention by the United States in the 1965 Dominican crisis and the Soviet Union in Czechoslovakia in 1968.

679 Garaudy, Roger. LA LIBERTE EN SURSIS, PRAGUE 1968. Paris: Fayard, 1968. 159 p.

A documentary volume with an introduction by a French Communist Politburo member criticized by the party leadership for his support of the Czechoslovak position.

679a Godwin, Paul H.B. "Communist Systems and Modernization: Sources of Political Crisis." STUDIES IN COMPARATIVE COMMUNISM 6 (Spring-Summer 1973): 107-34.

Good use of Czechoslovak examples.

680 Golan, Galia. THE CZECHOSLOVAK REFORM MOVEMENT: COMMUNISM IN CRISES 1962-1968. London: Cambridge University Press, 1971. viii, 349 p.

A thorough, careful presentation of the attempts at comprehensive reform in Czechoslovakia in 1968, focusing on the background conditions that were instrumental in determining type and scope of reform. Concludes with the invasion by "allied socialist states." Author is a lecturer in political science and Russian studies at Hebrew University of Jerusalem.

681 _____. "Prague's Spring: Root and Reasons--The Road to Reform." PROBLEMS OF COMMUNISM 20 (May-June 1971): 11-21.

682 _____. REFORM RULE IN CZECHOSLOVAKIA: THE DUBCEK ERA 1968-

1969. London and New York: Cambridge University Press, 1973. vii, 327 p.

A detailed analysis of reforms attempted during the brief Dubcek regime in Czechoslovakia. One of the best available sources for understanding why the winds of change in Prague brought such ill will from Moscow and the more orthodox East European Communist leaderships.

683 Goldmann, Josef, and Kouba, Karel. ECONOMIC GROWTH IN CZECHO-SLOVAKIA. New York: International Arts and Sciences Press, 1969. 150 p.

684 Griffith, William E. EAST EUROPE AFTER THE SOVIET INVASION OF CZECHOSLOVAKIA. Santa Monica, Calif.: RAND Memorandum P-3938, October 1968. 45 p.

Considers economic pull of West Germany to continue as an impetus for "normalization."

685 _____. "The Prague Spring and the Soviet Intervention in Czechoslovakia." In THE ANATOMY OF COMMUNIST TAKEOVERS, edited by Thomas T. Hammond, pp. 606-19. New Haven, Conn., and London: Yale University Press, 1975. Paperbound.

686 Hamsik, Dusan. WRITERS AGAINST RULERS. Translated by D. Orpington. Introduction by W.L. Webb. New York: Random House, 1971. 208 p. Paperbound. Appendix with selected speeches from the congress.

A fascinating account by one of the Czech writers who partici-pated in the Fourth Congress of the Czechoslovak Writers Union in June 1967.

687 Hejzlar, Zdenek, and Kusin, Vladimir V. CZECHOSLOVAKIA 1968-1969: CHRONOLOGY, BIBLIOGRAPHY, ANNOTATION. New York and London: Garland Publishing, 1975. 316 p.

A painstaking volume. Invaluable to students and scholars dealing with the dynamics of the Prague Spring, Soviet-Czecho-slovak relations, or repercussions in the broader arena of East European international relations.

688 Holesovsky, Vaclav. "Czechoslovakia's New Economic Model: Problems and Prospects." PROBLEMS OF COMMUNISM 14 (September 1965): 41-45.

Links the economic reforms to a powerful and constructive im-pact on the thinking of party intellectuals while remaining cautious about the actual progress toward liberalization.

689 _____ . "Prague's Economic Model." EAST EUROPE 16 (February 1967):
13-16.

690 _____ . "The Revolution Begins in Czechoslovakia." DISSENT 15
(May–June 1968): 202–4.

691 James, Robert Rhodes, ed. THE CZECHOSLOVAK CRISIS, 1968. London:
Weidenfeld and Nicolson, 1969. 203 p.

> Emphasis on the reaction of international organizations to the
> intervention in Czechoslovakia. Primarily concerned with the
> Warsaw Pact, NATO, and the United Nations. Uncritically
> accepts Moscow's view that the Warsaw Pact as an organiza-
> tion was involved in the intervention as a fundamental assump-
> tion, thereby weakening overall analysis.

692 Jancar, Barbara Wolfe. CZECHOSLOVAKIA AND THE ABSOLUTE MO-
NOPOLY OF POWER. New York: Praeger, 1971. xv, 330 p.

> Sees the 1960s as a progressive erosion of the party's monopoly
> of power within Czechoslovakia. Considers the only viable
> political alternative to be revolution.

693 Korey, William. "The Comintern and the Genealogy of the 'Brezhnev
Doctrine.'" PROBLEMS OF COMMUNISM 18 (March–April 1969): 52–
58.

> A cursory explanation of the invasion, emphasizing historical
> aspects of Soviet control, suggesting a return to Stalinist prin-
> ciples of one model development of socialism.

694 Kusin, Vladimir V., ed. THE CZECHOSLOVAK REFORM MOVEMENT
1968. Santa Barbara, Calif.: ABC–Clio Press, 1973. ix, 358 p.

> Proceedings of a seminar held at the University of Reading,
> England, 12–17 July 1971. An extremely interesting collec-
> tion of analyses dealing with both domestic and international
> aspects of the Czechoslovak crisis of 1968. Those taking part
> in the seminar included a cross-section of Czechs and Slovaks
> who left Czechoslovakia as a result of the Soviet intervention,
> professional observers, and political scientists from other coun-
> tries.

695 _____ . THE INTELLECTUAL ORIGINS OF THE PRAGUE SPRING: THE
DEVELOPMENT OF REFORMIST IDEAS IN CZECHOSLOVAKIA 1956-1967.
London: Cambridge University Press, 1971. 153 p.

> A brief, useful background to understanding the Czechoslovak
> experiment of 1968, Moscow's role in determining the direction
> of Czechoslovak communism prior to the fall of Novotny, and

the Kremlin's reaction to the Prague Spring. Kusin is lecturer at the Institute of Soviet and East European Studies, University of Glasgow.

696 _____. POLITICAL GROUPINGS IN THE CZECHOSLOVAK REFORM MOVEMENT. Political and Social Processes in Eastern Europe Series, sponsored by the Social Science Research Council. New York: Columbia University Press, 1972. xii, 244 p.

A study of the nongovernmental groups and organizations in Czechoslovakia during 1968. Includes trade unions, farmers, the intelligentsia, students, nationalities, semi-political groups such as the Club of Committed Non-Party Activists (KAN), and churches. Particularly useful to students of interest group activity within Communist systems. Also helpful for those studying multiethnic federalisms.

697 Liehm, Antonin J. THE POLITICS OF CULTURE. Translated by Peter Kussi. Introduction by Jean-Paul Sartre. Translated by Helen R. Land. Illustrations by Adolf Hoffmeister. New York: Grove Press, 1968. 412 p. Paperbound.

Intellectual biographies of fifteen Czech and Slovak writers and intellectuals who took active part in creating the atmosphere known as the Prague Spring. Based on interviews.

698 Littell, Robert, ed. THE CZECH BLACK BOOK. New York: Avon Books, 1969. x, 318 p. Paperbound.

Prepared by the Institute of History of the Czechoslovak Academy of Sciences. This book was first published in Czechoslovakia under the title SEVEN DAYS IN PRAGUE as a response to a justification of the Soviet intervention that was compiled by a "group of Soviet journalists." A gripping account of the mood and reaction of the Czechoslovak capital during the first week of the invasion. Contains valuable material on Soviet behavior as well as on both organized and spontaneous resistance of the populace.

699 Loebl, Eugen. STALINISM IN PRAGUE: THE LOEBL STORY. Introduction by Herman Starobin. New York: Grove Press, 1969. 327 p.

Memoirs and analysis of the former deputy minister of foreign trade in Czechoslovakia. The first official arrested in the Slansky trials, and one of its few survivors. Shows the intense anti-Semitism intertwined with charges of Titoism.

700 London, Arthur. THE CONFESSIONS. Translated by Alastair Hamilton. New York: William Morrow, 1970. xix, 442 p.

A gripping account of one of the three defendents to survive
the Slansky trials in Czechoslovakia in the early 1950s.
Author was under-secretary of foreign affairs at the time of
his arrest in January 1951. Sentenced to life but was released
in 1956 after Khrushchev's attack on Stalin at the CPSU 20th
Congress.

701 Lukaszewski, Jerzy, ed. LES DEMOCRATIES POPULAIRES APRES PRAGUE.
Bruges, Belg.: de Tempel, 1970. 330 p.

A compilation of the proceedings of a symposium held 27-29
March 1969 on Soviet hegemony, national and regional integration, the invasion of Czechoslovakia, European detente,
Eastern Europe, and its relations with the superpowers, economic integration, CMEA, and nationalism.

702 Mackintosh, Malcolm. "The Soviet Military: Influence on Foreign Policy."
PROBLEMS OF COMMUNISM 22 (September-October 1973): 1-11.

Speculates on role of the military in the decision-making
process that led to the invasion of Czechoslovakia in 1968.

703 Marcelle, Jacques. LE DEUXIEME COUP DE PRAGUE. Brussels: Editions
vie ouvriere, 1968. 295 p. Illus.

A history of Czechoslovakia from the 1948 Soviet takeover and
its transformation into a Socialist state under the influence of
the Soviet Union. Considers 1968 a "second coup" in Prague.

704 Mastny, Vojtech, ed. CZECHOSLOVAKIA: CRISIS IN WORLD COM-
MUNISM. New York: Facts on File, 1972. iii, 392 p.

705 Menges, C. PRAGUE RESISTANCE, 1968: THE INGENUITY OF CON-
VICTION. Santa Monica, Calif.: RAND Memorandum P-3930, September 1968. 15 p.

706 Mudry-Sebik, Michael. "Czechoslovakia: Husak Takes the Helm."
EAST EUROPE 18 (May 1969): 2-7.

707 Olivova, Vera. THE DOOMED DEMOCRACY: CZECHOSLOVAKIA IN
A DISRUPTED EUROPE, 1914-1938. Translated by George Theiner. Introduction by Sir Cecil Parrott. London: Sedwick and Jackson, 1972.
276 p.

Published in Prague in 1968 and is an example of Czech historiography attempting to combine a Marxist interpretation
with careful, historical fact. Author subsequently lost position
as lecturer of history at Charles University.

708   ON EVENTS IN CZECHOSLOVAKIA: FACTS, DOCUMENTS, PRESS RE-
      PORTS, AND EYE-WITNESS ACCOUNTS. Moscow: 1968. 168 p.
      Paperbound. Black and white illus.

      An English-language justification of the Soviet intervention in
      Czechoslovakia compiled by unidentified Soviet journalists.
      For the most part, a propaganda whitewash, stressing the kind
      of incidents that led the Kremlin to conclude that socialism
      was endangered by counterrevolutionary activity in Czechoslo-
      vakia. Interesting in terms of both individuals attacked and
      the rationale. Not easily available.

709   Oxley, Andrew, et al. CZECHOSLOVAKIA: THE PARTY AND THE
      PEOPLE. London and New York: Allen Lane and St. Martin's Press,
      1973. xxxvi, 303 p.

      Primarily domestic focus. Some attention to Soviet-Czechoslo-
      vak relations.

710   Page, Benjamin B. THE CZECHOSLOVAK REFORM MOVEMENT 1963-
      1968: A STUDY IN THE THEORY OF SOCIALISM. Amsterdam: B.R.
      Gruner, 1973. x, 127 p.

711   Paul, David W. "Soviet Foreign Policy and the Invasion of Czechoslo-
      vakia." INTERNATIONAL STUDIES QUARTERLY 15 (1971): 159-202.

712   Pelikan, Jiri, ed. THE CZECHOSLOVAK POLITICAL TRIALS 1950-1954:
      THE SUPPRESSED REPORT OF THE DUBCEK GOVERNMENT'S COMMIS-
      SION OF INQUIRY, 1968. Stanford, Calif.: Stanford University Press,
      1971. 360 p.

      An important document for understanding both the purges of
      the 1950s and the direction of the 1968 reforms with respect
      to rehabilitating the past. Examines the consequences of
      Stalinism in Czechoslovakia, leading the editor to reject
      Moscow's official version that the cult of the personality was
      a Stalinist abberation. Editor himself a Dubcek supporter and
      director of television in Prague during 1968.

713   _____, ed. ICI PRAGUE. Paris: Seuil, 1973. 426 p.

      A survey of various texts reflecting internal resistance to the
      Soviet occupation and the government of Gustav Husak. Dis-
      seminated secretly within the country and then exported for
      publication.

714   Piekalkiewicz, Jaroslaw A. PUBLIC OPINION POLLING IN CZECHO-
      SLOVAKIA 1968-1969: RESULTS AND ANALYSIS OF SURVEYS CON-
      DUCTED DURING THE DUBCEK ERA. New York: Praeger, 1972.
      xxix, 357 p.

Research for this study done during late 1968 and early 1969
in Czechoslovakia, where the situation still so much in flux,
the author was able to quietly continue his work. Based on
twenty public opinion polls conducted in Czechoslovakia from
March 1968 to March 1969. A valuable reference with much
information now otherwise unavailable, despite some difficulties
caused by topical organization of the subject matter.

715 Potichnyj, Peter J., and Hodnett, Greg. THE UKRAINE AND THE
CZECHOSLOVAK CRISIS. Occasional Paper no. 6. Canberra: Austra-
lian National University, Department of Political Science and Research
School of Social Sciences, 1970. v, 154 p. Paperbound.

716 Pravda, Alex. REFORM AND CHANGE IN THE CZECHOSLOVAK PO-
LITICAL SYSTEM: JANUARY-AUGUST 1968. Beverly Hills, Calif.,
and London: Sage Publications, 1975. 96 p. Paperbound.

A useful, concise analysis of the Czechoslovak search for a
new model of contemporary communism. Emphasis on actual
changes in the political system in relation to theory.

716a Remington, Robin Alison. "Czechoslovakia: Multilateral Intervention."
In COMPARATIVE DEFENSE POLICY, edited by Frank B. Horton III
et al., pp. 511-23. Baltimore, Md., and London: Johns Hopkins Press,
1974.

An examination of the role of military pressure in the foreign
policy maneuvering that led up to the intervention of Czechoslovakia in 1968, and the relationship of the Warsaw Pact to
use of force by five member states against another member of
the alliance.

717 _____, ed. WINTER IN PRAGUE: DOCUMENTS ON CZECHOSLOVAK
COMMUNISM IN CRISIS. Introduction by William E. Griffith. Cambridge, Mass.: MIT Press, 1969. xxvii, 473 p. Paperbound.

A collection of seventy-two documents telling the story of the
Prague Spring in the words of those who participated, with specific attention to the increasingly dismayed response of the
Soviets and other East European regimes who feared "contami-
nation" of their own societies from the Czechoslovak reforms.

718 Roberts, Adam. "Socialist Conservatism in Czechoslovakia." THE WORLD
TODAY 26 (November 1970): 478-88.

719 Robinson, William F. "Czechoslovakia and its Allies: Part I January-
June 1968." STUDIES IN COMPARATIVE COMMUNISM 1 (July-October
1968): 141-70.

A study of the attitudes, activity, and communications media of Czechoslovakia's six Warsaw Pact allies during the first six months of Dubcek's government. Indicates rising nervousness but no coordinated campaign against Czechoslovakia. Followed by 167 pages of documents dealing with the escalating confrontation.

720 Salomon, Michel. PRAGUE NOTEBOOK: THE STRANGLED REVOLUTION. Translated by Helen Eustis. Boston: Little, Brown, 1971. xi, 361 p.

Among the increasing number of journalists' accounts of what they saw and heard in Prague during the spring of 1968. Supplements other more analytical sources.

721 Schwartz, Harry. PRAGUE'S 200 DAYS: THE STRUGGLE FOR DEMOCRACY IN CZECHOSLOVAKIA. New York: Praeger, 1969. x, 274 p.

A journalistic analysis of the Czechoslovak experiment and the reasons for Soviet intervention. An interesting, if undocumented, book for the general reader. Author a working journalist for the NEW YORK TIMES who visited Czechoslovakia in February, March, and July 1968.

722 Schwartz, Morton. "Czechoslovakia's New Political Model: A Design for Renewal." JOURNAL OF POLITICS 30 (November 1968): 966-84.

Czech and Slovak interest group theories.

723 Selucky, Radoslav. CZECHOSLOVAKIA: THE PLAN THAT FAILED. Introduction by Kamil Winter. London: Thomas Nelson, 1970. xvi, 150 p.

723a _____. ECONOMIC REFORMS IN EASTERN EUROPE. New York: Praeger, 1972. x, 179 p.

Analysis by a leading Czech economist involved in both the reform process and the disillusionment of the Prague Spring. See also no. 287.

724 Shaffer, Harry G. "Czechoslovakia's New Economic Model: Out of Stalinism." PROBLEMS OF COMMUNISM 14 (September-October 1965): 31-40.

Outlines the background of the new model, focusing on its main features and the goals of the reforms.

725 Shawcross, William. DUBCEK. New York: Simon and Schuster, 1971. xvi, 317 p.

A British journalist's political biography of Alexander Dubcek.
A negative treatment that makes little allowance for the external pressures under which Dubcek's government operated
both before and after the 1968 intervention.

726 Sik, Ota. CZECHOSLOVAKIA: THE BUREAUCRATIC ECONOMY.
White Plains, N.Y.: International Arts and Sciences Press, 1972. 138 p.

Based on a series of television talks given by the author in
1968 to demonstrate the negative impact of imposing the Soviet
economic model on the Czechoslovak economy for the past
twenty years. Introduction to the American edition places
the economic reforms attempted in 1968 political context.

727 _____. PLAN AND MARKET UNDER SOCIALISM. New York: International Arts and Sciences Press, 1968. 382 p.

728 _____. "Prague's Spring: Roots and Reasons--The Economic Impact
of Stalinism." PROBLEMS OF COMMUNISM 20 (May-June 1971): 1-
10.

729 Simes, Dimitri K. "The Soviet Invasion of Czechoslovakia and the Limits
of Kremlinology." STUDIES IN COMPARATIVE COMMUNISM 8 (Spring-
Summer 1975): 174-80.

730 Skilling, H. Gordon. "Czechoslovakia." In THE COMMUNIST STATES
IN DISARRAY 1965-1971, edited by Adam Bromke and Teresa Rakowska-
Harmstone, pp. 43-75. Minneapolis: University of Minnesota Press,
1972.

Discusses internal conflict in the party under Novotny and
Dubcek, as well as an assessment of Dubcek's attempts to
walk the line between reforms and external Soviet pressures.
Treats the development of Soviet attitudes leading up to the
Czech invasion, and subsequent developments through 1970.

731 _____. "Czechoslovakia's Interrupted Revolution." In REGIMES AND
OPPOSITIONS, edited by Robert A. Dahl, pp. 121-42. New Haven,
Conn., and London: Yale University Press, 1973. Paperbound.

An insightful analysis of the changes in leadership, policy,
and political procedures underway in Czechoslovakia during
the Prague Spring. Emphasis on the uniqueness of the attempt
at broad scale "democratization" of a Communist polity. This
chapter provides preview to book by author that was subsequently published under the same title.

732 _____. CZECHOSLOVAKIA'S INTERRUPTED REVOLUTION. Princeton, N.J.: Princeton University Press, 1976. xvi, 924 p. Paperbound.

> The most comprehensive analysis of the 1968 Czechoslovak reform by a leading scholar in the field.

733 _____. "The Fall of Novotny in Czechoslovakia." CANADIAN SLA-VONIC PAPERS 13 (Fall 1970): 225-42.

734 _____. "Opposition in Communist East Europe." In REGIMES AND OPPOSITIONS, edited by Robert A. Dahl, pp. 89-120. New Haven, Conn., and London: Yale University Press, 1973. Paperbound.

> An extremely useful analysis of types, phases, and changing political context of East European oppositions. Uses Czechoslovakia as a special case and draws widely on other East European examples.

734a Steiner, Eugen. THE SLOVAK DILEMMA. New York and London: Cambridge University Press, 1973. ix, 229 p.

> See no. 387.

735 Svitak, Ivan. "The Czechoslovak Experiment, 1968-1969." New York: Columbia University Press, 1971. xi, 243 p.

> Essays by a leading Czech philosopher, originally published during the Prague Spring. Author a key figure among the radical intellectuals and his writings a part of the political controversy of the time. Useful to students interested in ex-post-facto understanding of the events leading to the Soviet decisions to use troops to resolve Moscow's differences with the Dubcek regime.

736 Szulc, Tad. CZECHOSLOVAKIA SINCE WORLD WAR II. New York: Viking Press, 1971. viii, 503 p. Paperbound.

> A sophisticated journalistic analysis of postwar Czechoslovakia dating from its "liberation" in 1945 through the aftermath of the 1968 invasion. Effectively drawn from author's personal experiences as the NEW YORK TIMES representative in Prague during Dubcek's tension-ridden last few months in power.

737 Taborsky, Edward. "Czechoslovakia's Abnormal 'Normalization.'" CURRENT HISTORY 65 (May 1973): 207-12.

> Analysis of post-1968 developments based on the assumption that "normalization" following the invasion of Czechoslovakia went forward according to Soviet design and that moderation toward the West by the Husak regime was also decided in Moscow.

738 Tatu, Michel. L'HERESIE IMPOSSIBLE. Paris: Bernard Grasset, 1967-1968. xi, 289 p. Paperbound.

A collection of articles written for LE MONDE between March 1967 and August 1969 when author was the correspondent on Czech developments stationed in Vienna. A reflection of the climate of events in Czechoslovakia at that time.

739 Tigrid, Pavel. "Czechoslovakia: A Post-Mortem, II." SURVEY: A JOURNAL OF EAST AND WEST STUDIES, nos. 74-75 (Winter-Spring 1970): 112-42.

A description of Soviet-Czechoslovak negotiations and relations from the signing of the Bratislava agreement on 3 August 1968 until the fall of Dubcek in April 1969. Based on extensive testimony of Czechoslovak Communist party officials as well as documents and personal records both public and confidential.

740 _____. LE PRINTEMPS DE PRAGUE. Paris: Seuil, 1968. 280 p.

Viewed within the context of the history, evolution, and crisis of the Czech Party, an examination of the Prague Spring and its relation to the crisis in international communism, and the decadence of the Soviet empire. Czech documents from the period in last two-thirds of the book.

741 _____. WHY DUBCEK FELL. London: Macdonald, 1971. 229 p.

An insightful analysis of the rise and fall of Alexander Dubcek as head of the Communist party of Czechoslovakia from January 1968 to April 1969 by a distinguished journalist, editor of the Czech-language SVEDECTVI in Paris. Unparalleled access by author both to documents and persons intimately involved in the political process of the Prague Spring.

742 Triska, Jan F. "Messages from Czechoslovakia." PROBLEMS OF COMMUNISM 24 (November-December 1975): 26-42.

A disquieting analysis of Czechoslovak dissident protest at the complete dependence of the present Czechoslovak leadership and apparat on the Soviet Union.

743 Ulc, Otto. POLITICS IN CZECHOSLOVAKIA. Foreword by Jan F. Triska. San Francisco: W.H. Freeman, 1974. xi, 181 p. Black and white illus.

Discussion of socioeconomic processes, political developments, conditions, and trends that culminated in Czechoslovakia of 1968. Primarily for advanced students of comparative government, Communist studies, and political science. Good use of cartoons.

744 U.S. Senate. Committee on Government Operations. CZECHOSLOVAKIA AND THE BREZHNEV DOCTRINE. Prepared by the Subcommittee on National Security and International Operations, 91st Congress, 1st sess., Washington, D.C.: Government Printing Office, 1969.

745 Urban, G.R. "East Europe After Czechoslovakia." STUDIES IN COMPARATIVE COMMUNISM 2 (January 1969): 50–68.

   Reflections on a tour of Hungary, Czechoslovakia, and Rumania in September 1968. Emphasis on the problems created by the Czechoslovak crisis for other East European Communist regimes.

746 Valenta, Jiri. "Soviet Decisionmaking and the Czechoslovak Crisis of 1968." STUDIES IN COMPARATIVE COMMUNISM 8 (Spring–Summer 1975): 147–73.

747 Viney, Deryck. "Alexander Dubcek." STUDIES IN COMPARATIVE COMMUNISM 1 (July–October 1968): 17–39.

   A good biographical sketch of the Slovak leader to replace Novotny as first secretary of the Czechoslovak Communist party. Emphasis on childhood in the Soviet Union, his rise in the party, and the maneuvering involved in getting rid of Novotny.

748 Wallace, William V. CZECHOSLOVAKIA. Boulder, Colo.: Westview Press, 1976. xv, 474 p.

749 Weit, Erwin. AT THE RED SUMMIT: INTERPRETER BEHIND THE IRON CURTAIN. Translated by Mary Schofield. Preface by Harry Schwartz. New York: Macmillan, 1973. 226 p. Black and white illus.

   Story of the July 1968 Warsaw meeting prior to the invasion of Czechoslovakia as recorded by former Polish party leader Gomulka's interpreter who subsequently defected to the West. Interesting, if biased, insights into Polish–East German relations during this period.

750 Wheeler, George Shaw. THE HUMAN FACE OF SOCIALISM: POLITICAL ECONOMY AND CHANGE IN CZECHOSLOVAKIA. New York: Lawrence Hill, 1973. xiv, 174 p.

   A poignant defense of the socialist principles underlying Czechoslovak economic reforms of 1968 by an American economist who had lived in Prague since 1947. Author elected as a corresponding member of the Czechoslovak Academy of Sciences in 1962.

751 Windsor, Philip, and Roberts, Adam. CZECHOSLOVAKIA 1968: REFORM,

REPRESSION AND RESISTANCE. New York: Columbia University Press for Institute of Strategic Studies-London, 1969. vii, 199 p. Paperbound.

A concise two-part study in which Windsor analyzes the political dynamics of the situation leading to the August 1968 invasion of Czechoslovakia, emphasizing the extent to which that process was directly tied to political crisis within the Soviet Union itself. Part 2 gives a detailed picture by Roberts of civilian resistance within Czechoslovakia following the entry of troops. Key documents included.

751a Wolfe, Thomas W. SOVIET POWER AND EUROPE, 1945-1970. Baltimore, Md.: Johns Hopkins Press, 1970. x, 534 p. Paperbound.

Includes analysis of the impact of the Czechoslovak intervention on Soviet European policy. See also no. 258.

752 Zaninovich, M. George, and Brown, Douglas A. "Political Integration in Czechoslovakia: Implications of the Prague Spring and Soviet Intervention." JOURNAL OF INTERNATIONAL AFFAIRS 27, no. 1 (1973): 66-79.

Provocative analysis of the ethnic dimension.

753 Zartman, I. William, ed. CZECHOSLOVAKIA, INTERVENTION AND IMPACT. New York: New York University Press, 1970. xiv, 127 p.

Papers based on a conference at the Center for International Studies at NYU held in December 1968 on the causes of the Soviet intervention in Czechoslovakia and its impact on world politics and international relations. Considers the effects of the U.S. reactions and the implications of Western reactions as a whole; Czechoslovakia as a predictor for future Soviet actions.

754 Zeman, Z[bynek].A.B. PRAGUE SPRING: A REPORT ON CZECHOSLOVAKIA 1968. Middlesex, Engl.: Penguin Books, 1969. 169 p. Paperbound.

A brief, sensitive analysis of the Communist reform movement in Czechoslovakia by a scholar who returned to his native country after an absence of twenty years during the spring of 1968. Good discussion of Soviet policy motivation.

Chapter IV
EAST GERMANY

755 Anderson, Evelyn. "East Germany." SURVEY: A JOURNAL OF SOVIET AND EAST EUROPEAN STUDIES, no. 42 (June 1962): 96-106.

A useful analysis of Soviet-East German relations on the issue of the policy switch from support for German reunification to "separatism" as a solution. Insight into Khrushchev-Ulbricht mutually supportive gestures.

756 Bares, Victor. "Beria's Fall and Ulbricht's Survival." SOVIET STUDIES 27 (July 1975): 381-95.

A provocative analysis of the impact of Soviet party faction-alism after Stalin's death on the East German leadership.

757 Baylis, Thomas A. "East Germany--In Quest of Legitimacy." PROBLEMS OF COMMUNISM 21 (March-April 1972): 46-55.

Focus on the problems of mature communism. A useful source for students concerned with the "red" vs. "expert" dilemma in Communist political systems.

758 _____. THE TECHNICAL INTELLIGENTSIA AND THE EAST GERMAN ELITE: LEGITIMACY AND SOCIAL CHANGE IN MATURE COMMUNISM. Berkeley and Los Angeles: University of California Press, 1974. xix, 314 p.

A pioneering contribution to the study of Communist elites use-ful to scholars of Communist systems and to mainstream politi-cal science as well. Explores the political characteristics of technical intelligentsia, recruitment, and career patterns. An important case study.

759 Bender, Peter. "The Special Case of East Germany." STUDIES IN COMPARATIVE COMMUNISM 2 (April 1969): 14-33.

A survey of East Germany's role in the Eastern bloc, the

unique problems created for the East Germans by West Germany, and East German foreign policy.

760 Birnbaum, Karl E. EAST AND WEST GERMANY: A MODUS VIVENDI. Lexington, Mass.: Lexington Books, 1973. xiii, 157 p.

761 Bleimann, Robert. "Ostpolitik and the GDR." SURVEY: A JOURNAL OF EAST & WEST STUDIES 18 (Summer 1972): 36-53.

762 Brandt, Heinz. THE SEARCH FOR A THIRD WAY. Foreword by Erich Fromm. Translated from German. New York: Doubleday, 1970. xvii, 333 p.

Artistic, gripping story of a German socialist and editor of a West German trade union newspaper who was kidnapped by East German security forces and spent three years in prison before his release in 1964. Valuable commentaries on Robert Havemann and Karl Schiedewan. Insightful analysis of Ulbricht's difficulties in coping with Soviet pressure for de-Stalinization.

763 Bromke, Adam, and von Riekhoff, Harald. "The West German-Polish Treaty." THE WORLD TODAY 27 (March 1971): 124-31.

764 Bryson, Phillip J. "The Red Miracle in the International Arena: Economic Foundations of East German Foreign Policy." EAST CENTRAL EUROPE 3, part 1 (1976): 84-96.

765 Childs, David. EAST GERMANY. Nations and Modern World Series. New York and Washington, D.C.: Praeger, 1969. 286 p. Black and white illus.

An uneven but useful study; focus primarily on domestic politics, concluding with a chapter on East Germany's international position. Author a British scholar at Nottingham University, substantially sympathetic to the East German demand for international recognition. Based on both Eastern and Western sources.

766 _____. "East Germany: Towards the Twentieth Anniversary." THE WORLD TODAY 25 (October 1969): 440-50.

767 Croan, Melvin. "After Ulbricht: The End of an Era?" SURVEY: A JOURNAL OF EAST & WEST STUDIES 17 (Spring 1971): 74-92.

Analysis of domestic and foreign policy, emphasizing the slow reconciliation of the East German population and regime during the last decade.

768   . "Czechoslovakia, Ulbricht, and the German Problem." PROB-
LEMS IN COMMUNISM 28 (January-February 1969): 1-7.

An examination of East German relations with Czechoslovakia
just prior to the Czech invasion, with emphasis on the intentions and roles played by Ulbricht and Dubcek in the light of
East German fears of West German ascendency.

769   . "East Germany" In THE COMMUNIST STATES IN DISARRAY
1965-1971, edited by Adam Bromke and Teresa Rakowska-Harmstone,
pp. 73-94. Minneapolis: University of Minnesota Press, 1972.

Assesses degree of economic development, diplomatic and international autonomy of East Germany since the early 1960s,
examines impact of West Germany "Ostpolitik," and the
nature of party controls.

770   . EAST GERMANY: THE SOVIET CONNECTION. Beverly Hills,
Calif.: Sage Publications, 1976. 71 p.

771   . "A Quarter of a Century of the Two Germanys." SURVEY: A
JOURNAL OF EAST & WEST STUDIES 21 (Winter-Spring 1975): 79-84.

Short analysis of the economic and political features and developments in both Germanys since 1945. Comments on the
enduring German national identifications.

772   . "Study of the DDR in the USA." EAST CENTRAL EUROPE   3,
part 1 (1976): 1-14.

772a Dean, Robert W. WEST GERMAN TRADE WITH THE EAST: THE PO-
LITICAL DIMENSION. New York: Praeger, 1974. xvi, 269 p.

See no. 316.

773 Feld, Werner. REUNIFICATION AND WEST GERMAN-SOVIET RELA-
TIONS: THE ROLE OF THE REUNIFICATION ISSUE IN THE FOREIGN
POLICY OF THE FEDERAL REPUBLIC OF GERMANY, 1949-1957, WITH
SPECIAL ATTENTION TO POLICY TOWARDS THE SOVIET UNION.
The Hague: Martinus Nijhoff, 1963. x, 204 p.

Useful for understanding the triangular relationship between
East and West Germany and the Soviet Union. Includes analysis of the Peace Treaty and the Oder-Neisse Line.

773a Forster, Thomas M. THE EAST GERMAN ARMY: A PATTERN OF A
COMMUNIST MILITARY ESTABLISHMENT. Introduction by Brigadier
W.K.F. Thompson. Translated by Anthony Buzek. London: Allen and
Unwin, 1967. 255 p. Black and white illus.

A specialized study of the East German armed forces, based primarily on official sources. Deals with organization, equipment, training, and maneuvers. Important for interaction with Soviet military.

774 Gyorgy, Andrew. "East Germany." In EASTERN EUROPEAN GOVERNMENT AND POLITICS, edited by Vaclav [L.] Benes et al., pp. 100-139. New York: Harper and Row, 1966.

Views the absence of "thaw" in East Germany as a function of Ulbricht's particular controls; a summary of foreign policy attitudes and trends toward various areas of the world, particularly interbloc nations, during the mid-1960s.

775 Haftendorn, Helga. "Ostpolitik Revisited 1976." THE WORLD TODAY 32 (June 1976): 22-229.

See regarding Polish-German relations since renunciation of force treaty December 1970.

776 Hangen, Welles. THE MUTED REVOLUTION: EAST GERMANY'S CHALLENGE TO RUSSIA AND THE WEST. New York: Knopf, 1966. ix, 231 p.

Survey of progress made by East Germany in the postwar period. Written in a readable fashion for the general reader by a former NEW YORK TIMES correspondent.

777 Hanhardt, Arthur M. THE GERMAN DEMOCRATIC REPUBLIC. Integration and Community Building in Eastern Europe Series. Baltimore, Md.: Johns Hopkins University Press, 1968. xxi, 126 p. Paperbound.

Traces the role of East Germany in the Communist system, its entry into the Socialist community.

778 _____. "Political Socialization in Divided Germany." JOURNAL OF INTERNATIONAL AFFAIRS 27, no. 2 (1973): 187-203.

779 Havemann, Robert. DIALEKTIK OHNE DOGMA? NATURWISSENSCHAFT UND WELTANSCHAUUNG. Hamburg: Rowohlt Verlag, 1964. 168 p.

780 Herspring, Dale R. EAST GERMAN CIVIL-MILITARY RELATIONS: THE IMPACT OF TECHNOLOGY, 1949-1972. Foreword by Peter C. Ludz. New York: Praeger, 1973. xxxvii, 216 p.

A provocative application of political science techniques to East German civil-military relations based on the assumption that as technology becomes more sophisticated the extent to which the party can control, i.e., interfere in the daily life of the army declines. Includes interesting comparisons with Soviet counterpart situation. Extremely useful for comparative analysis of the military and politics.

780a Hirsch, Gisela, comp. A BIBLIOGRAPHY OF GERMAN STUDIES, 1945–1971: GERMANY UNDER OCCUPATION, FEDERAL REPUBLIC OF GERMANY, GERMAN DEMOCRATIC REPUBLIC. Bloomington and London: Indiana University Press, 1972. xvi, 603 p.

781 Jones, W. Treharne. "East Germany Under Honecker." THE WORLD TODAY 32 (September 1976): 339–46.

> Deals with the problem of Eurocommunism for the Honecker regime in the context of increased dependence on the USSR.

782 Keren, Michael. "The New Economic System in the G.D.R.: An Obituary." SOVIET STUDIES 24 (April 1973): 554–87.

> Considers the recentralization of the East German economy a more or less permanent abandoning of the New Economic System.

783 Kiss, Sandor. "Hungary's 'Gastarbeiter' in East Germany." EAST EUROPE 18 (October 1969): 8–10.

> An interesting insight into intrabloc labor migration. Discusses the initial reaction to using Hungarian workers in East Germany, governmental attitudes, and institutional involvement.

784 Klimov, Gregory. THE TERROR MACHINE: THE INSIDE STORY OF SOVIET ADMINISTRATION IN GERMANY. Translated by H.C. Stevens. Introduction by Edward Crankshaw and Ernst Reuter. New York: Praeger, 1953. 400 p.

> Soviet Army officer's personal account of his life inside the Soviet bureaucracy in Berlin until his defection. Dramatic, well-written. May or may not be reliable.

784a Kohler, Heinz. ECONOMIC INTEGRATION IN THE SOVIET BLOC: WITH AN EAST GERMAN CASE STUDY. New York: Praeger, 1965. xxi, 402 p.

> See no. 441.

785 Korbel, Josef. DETENTE IN EUROPE: REAL OR IMAGINARY? Princeton, N.J.: Princeton University Press, 1972. viii, 302 p. Paperbound.

> Detailed discussion of intra-German relations and Brandt's "Ostpolitik." See also no. 274.

785a Krisch, Henry. GERMAN POLITICS UNDER SOVIET OCCUPATION. New York: Columbia University Press, 1974. xii, 312 p.

A valuable study of the creation of the Communist–dominated Socialist Unity Party in the Soviet zone of Germany in 1945–46. Strongly indicates the Soviet role in early domestic and foreign policy of East Germany.

786 Kuhlman, James A. "European Realpolitic I: East Berlin's Westpolitik." In THE FUTURE OF INTER–BLOC RELATIONS IN EUROPE, edited by Louis J. Mensonides and James A. Kuhlman, pp. 145–61. New York; Washington, D.C.; London: Praeger, 1974.

Discusses the German problem with specific attention to the problems of national and regional integration.

787 Kulski, W.W. GERMANY AND POLAND: FROM WAR TO PEACEFUL RELATIONS. Syracuse, N.Y.: Syracuse University Press, 1976. xii, 336 p.

A valuable, scholarly analysis written by a former Polish diplomat now professor of Russian affairs at Duke University.

788 Legters, Lyman H., ed. THE GERMAN DEMOCRATIC REPUBLIC: THE CHANGING ORDER AND ORDERLY CHANGE. Boulder, Colo.: Westview Press, 1977. 284 p.

789 Leonhard, Wolfgang. CHILD OF THE REVOLUTION. Translated by C.M. Woodhouse. London: Collins, 1957. 447 p.

The unique memoir of an East German party member who broke with the party over the expulsion of Yugoslavia from the Cominform and defected first to Belgrade, then to the West. Particularly useful for understanding Soviet–East German interparty relations in the early postwar period. A gripping, psychological study of ideological "falling away."

790 Lippmann, Heinz. "East Germany Today: The Limits of Reform Communism." PROBLEMS OF COMMUNISM 19 (May–June 1970): 15–22.

Dubious of piecemeal measures to adapt East Germany to the conditions of a modern industrial society without compromising the leading role of the party. Written by a former high official in the East German Youth Organization and personal deputy to then Politburo member Erich Honecker.

791 _____. HONECKER AND THE NEW POLITICS OF EUROPE. Translated by Helen Sebba. New York: Macmillan, 1972. xiii, 272 p.

A serious study for students concerned with the evolution of Honecker's thinking and the extent to which his personality influences current policy choices.

792   Ludz, Peter C. THE CHANGING PARTY ELITE IN EAST GERMANY.
       Foreword by Zbigniew [K.] Brzezinski. London and Cambridge, Mass.:
       MIT Press, 1968. xxi, 509 p.

> Unique, detailed study of the party organization and elites in
> East Germany. Provides a theoretical framework for the anal-
> ysis of the role of political elites in Communist political sys-
> tems, a wealth of information on the relation of the Socialist
> Unity Party of Germany (SED) to social and economic change,
> and a stimulating analysis of the role of ideology in that pro-
> cess. Written by professor of political science and sociology
> at the University of Bielefeld, West Germany.

793   _____. "Continuity and Change Since Ulbricht." PROBLEMS OF COM-
       MUNISM 21 (March-April 1972): 56-67.

> Section dealing with shift in East German foreign policy dis-
> cusses both relations with the Soviet Union and the West.
> Expects closer ties with CMEA, firm support for Moscow on
> international issues such as the Sino-Soviet confrontation and
> the Middle East, to be combined with all possible tactics to
> upgrade East Germany's international status.

794   _____. "East Germany Today: The SED Leadership in Transition."
       PROBLEMS OF COMMUNISM 19 (May-June 1970): 23-31.

795   _____. "Ostpolitik and the Present State and Future Course of Inner-
       German Contacts." In THE POLITICAL IMPLICATIONS OF SOVIET
       MILITARY POLICY, edited by Lawrence L. Whetten, pp. 65-80. New
       York: Crane, Russak, 1977. Paperbound.

795a   Merkl, Peter H. GERMAN POLICIES, EAST AND WEST; ON THE
       THRESHOLD OF A NEW EUROPEAN ERA. Santa Barbara, Calif.: ABC-
       Clio Press, 1974. ix, 232 p.

796   Nettl, John P. THE EASTERN ZONE AND SOVIET POLICY IN GER-
       MANY, 1945-1950. London and New York: Oxford University Press,
       1951. xix, 324 p.

> Valuable scholarly reference for early period of Communist
> consolidation of power in East Germany. Emphasis on the
> interaction of Soviet policy with both the international aspects
> of the German problem and internal developments in the East-
> ern Zone.

797   Ortmayer, Louis L. CONFLICT, COMPROMISE, AND CONCILIATION:
       WEST GERMAN-POLISH NORMALIZATION, 1966-1967. Denver:
       University of Denver Graduate School of International Studies, 1975.
       xxiii, 162 p. Paperbound.

798   "The Role of the German Democratic Republic Within Eastern Europe."
       In EASTERN EUROPE IN THE 1970'S, edited by Sylva Sinanian et al.,
       pp. 242-57. New York: Praeger, 1972.

       A roundtable discussion of experts on East German affairs from
       the United States and West Germany. Emphasizes that East
       Germany views itself as a part of the East European bloc
       rather than as a part of Germany. Not optimistic about the
       content of "normalization."

799   Scharf, C. Bradley. "East Germany's Approach to Industrial Democracy."
       EAST CENTRAL EUROPE 3, part 1 (1976): 44-57.

800   Schnitzer, Martin. EAST AND WEST GERMANY: A COMPARATIVE
       ECONOMIC ANALYSIS. New York and London: Praeger, 1972. xiii,
       446 p.

801   Schoenhals, Kai. "The 'Free Germany' Movement and Its Impact on the
       German Democratic Republic." EAST CENTRAL EUROPE 1, part 2
       (1974): 115-31.

802   Slusser, Robert [M.], ed. SOVIET ECONOMIC POLICY IN POST-WAR
       GERMANY. New York: Research Program on the USSR, 1953. xv,
       184 p.

       A collection of papers by a group of former Soviet officials.
       Insight into Soviet economic policy toward East Germany, also
       regarding administrative apparatus for implementation.

803   Smith, Jean Edward. GERMANY BEYOND THE WALL: PEOPLE, POLI-
       TICS, AND PROSPERITY. Boston and Toronto: Little, Brown, 1967.
       xiii, 338 p.

       A personalized account of the author's experience in East
       Germany as a visiting scholar. Includes political analysis
       of Ulbricht's approach to the problem of ruling "a country
       that does not exist" in an international environment split as
       to whether it should ever exist.

804   Spittmann, Ilse. "The Soviet Union and the DDR." SURVEY: A JOUR-
       NAL OF SOVIET AND EAST EUROPEAN STUDIES, no. 61 (October 1966):
       165-76.

       One of the earlier articles to recognize the gradual evolution
       of East German-Soviet relations toward a more balanced foot-
       ing. By 1966 East Germany was no longer "a vassal," al-
       though to consider the East German leaders "partners" with
       Moscow leans toward overstatement.

805 Starrels, John M., and Mallinckrodt, Anita M. POLITICS IN THE GER-
MAN DEMOCRATIC REPUBLIC. New York: Praeger, 1975. ix, 396 p.

Applies the systems-functional conceptual model as a framework for analyzing East Germany. Interesting regarding domestic inputs into East German policy positions on intra-German
relations, detente, and ongoing Mutual Force Reduction (MFR)
and SALT negotiations.

806 Stern, Carola [pseud.]. "Relations between the DDR and the Chinese
People's Republic, 1949-1965." In COMMUNISM IN EUROPE, vol. 2,
edited by William E. Griffith, pp. 97-156. Cambridge, Mass.: MIT
Press, 1964. Paperbound.

807 _____. ULBRICHT: A POLITICAL BIOGRAPHY. Translated by Abe
Farbstein. New York; Washington, D.C.; London: Praeger, 1965. xi,
231 p.

Written by an East German who fled to the West. The book
not only provides insight into Ulbricht's rise to power but is a
history of the German Communist movement. International aspects include Ulbricht's delicately negotiated relations with
Moscow, his position during the Berlin crises, East-West pressures,
and the East German leader's attitudes toward other East
European nations.

808 Stolper, Wolfgang F. THE STRUCTURE OF THE EAST GERMAN ECON-
OMY. Cambridge, Mass.: Harvard University Press, 1960. xxv, 478 p.

Extensive analysis of the East German economy broken down into
different sectors of development. Concluding chapter on gross
national product compares performance to that of West Germany.

809 Szaz, Zoltan Michael. GERMANY'S EASTERN FRONTIERS: THE PROB-
LEM OF THE ODER-NEISSE LINE. Foreword by Harold Zink. Chicago:
Henry Regnery, 1960. xi, 256 p.

A focused account of a key problem in Polish-West German
relations within the context of Russian aspirations at the end
of World War II.

810 Thalheim, Karl C. "The Development of the East German Economy in
the Framework of the Soviet Bloc." In EASTERN EUROPE IN TRANSI-
TION, edited by Kurt London, pp. 145-72. Baltimore, Md.: Johns
Hopkins Press, 1966. Paperbound.

811 Tudyka, Kurt P. "The Foreign Policy of the DDR." SURVEY: A JOUR-
NAL OF SOVIET AND EAST EUROPEAN STUDIES, no. 61 (October 1966):
56-69.

Discusses options for East German policy in light of the problem

of being a divided nation subject to overwhelming Soviet influence with major, if latent, conflicts of interest with Moscow.

812   von Riekhoff, Harald.   GERMAN-POLISH RELATIONS 1918-1933.   Baltimore, Md., and London: Johns Hopkins Press, 1971.   xii, 421 p.

A detailed, somewhat overly optimistic diplomatic history.

812a Weit, Erwin.   AT THE RED SUMMIT: INTERPRETER BEHIND THE IRON
CURTAIN.   Translated by Mary Schofield.   Preface by Harry Schwartz.
New York: Macmillan, 1973.   226 p.   Black and white illus.

Shows Ulbricht's influence on Gomulka's attitude toward what
should be done about the Czechoslovak experiment with reform
communism in 1968.   See also no. 749.

813   Wettig, Gerhard.   COMMUNITY AND CONFLICT IN THE SOCIALIST
CAMP: THE SOVIET UNION, EAST GERMANY AND THE GERMAN
PROBLEM 1965-1972.   Translated by Edwina Moreton and Hannes Adomeit.
New York: St. Martin's Press, 1975.   xiv, 161 p.

A major contribution to understanding Soviet-East German relations and the impact of East-West interactions on that process.
Contains a careful account of negotiations.

814   Whetten, Lawrence L.   "The Role of East Germany in West German-Soviet
Relations."   THE WORLD TODAY   25 (December 1969):   507-20.

One of the first academic analyses to pinpoint East Germany's
deliberate attempts to control Soviet policy initiatives toward
West Germany.

814a Windsor, Philip.   GERMANY AND THE MANAGEMENT OF DETENTE.
London: Chatto and Windus for the Institute for Strategic Studies, 1971.
207 p.

Includes an excellent discussion of intra-German relations.

815   Wolfe, Thomas W.   "The Soviet Union's Strategic Stake in the G.D.R."
THE WORLD TODAY   27 (August 1971):   340-50.

815a Zauberman, Alfred.   INDUSTRIAL PROGRESS IN POLAND, CZECHO-
SLOVAKIA, AND EAST GERMANY 1937-1962.   Oxford: Oxford University Press, 1964.   xiv, 338 p.

See no. 491.

A.   UPRISING OF 1953

816   Baring, Arnulg.   UPRISING IN EAST GERMANY: JUNE 17, 1953.

Translated by Gerald Onn. Introduction by David Schoenbaum. Foreword by Richard Lowenthal. Ithaca, N.Y., and London: Cornell University Press, 1972. xxvii, 194 p.

A West German account of the 17 June uprising, its historical aspects as well as causes and consequences for East German domestic and foreign policy.

817   Hidebrant, Rainer. THE EXPLOSION: THE UPRISING BEHIND THE IRON CURTAIN. Translated by E.B. Ashton. Introduction by Norbert Muhlen. Boston and Toronto: Little, Brown, 1955. xxxvi, 198 p. Black and white illus.

Nine personal histories of people swept forward in the uprising. A dramatic, emotional account for the general reader.

818   Kraus, Wolfgang H. "Crisis and Revolt in a Satellite: The East German Case in Retrospect." In EASTERN EUROPE IN TRANSITION, edited by Kurt London, pp. 41-65. Baltimore, Md.: Johns Hopkins Press, 1966. Paperbound.

Analysis of the causes for the June 1953 uprising in East Germany; consequences and impact on the Party leadership.

819   Thomson, Stewart. THE BIALEK AFFAIR. London: Wingate, 1955. 203 p.

An interesting account of the circumstances surrounding the rise, disillusionment, and eventual defection of Robert Bialek, a founding member of the Communist youth movement in East Germany, who defected after the June 1953 Berlin rising. Subsequently was abducted by the Russians in West Berlin in 1956.

B. BERLIN

See also part I, chapter V, "Eastern Europe in the Cold War," p. 29.

820   Allemann, Fritz Rene. "Berlin in Search of a Purpose." SURVEY: A JOURNAL OF SOVIET AND EAST EUROPEAN STUDIES, no. 61 (October 1966): 129-38.

A sensitive discussion of the impact of the Berlin Wall on West Berlin's sense of mission.

821   Armstrong, Anne. BERLINERS: BOTH SIDES OF THE WALL. New Brunswick, N.J.: Rutgers University Press, 1973. xxi, 463 p. Black and white illus.

Insights into the lives of individuals who live in the shadow of the Berlin Wall. Based on ten years of interviews in the divided city.

822 Bark, Dennis L. AGREEMENT ON BERLIN: A STUDY OF THE 1970–72
     QUADRIPARTITE NEGOTIATIONS. Washington, D.C.: American Enter-
     prise Institute for Public Policy Research, 1974. 131 p. Paperbound.

823 Camp, Glen D., Jr. BERLIN IN THE EAST–WEST STRUGGLE 1958–1961.
     New York: Facts on File, 1971. ii, 252 p. Paperbound.

     A detailed factual survey. Useful as a reference.

824 Collier, David S., and Glaser, Kurt [W.], eds. BERLIN AND THE FU-
     TURE OF EASTERN EUROPE. Chicago: Henry Regnery, 1963. vi, 251 p.

     A collection of essays by scholars in the field. Most useful
     for section on responses to Soviet challenge in East Europe.

825 Davison, W. Phillips. THE BERLIN BLOCKADE: A STUDY IN COLD
     WAR POLITICS. Princeton, N.J.: Princeton University Press, 1958.
     423 p.

     An analytical, comprehensive study. Essential for understand-
     ing the role of Berlin in East–West relations.

826 Donner, Jorn. REPORT FROM BERLIN. Translation by Albin T. Ander-
     son. Foreword by Stephen Spender. Bloomington: Indiana University
     Press, 1961. xvi, 284 p.

     A readable, sensitive analysis of a young Finnish scholar's
     stay in Berlin. Includes material from conversations and inter-
     views.

827 Donovan, Frank. BRIDGE IN THE SKY. London: Robert Hale, 1970.
     xii, 209 p.

     A dramatic journalistic account of the Berlin airlift. Interest-
     ing for the general reader rather than scholars in the field.

828 Dulles, Eleanor L[ansing]. BERLIN: THE WALL IS NOT FOREVER. Fore-
     word by Chancellor Konrad Adenauer. Chapel Hill: University of North
     Carolina Press, 1967. xi, 245 p.

     A historical–political discussion of the Berlin problem, coupled
     with an emotional argument for reunification.

829 Embree, George D., ed. THE SOVIET UNION AND THE GERMAN
     QUESTION: SEPTEMBER 1958–JUNE 1961. The Hague: Martinus
     Nijhoff, 1963. xi, 330 p. Paperbound.

     A wide-ranging documentary tracing the Soviet attitude to-
     ward Germany, Berlin, and the interests of East Germany during
     two years of crisis.

830 Haffner, Sebastian. "The Berlin Crisis." SURVEY: A JOURNAL OF
SOVIET AND EAST EUROPEAN STUDIES, no. 57 (October 1962): 37-44.

831 Hartmann, Frederick H. GERMANY BETWEEN EAST AND WEST: THE
REUNIFICATION PROBLEM. Englewood Cliffs, N.J.: Prentice-Hall,
1965. ix, 181 p.

A thoughtful analysis of the consequences of the division of
Germany, the Berlin crises, and possible solutions. Policy
suggestions well-grounded in a realistic assessment of Soviet
domestic developments and Moscow's East European policies.
Research dates from 1959 with the cooperation of the West
German ministry for all-German affairs.

832 Heidelmeyer, Wolfgang, and Hindrichs, Guenter, eds. DOCUMENTS ON
BERLIN 1943-1963. Munich: R. Oldenbourg Verlag, 1963. xviii, 373 p.

833 Heller, Deane, and Heller, David. THE BERLIN WALL. Introduction by
Konrad Adenauer. New York: Walker, 1962. 242 p. Black and white
illus.

An intensely anti-East Germany history of the circumstances
surrounding the building of the Berlin Wall. Most interesting
for the interview with Gen. Lucius D. Clay.

834 Keller, John W. GERMANY, THE WALL, AND BERLIN: INTERNAL
POLITICS DURING AN INTERNATIONAL CRISIS. Foreword by Dr. Hans
Kohn. New York; Washington, D.C.; Hollywood, Calif.: Vantage Press,
1964. 437 p.

Primarily regarding West Germany but useful for interaction of
two Germanys.

835 Kennedy, John F. THE BERLIN CRISIS: REPORT TO THE NATION
JULY 25, 1961. Washington, D.C.: Department of State Office of
Public Services Bureau of Public Affairs, 1961. 21 p.

836 Mahncke, Dieter. "The Berlin Agreement: Balance and Prospects." THE
WORLD TODAY 27 (December 1971): 511-21.

837 Morris, Eric. BLOCKADE: BERLIN AND THE COLD WAR. New York:
Stein and Day, 1973. viii, 278 p. Black and white illus.

A fact-laden, somewhat cluttered analysis. Informative and
readable.

838 Pounds, Norman J.G. DIVIDED GERMANY AND BERLIN. Princeton,
N.J.: Van Nostrand, 1962. 128 p. Paperbound.

Useful background analysis.

839 Schick, Jack M. THE BERLIN CRISIS 1958-1962. Philadelphia: University of Pennsylvania Press, 1971. xix, 266 p.

> A solid, detailed account linking Berlin strategy to other major crises, such as the U-2 incident and the Cuban missile confrontation. Differentiates between local actions in Berlin by the United States and West Germany to which East Germany felt compelled to reply and the crises of 1948-49 and 1958-62, seen as a function of Soviet changing policy toward the West German government.

840 Schutz, Klaus. "Berlin in the Age of Detente." THE WORLD TODAY 31 (January 1975): 29-35.

841 Slusser, Robert M. THE BERLIN CRISIS OF 1961: SOVIET AMERICAN RELATIONS AND THE STRUGGLE FOR POWER IN THE KREMLIN, JUNE-NOVEMBER 1961. Baltimore, Md.: Johns Hopkins Press, 1973. xvi, 509 p. Paperbound.

> An exhaustive, scholarly study of the 1961 Berlin crisis demonstrating the importance of Eastern Europe for Moscow and Washington alike in the bipolar international system of the 1960s. Useful for students of communism, crisis management, and international intrigue.

842 Smith, Jean Edward. THE DEFENSE OF BERLIN. Baltimore, Md.: Johns Hopkins Press, 1963. ix, 431 p.

> Scholarly analysis of problems inherent in defending Berlin from the immediate postwar period until the building of the wall in 1961. Sets the stage for East German foreign policy.

843 Speier, Hans. DIVIDED BERLIN: THE ANATOMY OF SOVIET POLITICAL BLACKMAIL. New York: Praeger, 1961. 201 p.

> A study of the Berlin crisis from the Soviet ultimatum in November 1958 to the building of the wall in 1961. Analysis of Soviet diplomatic techniques and Western response. Originally written for the RAND corporation.

843a Tanter, Raymond. MODELLING AND MANAGING INTERNATIONAL CONFLICTS: THE BERLIN CRISES. Beverly Hills, Calif.: Sage Publications, 1974. 272 p.

> Largely theoretical.

844 Whetten, Lawrence L. "The Problem of Berlin." THE WORLD TODAY 27 (May 1971): 222-27.

845   Windsor, Philip. CITY ON LEAVE, A HISTORY OF BERLIN, 1945-1962.
New York: Praeger, 1963. 275 p.

A sensitive study of the Berlin crisis within its international
context.

Chapter V
HUNGARY

846 Alton, Thad Paul, et al. HUNGARIAN NATIONAL INCOME AND PROD-
UCT IN 1955. Columbia University East Central European Series. New
York and London: Columbia University Press, 1963. xv, 254 p.

Part of a larger study on the structure and growth of Soviet-
type economies by the Research Project on National Income
in East Central Europe. Valuable economic reference book,
also useful to scholars interested in a detailed picture of the
Hungarian economy shortly before the political unrest in 1956.

846a Ausch, Sandor D. THEORY AND PRACTICE OF CMEA COOPERA-
TION. Budapest: Akademiai Kiado, 1972. 279 p.

Hungarian analysis of intrabloc economic cooperation. See
also no. 396.

847 Balassa, Bela A. THE HUNGARIAN EXPERIENCE IN ECONOMIC PLAN-
NING. New Haven, Conn.: Yale University Press, 1959. xii, 285 p.

A study of the theoretical problems of economic planning,
evaluated with respect to the functioning of the Hungarian
model. Based primarily on the Hungarian experience before
the revolution, focusing on the planning methods rather than
a presentation of the economic structure.

848 Berend, I[van].T., and Ranki, G[yorgy]. HUNGARY: A CENTURY OF
ECONOMIC DEVELOPMENT. New York: Barnes & Noble, 1974. 263 p.

A general statement of the current Hungarian interpretation.
Less useful than the more specific Hungarian economic analysis
available in English.

849 Buky, Barnabas. "Hungary's NEM on a Treadmill." PROBLEMS OF
COMMUNISM 21 (September–October 1972): 31-39.

850 Deak, Istvan. "Hungary." In THE EUROPEAN RIGHT: A HISTORICAL
PROFILE, edited by Hans Rogger and Eugen Weber, pp. 364-407. Berkeley and Los Angeles: University of California Press, 1965.

851 Dreisziger, Nander A.F. HUNGARY'S WAY TO WORLD WAR II.
Toronto: Hungarian Helicon Society, 1968. 240 p.

    The origins of Hungary's involvement in World War II. Em-
    phasis on Hungarian-German relations and the search for a
    Danubian solution.

852 Fejto, Francois. "Hungarian Communism." In COMMUNISM IN EUROPE,
vol. 1, edited by William E. Griffith, pp. 177-300. Cambridge, Mass.:
MIT Press, 1964.

    Hungarian relations with Khruschev, Tito, and the Chinese are
    given some treatment, focusing on Kadar's dependence on the
    USSR, and the beginnings of a "thaw" in domestic programs
    and policies in the early 1960s.

853 Fenyo, Mario D. HITLER, HORTHY AND HUNGARY: GERMAN-HUN-
GARIAN RELATIONS 1941-1944. New Haven, Conn.: Yale University
Press, 1972. xii, 279 p.

    Based mainly on German documents.

854 Fischer, Lewis A., and Uren, Philip E. THE NEW HUNGARIAN AGRI-
CULTURE. Montreal and London: McGill-Queens University Press, 1973.
xxi, 138 p.

    Relates agricultural policy to the New Economic Mechanism (NEM).

855 Friss, Istvan, ed. REFORM OF THE ECONOMIC MECHANISM IN HUN-
GARY. Budapest: Akademiai Kiado, 1971. 160 p.

856 Gado, Otto, ed. REFORM OF THE ECONOMIC MECHANISM IN HUN-
GARY: DEVELOPMENT 1968-1971. Budapest: Akademiai Kiado, 1972.
314 p.

    A valuable source for the principles of the Hungarian economic
    system and its relation to foreign trade.

857 Gati, Charles. "Hungary: The Dynamics of Revolutionary Transformation."
In his THE POLITICS OF MODERNIZATION IN EASTERN EUROPE: TEST-
ING THE SOVIET MODEL, pp. 51-88. New York: Praeger, 1974.

858 _____. "The Kadar Mystique." PROBLEMS OF COMMUNISM 23
(May-June 1974): 23-35.

    Good discussion of courses and potential consequences of grass-
    roots worker opposition to economic reform.

859 Helmreich, Ernst, ed. HUNGARY. Published for the Free Europe Committee as part of the East Central Europe under the Communists Series.
New York: Praeger, 1957. xiv, 466 p. Appendix.

> A survey of Hungarian history, geography, government, litera-
> ture, education, and economy up until 1956, written before
> the eruption of the Hungarian revolution, with a final chapter
> later added tracing the chronology of the events of the Revolu-
> tion, summarizing the impact of the revolution on Hungarian
> affairs. Biographical sketches of the leading Hungarian figures
> as of August 1956 in appendix. Compiled by Hungarian refu-
> gees and American scholars.

860 Horvath, Laszlo. "Participation and Factory Democracy." EASTERN
EUROPEAN ECONOMICS 14 (Spring 1976): 59-83.

861 HUNGARY TODAY. New York: Praeger, 1962. 104 p.

> Papers from a symposium of scholars and journalists devoted
> to the changes in Hungary since the 1956 upheavals. Insights
> both into Kadar's style of leadership and Soviet-Hungarian re-
> lations.

862 Ignotus, Paul. "The First Two Communist Takeovers of Hungary: 1919
and 1948." In THE ANATOMY OF COMMUNIST TAKEOVERS, edited
by Thomas T. Hammond, pp. 385-98. New Haven, Conn., and London:
Yale University Press, 1975. Paperbound.

863 _____. HUNGARY. Nations of the Modern World Series. New York:
Praeger, 1972. 333 p. Black and white illus.

> A scholarly study of present day Hungary concerned with the
> interaction of contemporary ideology and historical trends.
> Deals with Soviet-Hungarian relations before and after 1956,
> the evolution in the 1960s and 1970s. Also shows the impact
> of Yugoslav experiments on Hungarian politics. Particularly
> useful to students of comparative politics and political culture.

864 Janos, Andrew C. "Nationalism and Communism in Hungary." EAST
EUROPEAN QUARTERLY 5 (March 1971): 74-103.

865 Janos, Andrew C., and Slottman, William. REVOLUTION IN PERSPEC-
TIVE: ESSAYS ON THE HUNGARIAN SOVIET REPUBLIC OF 1919.
Berkeley and Los Angeles: University of California Press, 1971. x, 185 p.

> Based on the papers given at a conference at Berkeley in
> 1969. Essays on the internal and external affairs of the re-
> public, its connections with previous Hungarian history, its
> internal political history, and Austrian reactions. Concluding
> essay by Richard Lowenthall attempts to establish the links

between the Hungarian Soviet Republic and the subsequent history of communism.

866 Jaszi, Oscar. REVOLUTION AND COUNTER-REVOLUTION IN HUNGARY. Introduction by R[obert].W[illiam]. Seton-Watson. New York: Howard Fertig, 1969. 239 p.

A detailed historical study of the short-lived Hungarian Soviet Republic in 1919. Shows the importance of the Russian revolution on East European thinking.

867 Kertesz, Stephen D. DIPLOMACY IN A WHIRLPOOL: HUNGARY BETWEEN NAZI GERMANY AND SOVIET RUSSIA. Notre Dame, Ind.: University of Notre Dame Press, 1953. xvi, 273 p.

A historical account of the circumstances leading to a Communist takeover in Hungary by a former official in the Hungarian ministry of Soviet affairs.

867a Kiss, Sandor. "Hungary's 'Gastarbeiter' in East Germany." EAST EUROPE 18 (October 1969): 8-10.

867b Kiss, Tibor. INTERNATIONAL DIVISION OF LABOUR IN OPEN ECONOMIES: WITH SPECIAL REGARD TO CMEA. Budapest: Akademiai Kiado, 1971. 322 p.

Analysis of an Hungarian official economist.

868 Kovrig, Bennett. THE HUNGARIAN PEOPLE'S REPUBLIC. Integration and Community Building in Eastern Europe Series. Baltimore, Md.: Johns Hopkins Press, 1970. xvii, 206 p. Paperbound.

Good background on the relations of the Hungarian People's Republic with the rest of East Europe and also relations with the Soviet Union, analyzing the influence of a superpower on a small nation-state.

869 Laszlo, Ervin. "Trends in East-European Philosophy: A Case Study on Hungary." STUDIES IN SOVIET THOUGHT 7 (June 1967): 130-41.

870 Laszlo, Leslie. "Towards Normalization of Church-State Relations in Hungary." In RELIGION AND ATHEISM IN THE U.S.S.R. AND EASTERN EUROPE, edited by Bohdan R. Bociurkiw and John W. Strong, pp. 292-313. London and Basingstoke, Engl.: Macmillan, 1975.

Discusses Vatican agreement of 1964, the fate of Cardinal Mindszenty, and subsequent developments.

871 Lauter, Geza Peter. THE MANAGER AND ECONOMIC REFORM HUN-

GARY. New York: Praeger, 1972. xv, 189 p.

A useful economic analysis of the Hungarian New Economic Mechanism (NEM). Particularly important for scholars dealing with the question of whether Hungarian reforms can serve as a model for other CMEA countries.

872 Macartney, C.A. HUNGARY: A SHORT HISTORY. Chicago: Aldine, 1962. ix, 262 p.

Useful for historical perspective. Good on the early period; somewhat weak regarding more contemporary developments until 1956.

873 Mueller, George, and Singer, Herman. "Hungary: Can the New Course Survive." PROBLEMS OF COMMUNISM 14 (January-February 1965): 32-38.

A succinct analysis of the prospects for Hungarian economic reform. Guarded optimism with the warning that the result ultimately depends not on Budapest but on Moscow.

874 Nagy, Ferenc. THE STRUGGLE BEHIND THE IRON CURTAIN. Translated by Stephen K. Swift. New York: Macmillan, 1948. xvi, 471 p.

Memoirs and interpretation of the former Hungarian prime minister concerning Communist consolidation of power in the immediate postwar period. Understandably biased but interesting account.

875 Pamlenyi, Ervin, ed. A HISTORY OF HUNGARY. Wellingborough, Engl.: Collet's, 1975. 676 p.

875a Porro, J.D. CONTROLLED PLURALISM: IS HUNGARY THE FUTURE OF EAST EUROPE? Santa Monica, Calif.: RAND Memorandum P-5386, February, 1975. 18 p.

See no. 243.

876 Racz, Barnabas. "Political Changes in Hungary After the Soviet Invasion of Czechoslovakia." SLAVIC REVIEW 29 (December 1970): 633-50.

Indicates Hungarian retreat on liberal reforms in response to interbloc crisis.

877 Robinson, William F. THE PATTERN OF REFORM IN HUNGARY: A POLITICAL, ECONOMIC AND CULTURAL ANALYSIS. New York: Praeger, 1973. xiv, 467 p.

Evaluates the significance of the pattern of change in the

nature of Hungarian society despite continuation of the leading role of the Communist party. Analysis of the reform situation in Hungary as of spring 1972.

878   Sandor, E. [pseud.]. "Hope and Caution." PROBLEMS OF COMMUNISM 19 (January–February 1970): 60–66.

A journalistic analysis of post-1968 attempts at economic reform in Hungary in the context of the implications stemming from the intervention in Czechoslovakia.

879   Schopflin, George. "Hungarian Intellectuals under Pressure." THE WORLD TODAY 30 (1974): 73–79.

879a Shaffer, Harry G. "Progress in Hungary." PROBLEMS OF COMMUNISM 19 (January–February 1970): 48–59.

880   Shawcross, William. CRIME AND COMPROMISE: JANOS KADAR AND THE POLITICS OF HUNGARY SINCE REVOLUTION. New York: E.P. Dutton, 1974. 311 p.

A British journalist's somewhat dramatized description of the evolution of Hungarian politics since 1956. Author on the staff of THE SUNDAY TIMES, London.

881   Shonfield, Andrew. "Hungary and Poland: The Politics of Economic Reform." THE WORLD TODAY 26 (March 1970): 94–102.

882   Siman, Miklos. "Sources of Economic Growth in Hungary, 1967–1972." EASTERN EUROPEAN ECONOMICS 13 (Fall 1974): 25–58.

883   Szasz, Bela. VOLUNTEERS FOR THE GALLOWS. Translated by Kathleen Szasz. New York: Norton, 1971. vii, 244 p.

A narrative about the trial of Laszlo Rajk in Budapest, translated from the Hungarian.

884   Tokes, Rudolf L. BELA KUN AND THE HUNGARIAN SOVIET REPUBLIC. New York: Praeger, 1967. xii, 292 p.

The origins of the Hungarian Communist party and a background to its first short rule in Hungary, especially its organization, ideology, and Russian origins. Concludes with an analysis of the factors that contributed to the breakdown of discipline within the party and the fall of the republic. Appendix includes correspondence between the Hungarian group and the Russian Communist party.

885 Toma, Peter A. "The Case of Hungary." STUDIES IN COMPARATIVE COMMUNISM 4 (April 1971): 43-46.

886 Vajda, Imre, and Simai, Mihaly. FOREIGN TRADE IN A PLANNED ECONOMY. Cambridge, Engl.: At the University Press, 1971. xii, 221 p. Illus.

Written by a number of Hungarian economists, a valuable reference for students of either Hungarian economic relations or intra-Communist trade. Papers do not cover recent Hungarian reforms, but useful in understanding the climate for such changes.

887 Vali, Ferenc A. "Hungary." In THE COMMUNIST STATES AT THE CROSSROADS: BETWEEN MOSCOW AND PEKING, edited by Adam Bromke, pp. 71-86. New York; Washington, D.C.; London: Praeger, 1965.

888 _____. "Hungary." In THE COMMUNIST STATES IN DISARRAY 1965-1971, edited by Adam Bromke and Teresa Rakowska-Harmstone, pp. 121-35. Minneapolis: University of Minnesota Press, 1972.

Discusses Kadar's commitment to Soviet structures in foreign policy and defense, and to strict internal party controls. Also treats the New Economic Mechanism.

889 Volgyes, Ivan. "Hungary in the Seventies: The Era of Reform." CURRENT HISTORY 65 (May 1973): 216-20.

890 _____, ed. HUNGARY IN REVOLUTION 1918-1919. Lincoln: University of Nebraska Press, 1971. x, 219 p.

Nine essays on revolutionary changes in Hungary during the period of 1918-19: the background and causes of the revolution, the contribution of modernization, domestic reforms, the nationalities problems, foreign policy problems (based on the minutes of the Revolutionary Governing Council), and the differences between the Soviet Union and the Hungarian Soviet Republic in accession to power, makeup, and policies.

890a Zsoldos, Laszlo. THE ECONOMIC INTEGRATION OF HUNGARY INTO THE SOVIET BLOC. Columbus: Ohio University Press, 1963. xvii, 149 p.

See no. 492.

A. THE HUNGARIAN UPRISING OF 1956

See also part II, chapter VI, section A, "The Polish October, 1956," p. 175.

891 Aczel, Tamas, and Meray, Tibor. THE REVOLT OF THE MIND: A CASE HISTORY OF INTELLECTUAL RESISTANCE BEHIND THE IRON CURTAIN. New York: Praeger, 1959. xiv, 449 p.

A study of the intellectual resistance during the Hungarian Revolution. An account of the struggles of the Communist writers and the Hungarian Writers Association. (Both authors celebrated novelists who fled Hungary after the revolution.)

892 Aczel, Tamas, ed. TEN YEARS AFTER: THE HUNGARIAN REVOLUTION IN THE PERSPECTIVE OF HISTORY. New York: Holt, Rinehart and Winston, 1966. 253 p.

A study of the Hungarian revolution in historical perspective; eleven essays on "Hungary and the World" and "Hungary Ten Years After." Trends in Hungary in the ten years immediately following the revolution.

893 Aptheker, Herbert. THE TRUTH ABOUT HUNGARY. New York: Mainstream Publishers, 1957. 256 p.

An American Communist's justification of the Soviet 1956 invasion. Useful in understanding the CPUSA pro-Soviet stance and Moscow's version of its role as put forward within interparty circles.

894 Bain, Leslie B. THE RELUCTANT SATELLITES: AN EYE-WITNESS REPORT ON EASTERN EUROPE AND THE HUNGARIAN REVOLUTION. New York and London: Macmillan, 1960. 233 p.

An account of the author's life in Budapest during the "events of 1956," set in the context of postwar Hungarian circumstances. A vivid description, including a brief discussion of Yugoslavia, by a professional journalist for THE REPORTER.

895 Barber, Noel. SEVEN DAYS OF FREEDOM: THE HUNGARIAN UPRISING 1956. New York: Stein and Day, 1974. 26 p.

A somewhat belated journalistic account of the Hungarian uprising. A well-written analysis with the benefits of hindsight.

896 Beke, Laszlo [pseud.]. A STUDENT'S DIARY: BUDAPEST OCTOBER 16-NOVEMBER 1, 1956. Translated from the Hungarian by Leon Kossar and Ralph Zoltan. New York: Viking Press, 1957. 125 p. Illus.

The story of a student who participated in the Budapest up-

rising. Particularly interesting for those studying student political activities in the late 1960s. Shows the extent to which
students both served as a catalyst and were swept forward by
events.

897   Benes, Vaclav [L.]. "Hungary." In EASTERN EUROPEAN GOVERNMENT
AND POLITICS, edited by Vaclav Benes et al., pp. 140-77. New York:
Harper and Row, 1966.

Considers the Rakosi-Nagy struggle as an ideological dispute
parallel to the Malenkov-Khrushchev struggle, with the Soviet
Party as umpire.

898   Fetjo, Francois. BEHIND THE RAPE OF HUNGARY. Translated from
French by Norbert Guterman. Foreword by Jean-Paul Sartre. New York:
McKay, 1957. xv, 335 p.

A study of the Sovietization of Hungary, circumstances that
led to the uprising in 1956, and personalities involved, by a
French historian and journalist of Hungarian origin.

899   Fryer, Peter. HUNGARIAN TRAGEDY. London: Dobson, 1956. 96 p.
Illus.

Brief analysis written by the correspondent for the DAILY
WORKER in Hungary is a rejection of the various Soviet justifications for invasion. Not only provides a succinct version
of the Soviet line, but shows the depth of disaffection that
the intervention in Hungary caused among other Communist
parties.

900   Gyorgy, Andrew. "The Hungarian Revolution of 1956." In THE ANAT-
OMY OF COMMUNIST TAKEOVERS, edited by Thomas T. Hammond,
pp. 596-605. New Haven, Conn., and London: Yale University Press,
1975. Paperbound.

901   Kecskemeti, Paul. THE UNEXPECTED REVOLUTION: SOCIAL FORCES
IN THE HUNGARIAN UPRISING. Stanford, Calif.: Stanford University
Press, 1961. vi, 178 p.

A sophisticated analysis of the strains in Hungarian society
that contributed to the abortive uprising in 1956. Shows
clearly the impact of Moscow's decision to force de-Stalinization on the reluctant Rakosi.

902   Kovage, Jozsef. YOU ARE ALL ALONE. New York: Praeger, 1959.
295 p.

Personalized story of the Hungarian uprising by a one-time
mayor of Budapest from just after the war. After his arrest,

spent six years in prison, then was released in the wave of
rehabilitations that set the stage for the uprising of 1956.

903   Lasky, Melvin J., ed. THE HUNGARIAN REVOLUTION: THE STORY
OF THE OCTOBER UPRISING AS RECORDED IN DOCUMENTS, DISPATCHES,
EYEWITNESS ACCOUNTS, AND WORLD-WIDE REACTIONS. Introduction
by Hugh Seton-Watson. New York: Praeger, 1957. 318 p.

A useful collection for those interested in the daily and hourly
details of the Hungarian crisis from its beginning until the
Soviet intervention on 4 November 1956. Shows the pattern
of escalating political tension and chaos.

904   Lettis, Richard, and Morris, W.E. THE HUNGARIAN REVOLT, OCTOBER
23-NOVEMBER 4, 1956. New York: Charles Scribner's Sons, 1961.
xx, 219 p. Paperbound.

A day-by-day account.

905   Marton, Endre. THE FORBIDDEN SKY: INSIDE THE HUNGARIAN
REVOLUTION. Boston: Little, Brown, 1971. xii, 306 p.

906   Meray, Tibor. THIRTEEN DAYS THAT SHOOK THE KREMLIN. Translated
from the Hungarian by Howard L. Katzander. New York: Praeger,
1959. vi, 290 p.

A gripping account by a Hungarian novelist who fled after the
failure of the uprising of the 13 days from 23 October to 4
November 1956, as seen from the Hungarian Communist party
headquarters. Includes analysis of the aftermath of Soviet
intervention and ends with the execution of Imre Nagy.

907   Molnar, Miklos. VICTOIRE D'UNE DEFAITE. BUDAPEST 1956. Paris:
Fayard, 1968. 365 p. Illus.

Written by the editor-in-chief of the GAZETTE LITTERAIRE in
Budapest who witnessed the evolution leading up to the October Revolution of 1956. Sees the events of 1956 as a continuation of the national struggle to gain independence; its
anti-Stalin character as only one dimension among the political, social, and national components that were also important.

908   Molnar, Miklos, and Nagy, Laszlo. IMRE NAGY: REFORMATEUR OU
REVOLUTIONNAIRE? Geneva: Librarie Droz, 1959. 256 p.

An analysis of Nagy's attempted reform and revolt, comparing
him to Tito, Malenkov, and Gomulka, and a treatment of his
role in the Hungarian revolution.

909   Nagy, Imre. ON COMMUNISM: IN DEFENCE OF THE NEW COURSE.

Foreword by Hugh Seton-Watson. New York: Praeger, 1957. xliv, 306 p.

> Author's defense of his policy as premier from July 1953 until his fall in April 1955. Written before his star-crossed rise in 1956, is particularly interesting both for references to the USSR and for evident Yugoslav influence on his thinking. Used as a basis for the indictment during his trial in 1958.

910 Paloczi-Horvath, George. THE UNDEFEATED. London: Seeker and Warburg, 1959. 288 p.

> Autobiography of an articulate Hungarian journalist who became a member of the Communist party, spent several years in prison, then left the country during the uprising of 1956.

911 Radvanyi, Janos. HUNGARY AND THE SUPERPOWERS: THE 1956 REVOLUTION AND REALPOLITIK. Stanford, Calif.: Hoover Institution Press, 1972. xvii, 197 p.

> Written by a former diplomat of the Hungarian Communist government who participated in the Hungarian-U.S. negotiations in 1962. Emphasizes the reaction of the other leaders to Hungarian events, and particularly the international implications of the revolution.

912 REPORT OF THE SPECIAL COMMITTEE ON THE PROBLEM OF HUNGARY. New York: The United Nations, 1957. 148 p.

> Full report of the special committee set up by the General Assembly of the United Nations to study the question of aggression in Hungary. A valuable official document for any student of the crisis.

912a Seton-Watson, Hugh. NATIONALISM AND COMMUNISM: ESSAYS, 1946-1963. New York: Praeger, 1964. x, 253 p.

> Part 3 provides an analysis of the causes and aftermath of the Hungarian 1956 uprising. Concludes with a section devoted to intra-Communist tensions.

913 Stillman, Edmund [O.], ed. BITTER HARVEST: THE INTELLECTUAL REVOLT BEHIND THE IRON CURTAIN. Introduction by Francois Bondy. New York: Praeger, 1959. xxxiii, 313 p.

> An anthology of East European poems, essays, and stories showing the extent of intellectual unrest in that area primarily from 1955 to 1957. Includes a section on national communism and national identity with selections by both Nagy and Djilas. Important for an understanding of the events in Poland and Hungary in 1956. Also regarding balance of domestic vs. "international" complaints.

914 Szikszoy, Joseph Alexander. "The Legal Aspects of the Hungarian Question." Ph.D. thesis, University of Geneva, 1963. 219 p.

Detailed documentation regarding the Soviets' interpretations of the legality of their intervention in Hungary. A separate section deals with the relevance of the Warsaw Pact. Useful to students of regional defense alliances and the United Nations.

915 Tokes, Rudolf L. "Polycentrism: Central European and Hungarian Origins." STUDIES IN COMPARATIVE COMMUNISM 6 (Winter 1973): 414-28.

Insight into Hungarian-Soviet strategic, tactical, and ideological disagreements from 1953 to 1956.

916 Vali, Ferenc A. RIFT AND REVOLT IN HUNGARY: NATIONALISM VERSUS COMMUNISM. Cambridge, Mass.: Harvard University Press, 1961. xi, 590 p.

A scholarly analysis of the uneven course of Hungarian communism from 1945 to 1961. Emphasis on the uprising in 1956, both background and aftermath. Written by a former Hungarian jurist, now a professor at the University of Massachusetts, Amherst. One of the key books on the Hungarian crisis of 1956. See also for rising East European nationalism as a result of de-Stalinization and the New Course, and the changing nature of Soviet-East European relations in the late 1950s.

916a Welsh, William A. "A Game-Theoretic Conceptualization of the Hungarian Revolt: Toward an Inductuve Theory of Games." In COMMUNIST STUDIES AND THE SOCIAL SCIENCES: ESSAYS ON METHODOLOGY AND EMPIRICAL THEORY, edited by Frederic J. Fleron, Jr., pp. 420-66. Chicago: Rand McNally, 1971. Paperbound.

See no. 118.

917 Wiatr, Jerzy J. "Crisis of Internationalism." EAST EUROPE 6 (April 1957): 52-56.

Translated from the November-December 1956 issue of the Polish Communist theoretical journal, NOWE DROGI, this frank analysis of past and present differences among Communist parties and states is valuable for understanding Poland's attitudes toward interparty relations immediately following World War II, during the "Yugoslav affair," and the upheavals in Eastern Europe in 1956.

918 Zinner, Paul E. REVOLUTION IN HUNGARY. New York: Columbia University Press, 1962. xiii, 380 p.

Traces the developments in Hungary from 1945 to 1956, emphasizing the internal evolution of the Party, the popular reactions

to Communist rule there, and the factors that contributed to
the revolution.

919 _____, ed. NATIONAL COMMUNISM AND POPULAR REVOLT IN
EASTERN EUROPE: A SELECTION OF DOCUMENTS ON EVENTS IN
POLAND AND HUNGARY, FEBRUARY-NOVEMBER 1956. Foreword by
Henry L. Roberts. New York: Columbia University Press, 1956. xx,
561 p. Paperbound.

The best documentary collection dealing with these crises.
Communist analyses of the causes, dynamics, and repercussions
throughout Eastern Europe of the 1956 upheavals in Poland and
Hungary.

Chapter VI

POLAND

920 Anderson, Neal. "Poland's Place in Europe." THE WORLD TODAY 25
(December 1969): 520-29.

921 Benes, Vaclav L., and Pounds, Norman J.G. POLAND. Nations of
the Modern World Series. New York: Praeger, 1970. 416 p. Black
and white illus.

> A scholarly history of Poland including detailed analysis of
> Soviet-Polish relations in the postwar period, the Polish Octo-
> ber of 1956, and Polish foreign policy during the latter years
> of Gomulka's regime. Benes was a professor of political sci-
> ence at Indiana University; Pounds, professor of history and
> geography at Indiana University.

922 Bethell, Nicholas. GOMULKA. HIS POLAND AND HIS COMMUNISM.
2d ed., rev. Middlesex, Engl.: Penguin Books, 1972. 307 p. Paperbound. Black and white illus.

> A political biography with emphasis on the Polish leader's
> wartime and postwartime activity, especially during October
> 1956. Focuses more on the years before his regime and much
> less on the years of actual leadership.

923 Bromke, Adam. POLAND'S POLITICS: IDEALISM V. REALISM. Cambridge, Mass.: Harvard University Press, 1967. x, 316 p.

> A political history of Poland beginning in the late nineteenth
> century, but with the main emphasis on the last twenty-five
> years. Emphasis on the security dilemma for Poland. Deals
> with the foreign policy conflict generated by trying to balance
> between total independence and total dependence vis-à-vis the
> Soviet Union.

924 _____. "Poland's Role in the Loosening of the Communist Bloc." In
EASTERN EUROPE IN TRANSITION, edited by Kurt London, pp. 67-92.

Baltimore, Md.: Johns Hopkins Press, 1966. Paperbound.

925 _____. "Poland Under Gierek--A New Political Style." PROBLEMS OF COMMUNISM 21 (September-October 1972): 1-19.

926 _____. "Polish Foreign Policy in the 1970's." In GIEREK'S POLAND, edited by Adam Bromke and John W. Strong, pp. 192-204. New York: Praeger, 1973.

> Survey of Gierek's foreign policy toward both the Soviet Union and the West. Emphasis on coincidence of foreign policy as practiced in Bonn and Warsaw.

927 Bromke, Adam, and Strong, John W., eds. GIEREK'S POLAND. New York: Praeger, 1973. 219 p.

> A collection of articles on contemporary Polish domestic and foreign policy. Published in cooperation with Canadian Slavonic Papers; contributors include both Western and Polish scholars.

928 Buell, Raymond L[eslie]. POLAND: KEY TO EUROPE. 3d ed. New York: Knopf, 1939. vii, 406 p.

> Useful background for Polish interwar foreign policy. Concludes with Soviet-Nazi Pact and partition of Poland in 1939.

929 Campbell, John C. "Poland: A Special Case Within the Bloc." In his AMERICAN POLICY TOWARDS COMMUNIST EASTERN EUROPE: THE CHOICE AHEAD, pp. 58-67. Minneapolis: University of Minnesota Press, 1965.

> Deals with Polish-Soviet relations, Germany, and U.S. interests. Emphasis on the favorable repercussions of special treatment of Poland in other areas of the Communist world.

930 Chrypinski, V.C. "Poland." In THE COMMUNIST STATES IN DISARRAY 1965-1971, edited by Adam Bromke and Teresa Rakowska-Harmstone, pp. 95-129. Minneapolis: University of Minnesota Press, 1972.

> Discusses the country's domestic economic problems as functions, in part, of ideological priorities and CMEA demands.

931 Ciechanowski, Jan M. THE WARSAW RISING OF 1944. London and New York: Cambridge University Press, 1974. xi, 332 p.

> A study of Polish-Soviet relations putting forth the view that after Stalingrad the Poles should have been more realistic about coming to some sort of accommodation with the Soviet Union.

932 Cienciala, Anna M. POLAND AND THE WESTERN POWERS 1938-1939: A STUDY OF THE INTERDEPENDENCE OF EASTERN AND WESTERN EUROPE. London: Routledge and Kegan Paul, 1968. x, 310 p.

Excellent background for understanding the limitations on Polish foreign policy options before and during the Second World War. Use made of public Polish, German, British, and American foreign policy documents as well as some unpublished Polish documents.

933 Cieplak, Tadeusz N. "The Role and Function of Non-Communist Parties in the Polish People's Republic: The Case of the United Peasant Party." CANADIAN-AMERICAN SLAVIC STUDIES 6 (Spring 1972): 38-72.

Important for group theory and analysis of potential East European pluralism.

934 _____, ed. POLAND SINCE 1956. New York: Twayne Publishers, 1972. 482 p.

Essays on Polish government and politics (including the October upheaval), the position of the party, the intellectuals and the Catholic church, domestic and foreign policy, the economic sector, social attitudes, and U.S.-Polish relations.

935 Davies, Norman. WHITE EAGLE, RED STAR: THE POLISH-SOVIET WAR, 1919-1920. Foreword by A.J.P. Taylor. New York: St. Martin's Press, 1972. xviii, 318 p.

An English scholar's history of the war that influenced Polish foreign policy for twenty years after it officially ended and whose occurrence even today helps explain the emotions underlying Polish-Soviet relations. Based on extensive Polish sources.

936 Dean, Robert W. "Gierek's Three Years." SURVEY: A JOURNAL OF EAST & WEST STUDIES 20 (Spring-Summer 1974): 59-76.

A summary of developments, concluding that Polish foreign policy has been partially restructured to meet the needs of Gierek's program for economic development.

937 Debicki, Roman. FOREIGN POLICY OF POLAND 1919-1939. Foreword by Oscar Halecki. New York: Praeger, 1962. xi, 192 p.

A well-organized, well-written history of Polish foreign policy during the interwar years. Author a high ranking Polish diplomat before and during World War II; subsequently became professor of government at Georgetown University in Washington, D.C.

937a Drachkovitch, Milorad M. UNITED STATES AID TO YUGOSLAVIA AND
POLAND: ANALYSIS OF A CONTROVERSY. Washington, D.C.:
American Enterprise Institute for Policy Research, 1963. v, 124 p.

See no. 264.

938 Dziewanowski, M. Kamil. THE COMMUNIST PARTY OF POLAND:
AN OUTLINE OF HISTORY. 2d ed. Cambridge, Mass.: Harvard University Press, 1976. xii, 419 p.

First published in 1959. Expanded to include the Gomulka
era with an epilogue devoted to Gierek's leadership. Emphasis on the interaction of domestic and foreign policy developments.

939 _____. "Poland." In THE COMMUNIST STATES AT THE CROSSROADS:
BETWEEN MOSCOW AND PEKING, edited by Adam Bromke, pp. 56-70.
New York; Washington, D.C.; London: Praeger, 1965.

940 _____. POLAND IN THE TWENTIETH CENTURY. New York: Columbia
University Press, 1977. xiii, 309 p.

An historical survey putting Communist Poland in perspective.
Useful for undergraduates or a general reader.

941 Feiwel, George R. INDUSTRIALIZATION AND PLANNING UNDER
POLISH SOCIALISM. Vols. 1 and 2. New York: Praeger, 1971. xxv,
748 p. and xvii, 454 p.

Valuable data for students of planning and development. The
only study of this depth on the Polish economy available in
the West.

942 Flakierski, H. "Polish Postwar Economic Growth." SOVIET STUDIES
21 (July 1975): 460-76.

Continuation of academic polemics on the question of whether
or not Polish postwar growth patterns adhered to the Soviet
model.

943 Gamarnikow, Michael. "A New Economic Approach." PROBLEMS OF
COMMUNISM 21 (September-October 1972): 20-30.

Survey of the problems and prospects for Gierek's economic
reforms in relation to economic tensions that did not disappear
when Gomulka retired from the political scene.

944 _____. "The Polish Economy in Transition." PROBLEMS OF COMMU-
NISM 19 (January-February 1970): 40-47.

944a Gomulka, Wladyslaw. ON THE GERMAN PROBLEM. Warsaw: Ksiazka i. Wiedza, 1969. 431 p.

Translated from the German, a series of articles and speeches made between 1944 and 1969 by the Polish leader.

945 Groth, Alexander J. PEOPLE'S POLAND. GOVERNMENT AND POLITICS. San Francisco: Chandler, 1972. vii, 155 p. Paperbound.

An introduction to Polish politics in the 1970s; background survey including major institutions, policies, and problems. Focused on the interplay of international and domestic politics.

946 Halecki, Oscar. A HISTORY OF POLAND. Chicago: Henry Regnery, 1966. xii, 369 p. Paperbound.

947 _____, ed. POLAND. Published for the Mid-European Studies Center of the Free Europe Committee as part of the East Central Europe under the Communists Series. New York: Praeger, 1957. xviii, 601 p.

Emphasis on economic, political, and cultural changes produced by Communist takeover in Poland.

948 Heyman, Frederick G. POLAND AND CZECHOSLOVAKIA. Englewood Cliffs, N.J.: Prentice-Hall, 1966. viii, 181 p.

See no. 632.

949 Hiscocks, Richard. POLAND: BRIDGE FOR THE ABYSS? AN INTERPRETATION OF DEVELOPMENTS IN POSTWAR POLAND. London: Oxford University Press, 1963. viii, 359 p.

Covers relations with the Soviet Union during the Stalinist period, the importance of the 1956 demands for increased autonomy, and analysis of key foreign policy decisions from 1956 to 1961. Emphasis on the possibility of Poland serving as a bridge between East and West; generally optimistic about the direction of developments.

950 Horak, Stephan. POLAND'S INTERNATIONAL AFFAIRS 1919-1960. Russian and East European Series, vol. 31. Bloomington: Indiana University, 1964. xvii, 248 p. Paperbound.

A calendar of treaties, agreements, conventions, and other international acts with annotations, excerpts from documents and treaty texts, and useful references.

951 Johnson, A. Ross. "Poland: End of an Era?" PROBLEMS OF COMMUNISM 19 (January-February 1970): 28-39.

A prophetic forecast that the Gomulka era might be coming to an end nine months before the food riots and political chaos brought Gierek to power in December 1970.

952   _____ . "Polish Perspectives, Past and Present." PROBLEMS OF COMMUNISM   20 (July–August 1971):   59–72.

953   _____ . THE POLISH RIOTS AND GOMULKA'S FALL. Santa Monica, Calif.: RAND Memorandum P–4615, April 1971. 26 p.

Documents the Soviet long-term loan to Gierek in February 1971.

954   _____ . THE POWER STRUGGLE IN THE POLISH COMMUNIST LEADERSHIP: THE 'MARCH EVENTS'––END OF AN ERA. Santa Monica, Calif.: RAND Memorandum P–4238, November 1969. 26 p.

Reflects impact of the Czechoslovak crisis on Poland's internal power struggle.

955   Kleer, Jerzy. "Economic Reforms in the Socialist Countries in the Sixties." EASTERN EUROPEAN ECONOMICS   13 (Winter 1974):   3–30.

A Polish view of bloc developments.

956   Kodot, Jozef. THE LOGIC OF THE ODER–NEISSE FRONTIER. Poznan and Warsaw: Wydawnictwo Zachodnie, 1957. xx, 289 p.

A Polish scholar's defense of the territorial shift that took place at the end of World War II concerning Poland's western boundaries.

957   Korbel, Josef. POLAND BETWEEN EAST AND WEST: SOVIET–GERMAN DIPLOMACY TOWARDS POLAND 1919–1933. Princeton, N.J.: Princeton University Press, 1963. xi, 321 p. Paperbound.

A carefully researched study of interwar diplomacy showing the driving nationalistic forces on all sides of the Polish–German triangular relationship. Excellent background to contemporary Polish international relations.

958   Korbonski, Andrzej. POLITICS OF SOCIALIST AGRICULTURE IN POLAND, 1945–1960. New York: Columbia University Press, 1965. xii, 330 p.

959   Kornilowicz, Maria, ed. WESTERN AND NORTHERN POLAND. Warsaw: Zachodnia Agencja Prasowa, 1962. 534 p.

A Polish history of Poland's western territories designed to substantiate Polish postwar claims to that region.

960   Kot, Stanislaw. CONVERSATIONS WITH THE KREMLIN AND DISPATCHES FROM RUSSIA. Translated and arranged by H.C. Stevens. New York: Oxford University Press, 1963. xxx, 283 p.

Memoirs and papers of the Polish ambassador to the Soviet Union from 1941 to 1942.

961   Kruszewski, Z. Anthony. THE ODER-NEISSE BOUNDARY AND POLAND'S MODERNIZATION: SOCIOECONOMIC AND POLITICAL IMPACT. New York: Praeger, 1972. xviii, 245 p.

An important study for foreign policy-domestic process linkages.

962   Lane, David Stuart, and Kolankiewicz, George, eds. SOCIAL GROUPS IN POLISH SOCIETY. New York: Columbia University Press, 1973. xvi, 380 p.

A scholarly study of social groups in postwar Poland and their interaction with political forces. Particularly important for students of interest groups, elites, and comparative politics.

962a Laux, Jeanne Kirk. "Intra-Alliance Politics and European Detente: The Case of Poland and Rumania." STUDIES IN COMPARATIVE COMMUNISM 8 (Spring-Summer 1975): 98-122.

963   Lotarski, Susanne S. "The Communist Takeover in Poland." In THE ANATOMY OF COMMUNIST TAKEOVERS, edited by Thomas T. Hammond, pp. 339-67. New Haven, Conn., and London: Yale University Press, 1975. Paperbound.

964   Markiewicz, Wladyslaw. "Poland." In THE STATE OF SOCIOLOGY IN EASTERN EUROPE TODAY, edited by Jerzy J. Wiatr, pp. 97-138. Carbondale: Southern Illinois University Press, 1971.

964a Matejko, Alexander. SOCIAL CHANGE AND STRATIFICATION IN EASTERN EUROPE. New York: Praeger, 1974. xviii, 272 p.

Primarily Polish data.

965   Micewski, Andrzej. "Polish Foreign Policy: Historical Perspectives." In GIEREK'S POLAND, edited by Adam Bromke and John W. Strong, pp. 184-91. New York: Praeger, 1973.

A historical essay putting contemporary Polish foreign policy priorities into the perspective of past patterns. Written by a Polish publicist and historian living in Warsaw.

966 Monat, Pawel, and Dille, John. SPY IN THE U.S. New York: Harper and Row, 1961. 208 p.

967 Mond, George H. "The Student Rebels in Poland." EAST EUROPE 18 (July 1969): 1-7.

968 Montias, John Michael. CENTRAL PLANNING IN POLAND. New Haven, Conn., and London: Yale University Press, 1962. xv, 410 p.

A summary of the postwar economic development in Poland; planning institutions and methods, financial system and price setting policies, and reforms within the framework of the planning system. Good background for understanding integration prospects within the CMEA bloc.

969 Morawiecki, Wojciech. "Institutional and Political Conditions of Participation of Socialist States in International Organization: A Polish View." INTERNATIONAL ORGANIZATION 22, no. 2 (1968): 494-507.

970 Morrison, James F. THE POLISH PEOPLE'S REPUBLIC. Foreword by Jan F. Triska. Integration and Community Building in Eastern Europe Series. Baltimore, Md.: Johns Hopkins Press, 1968. xiii, 160 p. Paperbound.

Emphasis on attitude formation within the Communist system. Ongoing assessment of interaction of domestic and foreign policy developments.

971 Ortmayer, Louis L. CONFLICT, COMPROMISE, AND CONCILIATION: WEST GERMAN-POLISH NORMALIZATION 1966-1967. Denver: University of Denver Graduate School of International Studies, 1975. xxiii, 162 p. Paperbound.

972 Pastusiak, Login. "East West Relations and Arms Control: Achievements and Prospects." EAST EUROPEAN QUARTERLY 9 (Spring 1975): 1-13.

Evaluation by a Polish scholar affiliated with the Polish Institute of International Affairs, Warsaw.

973 Pelczynski, Zbigniew A. "The Downfall of Gomulka." In GIEREK'S POLAND, edited by Adam Bromke and John W. Strong, pp. 1-23. New York: Praeger, 1973.

Interesting analysis of Soviet inaction during the December 1970 crisis that led to Gomulka's replacement as head of the Polish party and government. Author a fellow of Pembroke College, Oxford Univeristy.

974 Piekalkiewicz, Jaroslaw [A.]. COMMUNIST LOCAL GOVERNMENT: A STUDY OF POLAND. Athens: Ohio University Press, 1975. xiv, 282 p.

974a Pirages, Dennis Clark. MODERNIZATION AND POLITICAL TENSION MANAGEMENT: A SOCIALIST SOCIETY IN PERSPECTIVE: CASE STUDY OF POLAND. New York: Praeger, 1972. xvi, 259 p.

975 Podolski, T.M. SOCIALIST BANKING AND MONETARY CONTROL: THE EXPERIENCE OF POLAND. London: Cambridge University Press, 1973. xii, 392 p.

975a Polonsky, Antony. "The History of Inter-War Poland Today." SURVEY: A JOURNAL OF SOVIET AND EAST EUROPEAN STUDIES (Winter-Spring 1970): 143-59.

   A bibliographic essay of historical works dealing with Poland since 1956.

976 _____. POLITICS IN INDEPENDENT POLAND, 1921-1939: THE CRISIS OF CONSTITUTIONAL GOVERNMENT. Oxford: Clarendon Press, 1972. xvi, 572 p.

   See chapter 10 devoted to economics, the national minorities, and foreign policy. Based on Polish sources.

977 Pravda, Alex. "Gierek's Poland: Five Years On." THE WORLD TO-DAY 32 (July 1976): 270-78.

   Deals with problems of foreign trade, relations with the West, and Soviet perspective.

978 Revesz, Laszlo. "Political Science in Eastern Europe: Discussion and Initial Steps." STUDIES IN SOVIET THOUGHT 7 (September 1967): 185-210.

   Indicates that, at least in Poland, such key problems as rela-tions between socialist states, problems of peaceful coexistence, and basic principles of foreign policy of socialist states are included in political science programs.

979 Roos, Hans. A HISTORY OF MODERN POLAND. Translated by J.R. Foster. New York: Knopf, 1966. xii, 303 p.

   A study of Polish society and political ideas from World War I to 1965. Includes Soviet-Polish relations following the Second World War, analysis of the Polish October in 1956, and for-eign policy under Gomulka.

980 Segal, Simon. THE NEW ORDER IN POLAND. Introduction by Raymond

Leslie Buell. New York: Knopf, 1942. viii, 286 p.

The frightening story of Nazi rule in Poland during World War
II. Good background to understanding Polish foreign policy
during and after the war.

981 Sharp, Samuel L. POLAND: WHITE EAGLE ON A RED FIELD. Cambridge, Mass.: Harvard University Press, 1953. vii, 338 p.

Puts the Polish problem in historical context. Survey of U.S.-
Polish relations from the perspective of possible policy objectives. Good use of maps.

982 Shonfield, Andrew. "Hungary and Poland: The Politics of Economic Reform." THE WORLD TODAY 26 (March 1970): 94-102.

983 Staar, Richard F. POLAND 1944-1962: THE SOVIETIZATION OF A
CAPTIVE PEOPLE. New Orleans: Louisiana State University Press, 1962.
xviii, 300 p.

A study of governmental dynamics, legislative structure, party
and nonparty pressures within Poland. Treats the development
of Polish domestic and foreign policies as an extension of
Soviet will within the context of "Sovietization."

984 Stehle, Hansjakob. "Polish Communism." In COMMUNISM IN EUROPE,
vol. 1, edited by William E. Griffith, pp. 85-176. Cambridge, Mass.:
MIT Press, 1964. Paperbound.

Analysis and comments on Polish-Soviet and Polish-bloc relations mixed in with an analysis of Polish politics that focuses
on the personality and consistency of programs of Gomulka.
Role of Gomulka as a mediating influence in the Sino-Soviet
rift given some attention.

985 Stern, H. Peter. THE STRUGGLE FOR POLAND. Washington, D.C.:
Public Affairs Press, 1953. 79 p.

A monograph dealing with the diplomatic manuevering that
went on from September 1939 until January 1947 between
Russia and the Western allies in their determination to influence the postwar political outcome in Poland.

985a Szaz, Zoltan Michael. GERMANY'S EASTERN FRONTIERS: THE PROB-
LEM OF THE ODER-NEISSE LINE. Foreword by Harold Zink. Chicago:
Henry Regnery, 1960. xi, 256 p.

986 Szczepanski, Jan. POLISH SOCIETY. New York: Random House, 1970.
ix, 214 p. Paperbound.

Written by an internationally-known Polish sociologist. Excellent background for undergraduates or general reader.

987 Sztyber, Wladyslaw. "Theoretical Basis for the Reform of Sale Prices in Socialist Countries." EASTERN EUROPEAN ECONOMICS 9 (Winter 1970-71): 91-131.

A Polish analysis.

988 Taylor, J. THE ECONOMIC DEVELOPMENT OF POLAND 1919-1950. Ithaca, N.Y.: Cornell University Press, 1952. xiv, 222 p.

Emphasis on economic achievements both between the World Wars and after 1945.

989 Trepczynski, Stanislaw. "Poland and European Security." In GIEREK'S POLAND, edited by Adam Bromke and John W. Strong, pp. 205-12. New York: Praeger, 1973.

A summary of Polish policy toward European security by a deputy minister of the Polish Ministry of Foreign Affairs. Useful restatement of oft-stated positions.

990 Trzeciakowski, Witold. "Polish Foreign Trade: A Retrospective View." In GIEREK'S POLAND, edited by Adam Bromke and John W. Strong, pp. 71-89. New York: Praeger, 1973.

A detailed analysis of past and present Polish foreign trade patterns by the director of research of the Polish Ministry of Foreign Trade, Warsaw. Valuable for specialists in the field.

991 Wandycz, Piotr S. CZECHOSLOVAK-POLISH CONFEDERATION: 1940-1943. Russian and East European Series, vol. 3. Bloomington: Indiana University Press, 1956. iii, 152 p. Paperbound.

A narrowly-focused insight into Polish-Czechoslovak relations and the great powers during World War II.

992 _____ . POLISH-SOVIET RELATIONS: 1917-1921. Cambridge, Mass.: Harvard University Press, 1969. ix, 403 p.

A scholarly study of diplomatic and military affairs during a dramatic period in the long history of troubled Russian-Polish relations. Useful in understanding present Polish-Soviet dealings.

992a Weit, Erwin. AT THE RED SUMMIT: INTERPRETER BEHIND THE IRON CURTAIN. Translated by Mary Schofield. Preface by Harry Schwartz. New York: Macmillan, 1973. 226 p. Black and white illus.

See no. 749.

993 Whalley, John. "Polish Postwar Growth from the Viewpoint of Soviet Experience." SOVIET STUDIES 24 (April 1973): 533-49.

A detailed economic analysis concluding that Poland did not follow the Soviet developmental model.

994 Wiatr, Jerzy J. "Political Parties, Interest Representation and Economic Development in Poland." THE AMERICAN POLITICAL SCIENCE REVIEW 64 (December 1970): 1239-45.

Unique analysis of the Polish party system and other societal interest representation written by a Polish scholar. Useful for students of comparative politics as well as those concerned with the extent of Soviet influence on Polish political institutions. Author a professor of sociology at the University of Warsaw.

995 Wiewiora, Boleslaw. POLISH-GERMAN FRONTIER FROM THE STAND-POINT OF INTERNATIONAL LAW. Preface by Dr. Alfons Klafkowski. Poznan and Warsaw: Wydawnictwo Zachodnie, 1959. xxxii, 224 p.

Translation of the author's doctoral dissertation, which gives a detailed analysis of the sensitive border issue from the Polish perspective. At the time of publication, was an assistant in the Department of Public Law at the Poznan University Law Faculty.

996 Woods, William. POLAND, EAGLE IN THE EAST. London: Andre Deutsch, 1969. xi, 272 p.

Based on research in Poland conducted with the cooperation of the Polish government.

997 Wynot, Edward D., Jr. POLISH POLITICS IN TRANSITION: THE CAMP OF NATIONAL UNITY AND STRUGGLE FOR POWER, 1935-1939. Athens: University of Georgia Press, 1974. xvi, 294 p.

A carefully written study of the post-Pilsudski years. Important for understanding interwar Polish foreign policy.

997a Zauberman, Alfred. INDUSTRIAL PROGRESS IN POLAND, CZECHOSLO-VAKIA, AND EAST GERMANY 1937-1962. Oxford: Oxford University Press, 1964. xiv, 338 p.

See no. 491.

998 Zielinski, Janusz G. ECONOMIC REFORMS IN POLISH INDUSTRY. New York: Oxford University Press, 1973. xxxiv, 333 p.

A detailed study of the Polish economy since 1956.

A. THE POLISH OCTOBER, 1956

See also part II, chapter V, section A, "The Hungarian Uprising of 1956," p. 156.

999 Gibney, Frank. THE FROZEN REVOLUTION, POLAND: A STUDY IN COMMUNIST DECAY. New York: Farrar, Straus, and Cudhy, 1959. xiv, 269 p.

> A journalist's highly negative interpretation of the results of Poland's independent stand in 1956. Based on travels in Poland during the following spring.

1000 Lewis, Flora. A CASE HISTORY OF HOPE: THE STORY OF POLAND'S PEACEFUL REVOLUTIONS. New York: Doubleday, 1958. xiv, 267 p.

> A well-written, journalistic account of events in Poland from Stalin's death until Gomulka's return to power in 1956. Interesting insights into the impact of the Soviet 20th party congress on Polish domestic politics. Also, a good discussion of Polish-Soviet confrontation over the expanding Polish independence signaled by the change in party leadership in 1956.

1001 Shneiderman, S.L. THE WARSAW HERESY. New York: Horizon Press, 1959. 253 p.

> A journalistic version of the events leading to, and consequences of, the Polish October of 1956. Author born in Poland and educated at Warsaw University before he emigrated to Paris. For general reader.

1002 Stehle, Hansjakob. THE INDEPENDENT SATELLITE: SOCIETY AND POLITICS IN POLAND SINCE 1945. Translated by O.J.S. Thompson. New York; Washington, D.C.; London: Praeger, 1965. xi, 361 p.

> Evaluates what in fact survived from the Polish October of 1956 with a view to understanding the failures of Western, particularly German, policy toward Poland. Written by a long-time correspondent of FRANKFURTER ALLGEMEINE ZEITUNG in Warsaw.

1002a Stillman, Edmund [O.], ed. BITTER HARVEST: THE INTELLECTUAL RE-VOLT BEHIND THE IRON CURTAIN. Introduction by Francois Bondy. New York: Praeger, 1959. xxxiii, 313 p.

> See no. 913.

1003 Syrop, Konrad. SPRING IN OCTOBER: THE STORY OF THE POLISH REVOLUTION OF 1956. New York: Praeger, 1957. xii, 207 p. Black and white illus.

A dramatically-written account of the process which culminated in Gomulka's return to power in Poland. Useful chronology of events for a general reader. Author a member of the European Service, British Broadcasting Company.

1003a Zinner, Paul E., ed. NATIONAL COMMUNISM AND POPULAR RE-
VOLT IN EASTERN EUROPE: A SELECTION OF DOCUMENTS ON
EVENTS IN POLAND AND HUNGARY, FEBRUARY-NOVEMBER 1956.
New York: Columbia University Press, 1956. xx, 561 p. Paperbound.

See no. 919.

Chapter VII

RUMANIA

1004 Bishop, Robert, and Crayfield, E.S. RUSSIA ASTRIDE THE BALKANS. New York: McBride, 1948. 287 p.

Detailed discussion of the Sovietization of Rumania.

1005 Brown, J[ames]. F. "Romania and Bulgaria." In THE COMMUNIST STATES AT THE CROSSROADS: BETWEEN MOSCOW AND PEKING, edited by Adam Bromke, pp. 106-25. New York; Washington, D.C.; London: Praeger, 1965.

1006 _____. "Rumania--The Strategy of Defiance." PROBLEMS OF COM-MUNISM 18 (March-April 1969): 32-38.

A perceptive analysis of Rumanian foreign policy through the late 1960s. Stresses the increasing independence with respect to Rumanian-Bonn relations, Arab-Israeli neutrality, Soviet pressures, and Rumanian open repudiation of the Czech invasion.

1007 _____. "Rumania Steps Out of Line." SURVEY: A JOURNAL OF SOVIET AND EAST EUROPEAN STUDIES, no. 49 (October 1963): 19-34.

One of the first Western analyses to pinpoint Soviet-Rumanian differences. Historically important for perspective on Rumania's cautious move toward an independent foreign policy.

1008 Burks, R.V. "The Rumanian National Deviation: An Accounting." In EASTERN EUROPE IN TRANSITION, edited by Kurt London, pp. 93-113. Baltimore, Md.: Johns Hopkins Press, 1966. Paperbound.

Basic survey of Soviet-Rumanian conflicts of interest, the role of the Sino-Soviet dispute in these developments, and the re-vival of minority and frontier issues with its implications for Rumanian relations with its East European neighbors as well as for the USSR.

1009   Campbell, John C. FRENCH INFLUENCE AND THE RISE OF ROUMA-
        NIAN NATIONALISM: THE GENERATION OF 1848. New York: Arno
        Press and New York Times, 1971. ii, 463 p.

        A detailed insight into historical French-Rumanian contacts,
        valuable for understanding contemporary Rumanian political
        culture. Author's dissertation, submitted to Harvard University
        in 1940.

1010   Cretzianu, Alexandre, ed. CAPTIVE RUMANIA: A DECADE OF SOVIET
        RULE 1945-1955. New York: Praeger, 1956. xvi, 424 p.

        An uneven study by a group of scholars on the consolidation
        period of the Rumanian party. As its title implies, this col-
        lection compiled on the assumption that Rumanian Communists
        operated as passive "catspaws" for Soviet interests.

1011   Farlow, Robert [L.]. "Romanian Foreign Policy: A Case of Partial Align-
        ment." PROBLEMS OF COMMUNISM 20 (November-December 1971):
        54-63.

        Examines Rumanian patterns of adherence-deviation from Soviet
        foreign policy objectives and the determinants of Rumanian
        policies. Stresses personal characteristics of the top leader-
        ship, changing international environment, and the internal
        cohesion of Bucharest's party-state apparatus.

1012   Fischer-Galati, Stephen [Z.]. "The Communist Takeover of Rumania: A
        Function of Soviet Power." In THE ANATOMY OF COMMUNIST TAKE-
        OVERS, edited by Thomas T. Hammond, pp. 310-20. New Haven, Conn.,
        and London: Yale University Press, 1975. Paperbound.

1013   _____ . "The Moldavian Soviet Republic in Soviet Domestic and Foreign
        Policy." In THE INFLUENCE OF EAST EUROPE AND THE SOVIET WEST
        ON THE USSR, edited by Roman Szporluk, pp. 229-50. New York:
        Praeger, 1975.

        Includes discussion of the Moldavian Republic and Soviet-
        Rumanian tensions in the 1960s.

1014   _____ . THE NEW RUMANIA: FROM PEOPLE'S DEMOCRACY TO
        SOCIALIST REPUBLIC. Cambridge, Mass.: MIT Press, 1967. ix, 126 p.

        An important reinterpretation of contemporary independent
        Rumanian foreign policy, stressing the impact of Sino-Soviet
        differences on Rumanian thinking long before such "differences"
        were accepted as real by Western analysts. Puts forward the
        hypothesis that the Rumanian party leader Gheorghiu-Dej's
        decision to move toward a more national policy was dictated
        by personal survival considerations as well as Rumanian eco-
        nomic interests. Much of the research for this volume done

in Rumania, and author had unusual access to Rumanian sources.

1015 _____. ROMANIA. East Europe Under the Communists Series. New York: Praeger, 1957. xv, 300 p.

A dated but good introductory reference. Author a professor of history at the University of Colorado.

1016 _____. "Rumanian and the Sino-Soviet Conflict." In EASTERN EUROPE IN TRANSITION, edited by Kurt London, pp. 261-75. Baltimore, Md.: Johns Hopkins Press, 1966. Paperbound.

1017 _____. TWENTIETH CENTURY RUMANIA. New York: Columbia University Press, 1970. ix, 248 p.

A sketch of the hobbled development of Moldavia-Wallachian-centered, Turk-Russo-Austrian-dominated nineteenth and twentieth-century Rumanian nationalism.

1018 Fisher, Gabriel. "Rumania." In THE COMMUNIST STATES IN DISARRAY 1965-1971, edited by Adam Bromke and Teresa Rakowska-Harmstone, pp. 158-79. Minneapolis: University of Minnesota Press, 1972.

Discusses the "Ceausescu era," focusing on feverish internal legal and administrative reforms. Especially on the deviance in foreign policy, including the denunciation of the invasion of Czechoslovakia, the successful resistance to the Brezhnev Doctrine, resistance to economic and military integration, and the balancing of Soviet and Chinese relations.

1019 Florescu, Radu R. "Ceauseschism: Rumania's Road to Communism." CURRENT HISTORY 65 (May 1973): 212-16.

Considers Rumanian diplomacy inseparable from domestic policy. Discusses briefly Bucharest's Westward initiatives as well as Ceausescu's maneuvering within the Communist world.

1020 _____. "Nicholas Balcescu: A Forgotten Diplomat." EAST EUROPEAN QUARTERLY 5 (June 1971): 165-76.

Considers Balcescu as a connecting link between the Rumanian revolution of 1848 and the broader European revolutionary process.

1021 Floyd, David. RUMANIA. RUSSIA'S DISSIDENT ALLY. New York: Praeger, 1965. xvi, 144 p.

A study of Rumanian-Russian relations, the moves toward autonomy in Rumania and the significance for the rest of Eastern Europe. Deals with the process of disintegration of relations from 1956.

1022   Gilberg, Trond. "Ceausescu's Romania." PROBLEMS OF COMMUNISM
        23 (July-August 1974): 29-43.

1023   _____. "Ethnic Minorities in Romania Under Socialism." EAST EURO-
        PEAN QUARTERLY 7 (January 1974): 435-58.

        Interesting regarding Hungarian-Rumanian relations. Deals with
        Hungarians, Gypsies, and Jews, suggesting that increasing ur-
        banization has eroded ethnicity among minority elites.

1024   _____. MODERNIZATION IN ROMANIA SINCE WORLD WAR II.
        New York: Praeger, 1975. xiii, 261 p.

        A wealth of data. Important background for understanding the
        roots of Soviet-Rumanian tensions so evident since the mid-
        1960s.

1025   _____. "Romania: Problems of the Multilaterally Developed Society."
        In THE POLITICS OF MODERNIZATION IN EASTERN EUROPE: TESTING
        THE SOVIET MODEL, edited by Charles Gati, pp. 117-59. New York:
        Praeger, 1974.

        Considers Communist power instrumental in shaping the scope
        and direction of Rumanian modernization. Discusses the process
        in detail, but does not deal with the impact of this process on
        Soviet-Rumanian relations. Useful to students of development
        and comparative politics.

1026   Gross, George. "Rumania: The Fruits of Autonomy." PROBLEMS OF
        COMMUNISM 15 (January-February 1966): 16-27.

        A perceptive tracing of Rumanian assertiveness in foreign policy
        as especially linked to economic integration efforts by the
        Soviets in the late 1950s, up through the mid-1960s.

1027   Hale, Julian. CEAUSESCU'S ROMANIA: A POLITICAL DOCUMENTARY.
        London; Toronto; Wellington, N.Z.; Sydney: George G. Harrap, 1971.
        208 p. Black and white illus.

        Chatty, journalistic account centered on Bucharest's efforts to
        maintain a balance of friendship and independence vis-à-vis
        the USSR. For a general reader.

1028   Ionescu, Ghita. COMMUNISM IN RUMANIA 1944-1962. New York:
        Oxford University Press, 1964. xvi, 378 p.

        Basic account of Rumanian foreign and domestic policy from
        World War II until 1960. Emphasis on Soviet influence in the
        early period, party history, and subsequent impact of the 1956
        upheavals in Eastern Europe.

1029 Jelavich, Barbara. RUSSIA AND THE RUMANIAN NATIONAL CAUSE
(1858-1859). Russian and East European Series, vol. 17. Bloomington:
Indiana University Press, 1959. xi, 169 p.

1029a Jelavich, Charles, and Jelavich, Barbara. THE BALKANS. Englewood
Cliffs, N.J.: Prentice-Hall, 1965. xi, 148 p.

Good summary of Rumanian post-World War II international
relations. See also no. 138.

1030 Jowitt, Kenneth. "Political Innovation in Rumania." SURVEY: A JOUR-
NAL OF EAST AND WEST STUDIES 20 (Autumn 1974): 132-51.

Rules out China as a model for Rumania, but sees North Korea
as salient for Bucharest in terms of both organizations and international policy.

1030a _____. REVOLUTIONARY BREAKTHROUGHS AND NATIONAL DE-
VELOPMENT: THE CASE FOR RUMANIA, 1944-1965. Berkeley and
Los Angeles: University of California Press, 1971. 317 p.

See no. 79.

1031 _____. "The Romanian Communist Party and the World Socialist System:
A Re-definition of Unity." WORLD POLITICS 23 (October 1970): 38-
60.

A key analysis of Rumanian interparty relations from the perspective of Bucharest's definition of the ideal character of the
world Communist movement. Ties the Rumanian conception of
bloc relations and conflict resolution to party institutionalization or "maturity" using Samuel Huntington's concept of adapt-
ability.

1032 King, Robert R. "The Problem of Rumanian Foreign Policy." SURVEY:
A JOURNAL OF EAST AND WEST STUDIES 20 (Spring-Summer 1974):
105-20.

Analysis of the implications of continued detente for Rumanian
autonomy. Also Sino-Soviet-Rumanian relations and Rumania's
increasing interest in the markets of developing countries.

1033 _____. "Rumania and the Sino-Soviet Conflict." STUDIES IN COM-
PARATIVE COMMUNISM 5 (Winter 1972): 373-93.

Emphasis on Rumanian-Chinese relations with its implications
for Bucharest's dealings with Moscow. Indications of declining closeness, perhaps as a result of Rumanian realization of
Chinese actual capability to defend Balkan allies in the event
of attack. Followed by relevant documents.

1034 Kristof, Ladis K.D. "The Case of Rumania." STUDIES IN COMPARA-
TIVE COMMUNISM 4 (April 1971): 36-42.

Discussion of the problems and advantages in applying Gabriel A.
Almond's comparative politics model to Rumania. Originally presented at an American Political Science Association Roundtable on
comparing East European political systems, September 1970.

1035 Larrabee, F. Stephen. "The Rumanian Challenge to Soviet Hegemony."
ORBIS 18 (Spring 1973): 227-46.

A summary of Soviet-Rumanian relations that divides Bucharest's
"differences" with Moscow into four phases: latent conflict,
1955-61; emergent conflict, 1961-64; expanded conflict, 1966-
67; and institutionalized conflict dating from 1968. Includes
discussion of Rumanian maneuvering vis-à-vis the European
Security Conference and related calls for Balkan cooperation.

1035a Laux, Jeanne Kirk. "Intra-Alliance Politics and European Detente: The
Case of Poland and Rumania." STUDIES IN COMPARATIVE COMMU-
NISM 8 (Spring-Summer 1975): 98-122.

1036 Lendvai, Paul. "Rumania: A Quiet Revolution." In his EAGLES IN
COBWEBS: NATIONALISM AND COMMUNISM IN THE BALKANS,
pp. 262-350. London: Macdonald, 1969.

Historical background to Rumanian independent foreign policy
maneuvering from the early 1960s. A good survey of the
reasons why Bucharest stepped out of line which includes
relevance to the Warsaw Pact.

1037 Markham, Reuben H. RUMANIA UNDER THE SOVIET YOKE. Boston:
Meador, 1949. 601 p.

One of the more exhaustive early treatments of Rumanian communism. Written by a former correspondent of the CHRISTIAN
SCIENCE MONITOR, focusing on Sovietization of Rumania
and Soviet control of that process. A typical example of the
"satellite" approach common to studies of East Europe during
the height of the cold war.

1038 Meier, Viktor. "The Political Dynamics of the Balkans in 1974." In
THE WORLD AND THE GREAT-POWER TRIANGLE, edited by William E.
Griffith, pp. 34-84. Cambridge, Mass.: MIT Press, 1975.

1039 Montias, J[ohn].M[ichael]. "Background and Origin of the Rumanian
Dispute with Comecon." SOVIET STUDIES 16 (October 1964): 125-51.

1040 _____. ECONOMIC DEVELOPMENT IN COMMUNIST RUMANIA.
Cambridge, Mass.: MIT Press, 1967. xiv, 327 p.

The most definitive study of its kind. Important chapters on both foreign trade and Rumanian role in CMEA. Based on Rumanian sources. Author a professor of economics at Yale University.

1041 Oldson, William O. "Romania and the Munich Crisis August–September 1938." EAST EUROPEAN QUARTERLY 11 (Summer 1977): 177–90.

1042 Paul, David W. "Romania's Special Diplomatic Position: A Case Study of China's Role." EAST EUROPEAN QUARTERLY 7 (Fall 1973): 311–30.

Standard survey. Emphasis on Bucharest's opposition to military blocs and resistence to "strengthening" the Warsaw Pact.

1043 Ratiu, Ion. CONTEMPORARY ROMANIA: HER PLACE IN WORLD AFFAIRS. Richmond, Engl.: Foreign Affairs Publishing Company, 1975. 138 p.

A well-written political tract that considers Rumania still a vassal state of the Soviet Union.

1044 Roberts, Henry L. RUMANIA: POLITICAL PROBLEMS OF AN AGRARIAN STATE. New Haven, Conn.: Yale University Press, 1951. xiv, 414 p.

Largely concerned with pre-Communist Rumania, although the author does deal with the early postwar period. Interesting speculation on relations of foreign trade patterns to political decisions.

1045 Roucek, Joseph Slabey. CONTEMPORARY RUMANIA AND HER PROBLEMS. New York: Arno Press, 1971. xxv, 422 p.

Updated from a 1932 study of developing Rumanian nationalism.

1046 Rura, Michael J. REINTERPRETATION OF HISTORY AS A METHOD OF FURTHERING COMMUNISM IN RUMANIA: A STUDY OF COMPARATIVE HISTORIOGRAPHY. Washington, D.C.: Georgetown University Press, 1961. xii, 123 p.

Interesting for version of Soviet-Rumanian history, particularly in light of the Rumanian subsequent rewriting of that period during intensified organizational maneuvering on Bucharest's part in the late 1960s.

1047 Schopflin, George. "Rumanian Nationalism." SURVEY: A JOURNAL OF EAST & WEST STUDIES 20 (Spring-Summer 1974): 77–104.

Analysis of key components of Rumanian reemerging sense of national identity since the mid-1960s: language, historiography, political-economic sovereignty, and territorial irredentas. Useful for understanding not only Soviet-Rumanian relations but also Bucharest's problems with some of its East European neighbors.

1048 Socor, Vladimir. "The Limits of National Independence in the Soviet Bloc: Rumania's Foreign Policy Reconsidered." ORBIS 20 (Fall 1976): 701-32.

Considers Bucharest's independent foreign policy line a Trojan horse for Soviet goals rather than a conflict of interest with Moscow.

1048a Spigler, Iancu. ECONOMIC REFORM IN RUMANIAN INDUSTRY. New York: Oxford University Press, 1973. xxi, 176 p.

A somewhat technical study, useful to economists dealing either with Rumania per se, CMEA, or comparative industrial analysis.

1049 Tufescu, V., and Pascu, S., et al. LA ROUMANIE ECONOMIQUE ET CULTURELLE. Geneva: Droz, 1970. xi, 206 p. Illus.

Sixteen essays on various aspects of economic and cultural life in Rumania written by people in the government and in the academies of Bucharest. Includes a chapter on foreign policy by the vice minister of foreign affairs dealing with Rumania's relations with the Communist and non-Communist world, its position in the United Nations, and its relations with underdeveloped nations.

1050 Vali, Ferenc. "Transylvania and the Hungarian Minority." JOURNAL OF INTERNATIONAL AFFAIRS 20, no. 1 (1966): 32-44.

1051 Weiner, Robert. "Albanian and Romanian Deviance in the U.N." EAST EUROPEAN QUARTERLY 7 (Spring 1973): 65-83.

Chapter VIII
YUGOSLAVIA

A. THE YUGOSLAV WAY

1052 Adizes, Ichak, and Mann Borgese, Elisabeth, eds. SELF-MANAGEMENT: NEW DIMENSIONS TO DEMOCRACY. Santa Barbara, Calif.: ABC-Clio Press, 1975. 162 p.

 A comparative politics perspective toward self-management. Important for students of ideological transfer.

1053 Arnez, John A. SLOVENIA IN EUROPEAN AFFAIRS: REFLECTIONS ON SLOVENIAN POLITICAL HISTORY. New York and Washington, D.C.: League of CAS, 1958. x, 204 p.

 A useful background to Slovene nationalism in contemporary Yugoslavia and impact on Yugoslav relations with Italy and Austria.

1054 Auty, Phyllis. TITO: A BIOGRAPHY. New York: McGraw-Hill, 1970. xvi, 343 p. Black and white illus. Paperbound.

 A biography of Tito by the first British journalist to interview the Yugoslav leader after the 1948 break with Moscow. Systematic insight into Tito's childhood and prison experiences in Yugoslavia. Interesting material on his years in Moscow during the purges of the late 1930s. Detailed coverage of the underlying causes of Soviet-Yugoslav differences, but only brief attention to the post-1945 period.

1055 _____. YUGOSLAVIA. London: Thames and Hudson, 1965. 251 p. Black and white illus.

 A historical survey from the formation of the Yugoslav state until Hitler's invasion, followed by a discussion of Communist Yugoslavia. Written for a general reader. Stronger on domestic than international developments, but does contain material on Soviet-Yugoslav relations.

1056 _____ . "Yugoslavia's International Relations 1945-1965." In CONTEM-
PORARY YUGOSLAVIA: TWENTY YEARS OF SOCIALIST EXPERIMENT,
edited by Wayne S. Vucinich, pp. 154-203. Berkeley and Los Angeles:
University of California Press, 1969.

A good survey of Yugoslav foreign policy, interparty relations,
and Western contacts. Useful to the general reader.

1057 Auty, Phyllis, and Clogg, Richard, eds. BRITISH POLICY TOWARDS
WARTIME RESISTANCE IN YUGOSLAVIA AND GREECE. New York:
Barnes & Noble, 1975. xii, 308 p.

1058 Avakumovic, Ivan. HISTORY OF THE COMMUNIST PARTY OF YUGO-
SLAVIA. Aberdeen, Scotland: University Press of Aberdeen, 1964.
xii, 207 p.

Especially useful treatment of Comintern-CPY relations emphasizing "satellite" status during the late 1930s and 1940s, and
an account of CPY efforts to forge a Popular Front with opposition parties during this period.

1059 Barker, E. "Fresh Insights on British Policy in Yugoslavia, 1942-43."
THE SLAVONIC AND EAST EUROPEAN REVIEW 54 (October 1976):
572-85.

1060 Barker, Elisabeth. MACEDONIA: ITS PLACE IN BALKAN POWER
POLITICS. London and New York: Royal Institute of International
Affairs, 1950. 129 p. Paperbound.

Valuable historical summary.

1061 Barton, Allen H., et al., eds. OPINION-MAKING ELITES IN YUGO-
SLAVIA. Foreword by Firdus Dzinic. New York; Washington, D.C.;
London: Praeger, 1973. xii, 344 p.

1062 Bertsch, Gary K. "Currents in Yugoslavia--The Revival of Nationalisms." PROBLEMS OF COMMUNISM 20 (November-December 1973):
1-15.

Emphasis on republican party elite manipulation of ethnic
nationalism for their own political gain, thereby intensifying
national frustrations and contributing to domestic crisis.

1062a _____ . NATION-BUILDING IN YUGOSLAVIA: A STUDY OF POLITI-
CAL INTEGRATION AND ATTITUDINAL CONSENSUS. Beverly Hills,
Calif.: Sage Publications, 1971. 48 p.

See no. 44.

1063 Bilainkin, George. TITO. New York: Philosophical Library, 1949.

287 p. Black and white illus.

A carefully researched biography of Tito focusing on the war
years. Covers the early postwar period through the 1948
Soviet-Yugoslav split. Includes Tito-Stalin correspondence.
A good part of author's research conducted in Yugoslavia with
the cooperation of the Yugoslav government.

1064 Burks, R.V. THE NATIONAL PROBLEM AND THE FUTURE OF YUGO-
SLAVIA. Santa Monica, Calif.: RAND Memorandum P-4761, October
1971. 85 p.

A sensitive analysis of the tensions created by rising ethnic
awareness with particular reference to the viability of confederation as a solution. Good background for the Croatian
crisis of 1971.

1065 _____. THE REMOVAL OF RANKOVIC: AN EARLY INTERPRETATION
OF THE JULY YUGOSLAV PLENUM. Santa Monica, Calif.: RAND
Memorandum RM-5132-PR, August 1966. 34 p.

1066 Byrnes, Robert Francis, ed. YUGOSLAVIA. East Central Europe under
the Communists Series. New York: Praeger for Mid-European Studies
Center of Free Europe Committee, 1957.

A background part of the East Central Europe under the Communists series.

1067 Campbell, John C. "Insecurity and Cooperation: Yugoslavia and the
Balkans." FOREIGN AFFAIRS 51 (July 1973): 778-93.

Emphasis on the importance for European security of containing
post-Tito destabilization in Yugoslavia. Considers Yugoslavia
able to weather the succession crisis despite the severity of
the coming test for the regime and the country.

1068 _____. TITO'S SEPARATE ROAD: AMERICA AND YUGOSLAVIA IN
WORLD POLITICS. New York: Harper and Row for the Council on
Foreign Relations, 1967. viii, 180 p.

A focused study of Yugoslav-American relations. Useful for
understanding the impact of the 1948 split on American policy
toward Yugoslavia.

1069 _____. "Yugoslavia." In THE COMMUNIST STATES IN DISARRAY
1965-1971, edited by Adam Bromke and Teresa Rakowska-Harmstone,
pp. 180-97. Minneapolis: University of Minnesota Press, 1972.

Focuses around the principle of autonomous foreign policy, and
the personality of Tito as the significant factor, with attention

to the fears generated by the Czech invasion.

1070 _____ . "Yugoslavia: A Special Case Outside the Bloc." In his AMERI-
CAN POLICY TOWARDS COMMUNIST EASTERN EUROPE: THE CHOICES
AHEAD, pp. 67-83. Minneapolis: University of Minnesota Press, 1965.

Cautions that Washington can not expect too much visible return for aid to Yugoslavia, but still considers that contributing
to the possibility for Yugoslav independence via trade is worth
the cost.

1071 Christman, Henry M., ed. THE ESSENTIAL TITO. New York: St.
Martin's Press, 1970. xviii, 197 p.

A collection of key Tito speeches from the period of partisan
struggle in 1941 until the twenty-fifth anniversary of the Communist regime in November 1968. The first documentary of
its type published by an American press. Less complete than
its Yugoslav counterparts but nonetheless a valuable reference.

1072 Clark, Cal, and Johnson, Karl F. DEVELOPMENT'S INFLUENCE ON
YUGOSLAV POLITICAL VALUES. Beverly Hills, Calif.: Sage Publications, 1976. 72 p.

1073 Clissold, Stephen. WHIRLWIND: AN ACCOUNT OF MARSHAL TITO'S
RISE TO POWER. New York: Philosophical Library, 1949. 345 p.

1074 Cviic, K.F. "The Outlook for Yugoslavia." THE WORLD TODAY 27
(December 1971): 522-30.

1075 _____ . "Turning the Clock back in Yugoslavia." THE WORLD TODAY
30 (May 1974): 206-13.

Discusses the nationality question in Croatia during the aftermath of the crisis of 1971. Considers Croat fears of a return
to Stalinism in Yugoslavia as realistic should recession in the
West force disasterous return of thousands of Yugoslavs working
abroad.

1076 _____ . "Yugoslavia After Tito." THE WORLD TODAY 32 (April
1976): 126-33.

1077 Dallin, Alexander, ed. "The Yugoslav Response." In his DIVERSITY IN
INTERNATIONAL COMMUNISM: A DOCUMENTARY RECORD, 1961-1963,
pp. 584-605. New York: Columbia University Press, 1963. Paperbound.

A number of documents recording Belgrade's reaction to Soviet-
Albanian polemics. Tito's speech of 13 November 1961 sets

the tone for a much more elaborate discussion of "polycentrism" in April of 1962, attacking Stalinism and Soviet primacy as the basis for relations among Communist countries.

1078 Dedijer, Vladimir, et al. HISTORY OF YUGOSLAVIA. New York: McGraw-Hill, 1974. 752 p.

Includes a detailed chronology of events 1945-73, particularly useful for understanding domestic-foreign policy linkages.

1079 Denitch, Bogdan Denis. THE LEGITIMATION OF A REVOLUTION: THE YUGOSLAV CASE. New Haven, Conn., and London: Yale University Press, 1976. xi, 254 p.

Provocative analysis questioning the relevance of contemporary theories of social change and modernization.

1080 _____. "Notes on the Relevance of Yugoslav Self-Management." BALKANISTICA: OCCASIONAL PAPERS IN SOUTHEAST EUROPEAN STUDIES 1 (1974): 126-60.

An extremely useful analysis of both the domestic and international importance of the Yugoslav experiment with "self-managing socialism." Touches on differences from Polish and Hungarian attempts in the mid-1950s and the Czechoslovak reforms of 1968. Speculates about applying the Yugoslav model to advanced industrial societies.

1081 Djilas, Milovan. LAND WITHOUT JUSTICE: AN AUTOBIOGRAPHY OF HIS YOUTH. New York: Harcourt, Brace, 1958. xvi, 366 p. Paperbound.

Author describes early childhood and youth in Montenegro. Important for understanding his later break with the Yugoslav Communist Party.

1082 _____. MEMOIR OF A REVOLUTIONARY. New York: Harcourt Brace Jovanovich, 1973. 402 p.

A sequel to LAND WITHOUT JUSTICE dealing with interwar Yugoslavia from the time the author came to Belgrade as a student in 1929 until the beginning of the war in 1941.

1082a Drachkovitch, Milorad M. UNITED STATES AID TO YUGOSLAVIA AND POLAND: ANALYSIS OF A CONTROVERSY. Washington, D.C.: American Enterprise Institute for Policy Research, 1963. v, 124 p.

See no. 264.

1083 _____. "Yugoslavia." In THE COMMUNIST STATES AT THE CROSS-

ROADS: BETWEEN MOSCOW AND PEKING, edited by Adam Bromke, pp. 179-98. New York; Washington, D.C.; London: Praeger, 1965.

1084 Dragnich, Alex N. SERBIA, NIKOLA PASIC AND YUGOSLAVIA. New Brunswick, N.J.: Rutgers University Press, 1974. xiii, 266 p.

A political biography focused on Pasic's influence and impact on the political institutions both of Serbia and interwar Yugoslavia. Intimately interwoven with the international maneuvering involved in creating the Yugoslav state.

1085 Dunn, William N. "Ideology and Organization in Socialist Yugoslavia: Modernization and Obsolescence of Praxis." NEWSLETTER ON COMPARATIVE STUDIES OF COMMUNISM 5 (August 1972): 21-56.

1086 _____. "Revolution and Modernization in Economic Organizations." In COMPARATIVE SOCIALIST SYSTEMS: ESSAYS ON POLITICS AND ECONOMICS, edited by Carmelo Mesa-Lago and Carl Beck, pp. 147-91. Pittsburgh, Pa.: University of Pittsburgh Center for International Studies, 1975. Paperbound.

Provocative comparison of Yugoslavia with Cuba and China.

1086a Enloe, Cynthia H. ETHNIC CONFLICT AND POLITICAL DEVELOPMENT. Boston: Little, Brown, 1973. xvii, 282 p. Paperbound.

Provocative use of Yugoslav examples.

1087 Fisher, Jack C. YUGOSLAVIA: A MULTINATIONAL STATE, REGIONAL DIFFERENCES AND ADMINISTRATIVE RESPONSE. San Francisco: Chandler, 1966. xxiii, 244 p.

A clearly written study making good use of demographic and statistical analysis to demonstrate the different levels of economic development throughout Yugoslavia. Concise description of the diffusion of decision making to commune and enterprise levels.

1088 Frey, Cynthia W. "Ethnicity in the Yugoslav Theory of International Relations." Paper delivered at the American Political Science Association annual meeting, 29 August-2 September 1974, at Chicago.

A provocative analysis linking Yugoslav international relations theory to both Austro-Marxist nationalism and Leninist internationalism. Largely based on the theories contained in Edvard Kardelj's pre-World War II study, THE DEVELOPMENT OF THE SLOVENIAN NATIONAL QUESTION.

1089 _____. "Yugoslav Nationalisms and the Doctrine of Limited Sovereignty." EAST EUROPEAN QUARTERLY 10 (Winter 1976): 427-57 and 11 (Spring

1977): 79-108.

A two-part article based on the author's earlier work dealing with ethnicity and international relations.

1090 Gazi, Stephen. A HISTORY OF CROATIA. New York: Philosophical Library, 1973. xv, 362 p.

Based on the text of leading Croatian historians and written by an emigré patriot. First ten chapters contain a narrative history of Croatia until the nineteenth century, followed by a discussion of Croatia's national awakening. The remainder of the book is an analysis of Croatian modern history that is useful for understanding contemporary Croatian nationalism.

1091 Halpern, Joel M. "Some Perspectives on Balkan Migration Patterns (With Particular Reference to Yugoslavia)." Paper presented at pre-congress conference on migration and ethnicity prior to ninth International Congress of International Union of Anthropological and Ethnological Sciences, 1-8 September 1973, at Chicago.

Excellent background for students interested in the impact of massive labor migration on Balkan international relations.

1092 _____. "Yugoslavia Modernization in an Ethnically Diverse State." In CONTEMPORARY YUGOSLAVIA; TWENTY YEARS OF SOCIALIST EXPERIMENT, edited by Wayne S. Vucinich, pp. 316-50. Berkeley and Los Angeles: University of California Press, 1969.

Insight into role of native political culture in process of modernization. Especially valuable to students of comparative politics in developing countries.

1093 Harriman, Helga H. "Slovenia as an Outpost of the Third Reich." EAST EUROPEAN QUARTERLY 5 (June 1971): 222-31.

A detailed look at the consequences of Hitler's policy of partition and Germanization in Slovenia.

1094 Heppell, Muriel, and Singleton, Fred B. YUGOSLAVIA. New York: Praeger, 1961. 236 p.

Introductory survey of Yugoslav history. Useful to undergraduate or general reader.

1095 Hoffman, George W. "Migration and Social Change." PROBLEMS OF COMMUNISM 22 (November-December 1973): 16-31.

Analysis of the impact of mass labor migration on Yugoslav society since the mid-1960s. Valuable background to Yugoslavia's foreign relations with host countries temporarily absorbing these foreign workers, especially West Germany.

1096   Hoffman, George W., and Neal, Fred Warner. YUGOSLAVIA AND THE NEW COMMUNISM. New York: Twentieth Century, 1962. xiii, 546 p.

Academic study of Yugoslav communism; its history, unique domestic experiments, and foreign policy. Considers the nature of Titoism as a system. Part 5 devoted to the impact of Titoism abroad. A good general source. Both authors spent time travelling and working in Yugoslavia. Hoffman a professor of geography at the University of Texas. Neal, professor of international relations and government, Claremont Graduate School, Claremont, California, a former journalist who worked in Eastern Europe.

1097   Hondius, Frits W. THE YUGOSLAV COMMUNITY OF NATIONS. The Hague and Paris: Mouton, 1968. 375 p. Paperbound.

Scholarly analysis of Yugoslav multinational federalism. Emphasis on constitutions. Useful for evolution from the 1946 constitution based on the Soviet model to the 1953 and 1963 documents.

1098   Hoptner, J.B. YUGOSLAVIA IN CRISIS, 1934-1941. New York: Columbia University Press, 1962. xvi, 328 p.

Covers the critical period before the German invasion of Yugoslavia in 1941. Excellent on the problems entailed in this small Balkan state's attempt to accommodate itself to an increasingly hostile international environment. Also useful material on the ways in which Yugoslavia's multiethnic population exacerbated its difficulties. Based on interviews with participants in many of the events described.

1099   Horvat, Branko. AN ESSAY ON YUGOSLAV SOCIETY. Translated by Henry F. Mins. White Plains, N.Y.: International Arts and Sciences Press, 1969. x, 245 p.

An interesting analysis of the Yugoslav experiment showing its theoretical and practical bases. Stresses the importance of expulsion from the Cominform on the nature of the Yugoslav road to socialism. Author, an internationally known Yugoslav economist, the former director of the Institute of Economic Studies, Belgrade.

1100   _____. "The Postwar Evolution of Yugoslav Agricultural Organization: Interaction of Ideology, Practice, and Results." EASTERN EUROPEAN ECONOMICS 12 (Winter 1973): 3-106.

1101 Iatrides, John O. BALKAN TRIANGLE: BIRTH AND DECLINE OF AN ALLIANCE ACROSS IDEOLOGICAL BOUNDARIES. Paris: Mouton, 1968. 211 p.

> One of the few book-length treatments of the Balkan Pact of the 1950s. Useful regarding Yugoslavia as a barometer of East-West relations.

1101a Jelavich, Charles, and Jelavich, Barbara. THE BALKANS. Englewood Cliffs, N.J.: Prentice-Hall, 1965. xi, 148 p.

> Excellent summary of Yugoslav post-World War II international relations. See also no. 138.

1102 Johnson, A. Ross. ITALY AND YUGOSLAV SECURITY. Santa Monica, Calif.: RAND Memorandum P-5898, June 1977. 8 p.

1103 _____. TOTAL NATIONAL DEFENSE IN YUGOSLAVIA. Santa Monica, Calif.: RAND Memorandum P-4746, December 1971. 13 p.

> Discusses impact of the invasion of Czechoslovakia on Yugoslav military strategy.

1104 _____. THE TRANSFORMATION OF COMMUNIST IDEOLOGY: THE YUGOSLAV CASE 1945-1953. Cambridge, Mass.: MIT Press, 1972. ix, 269 p.

> Deals with the ideological changes brought about in the Yugoslav system by the 1948 split, showing the impact of Soviet rejection on the development of Yugoslav self-managing socialism. Contains one of the best analyses to date of the "theory of peoples" democracy, used to describe the transitional stage of mixed governments in East Europe at the end of World War II until the combination of the emerging cold war and the Soviet-Yugoslav split led Stalin to demand rigid imitation of the Soviet model by 1948-49. Also valuable for an understanding of the dynamics of ideological change.

1105 _____. YUGOSLAVIA IN THE TWILIGHT OF TITO. Washington Papers, vol. 2. Beverly Hills, Calif., and London: Sage Publications, 1974. 67 p. Paperbound.

> A sensitive analysis of domestic and foreign policy problems facing Yugoslavia during Tito's declining years with an essentially favorable prognosis for the country's ability to absorb the shock of his passing from the political scene. Emphasis on the LCY and the army as integrating institutions.

1106 Jukic, Ilija. THE FALL OF YUGOSLAVIA. Translated by Dorian Cooke. New York and London: Harcourt Brace Jovanovich, 1974. 315 p.

The personal account of the Yugoslav assistant foreign minister during the last tense days of Prince Paul's attempt to avoid having Yugoslavia dragged into World War II.

1107 Kardelj, Edvard. SOCIALISM AND WAR: A SURVEY OF CHINESE CRITICISM OF THE POLICY OF COEXISTENCE. Translated from Serbo-Croatian by Alec Brown. London: Methuen, 1961. 238 p.

An important theoretical analysis by a key figure in the Yugoslav leadership.

1108 Kartun, Derek. TITO'S PLOT AGAINST EUROPE: THE STORY OF THE RAJK CONSPIRACY. New York: International Publishers, 1950. 127 p.

Written by the editor of the London DAILY WORKER. A succinct statement of the Soviet line of the Rajk trial. Interesting in historical perspective of de-Stalinization and Rajk's rehabilitation.

1109 Kofos, Evangelos. NATIONALISM AND COMMUNISM IN MACEDONIA. Salonika, Greece: Institute for Balkan Studies, 1964. xx, 254 p.

1110 Korbel, Josef. TITO'S COMMUNISM. Denver, Colo.: University of Denver Press, 1951. viii, 368 p.

Written by the Czech ambassador to Yugoslavia from 1945 to 1948. Most useful for discussion of Yugoslav communism before the break with Moscow in 1948.

1111 Lendvai, Paul. "Yugoslavia: Stormy Voyage into Unchartered Seas." In his EAGLES IN COBWEBS, pp. 51-173. London: Macdonald, 1969.

Covers Soviet-Yugoslav relations, problems of attempting a "mixed socialist" economy, importance of tourism, international and domestic implications of rising Croatian nationalism.

1112 McClellan, Woodford. "Postwar Political Evolution." In CONTEMPORARY YUGOSLAVIA: TWENTY YEARS OF SOCIALIST EXPERIMENT, edited by Wayne S. Vucinich, pp. 119-54. Berkeley and Los Angeles: University of California Press, 1969.

Impact of Tito-Stalin break on future Yugoslav domestic policy direction. Concludes with economic reforms of 1965 and subsequent fall of Alexander Rankovic.

1113 Mackenzie, David. THE SERBS AND RUSSIAN PAN-SLAVISM 1878-1885. Ithaca, N.Y.: Cornell University Press, 1967. xx, 365 p.

1114 Maclean, Fitzroy H. THE HERETIC: THE LIFE AND TIME OF JOSIP

BROZ-TITO. New York: Harper, 1957. 436 p.

A well-documented biography of Tito written by the chief British representative to Yugoslavia during World War II. Not surprisingly, strongest in its analysis of the war years.

1115 McVicker, Charles P. TITOISM: PATTERN FOR INTERNATIONAL COMMUNISM. New York: St. Martin's Press, 1957. xx, 332 p.

A scholarly study of Titoism; domestic and foreign policy priorities of the Yugoslav brand of communism. Author a former U.S. consul in Zagreb; subsequently a professor of political science at Yale University.

1116 Markham, Reuben H. TITO'S IMPERIAL COMMUNISM. Chapel Hill: University of North Carolina Press, 1947. xii, 292 p.

A dated, extremely negative interpretation of Tito's wartime strategy.

1117 Markovic, Mihailo. FROM AFFLUENCE TO PRAXIS: PHILOSOPHY AND SOCIAL CRITICISM. Foreword by Erich Fromm. Ann Arbor: University of Michigan Press, 1974. xiv, 265 p. Paperbound.

1117a Markovich, Stephen C. "American Foreign Aid and Yugoslav Internal Policies." EAST EUROPEAN QUARTERLY 9 (Summer 1975): 184-95.

1117b Marmullaku, Ramadan. ALBANIA AND THE ALBANIANS. Translated from the Serbo-Croatian by Margot and Bosko Milosavljevic. Hamden, Conn.: Archon Books, 1975. x, 178 p.

Written by a Yugoslav official of Albanian origin. Important regarding Yugoslav-Albanian relations. See also no. 578.

1117c Meier, Viktor. "The Political Dynamics of the Balkans in 1974." In THE WORLD AND THE GREAT-POWER TRIANGLE, edited by William E. Griffith, pp. 34-84. Cambridge, Mass., and London: MIT Press, 1975.

A sensitive, recent survey. Particularly good regarding Yugoslavia, including extra-Balkan influences on the region.

1118 _____. "Yugoslav Communism." In COMMUNISM IN EUROPE, vol. 1, edited by William E. Griffith, pp. 19-84. Cambridge, Mass.: MIT Press, 1964. Paperbound.

Survey of Soviet-Yugoslav relations, attempts at rapprochement, and the dilemmas of nonalignment.

1118a Milazzo, Mateo J. THE CHETNIK MOVEMENT AND THE YUGOSLAV RESISTANCE. Baltimore, Md.: Johns Hopkins Press, 1975. ix, 208 p.

Impressively researched, a balanced interpretation.

1119 Milenkovitch, Michael M.   "Soviet-Yugoslav Relations and the Brezhnev
      Doctrine." STUDIES FOR A NEW CENTRAL EUROPE, no. 4 (1968-1969):
      112-21.

> A good analysis of Belgrade's reaction to the Brezhnev Doctrine
> used to justify Soviet troops in Czechoslovakia in the context
> of long-term Yugoslav foreign policy objectives.

1120 Milenkovitch, Michael M., and Milenkovitch, Deborah [D.], eds.
      MILOVAN DJILAS: PARTS OF A LIFETIME. New York: Harcourt
      Brace Jovanovich, 1975. xiii, 442 p.

> A sensitive anthology of Djilas's work spanning his autobio-
> graphical writings, poetry, essays, and political analysis.
> Particularly valuable for the Yugoslav leader's reflections on
> the process that led to his expulsion from the Yugoslav Com-
> munist party. Also containing previously unpublished political
> analysis of contemporary problems within the international Com-
> munist movement.

1121 Moodie, A.E. THE ITALO-YUGOSLAV BOUNDARY: A STUDY IN
      POLITICAL GEOGRAPHY. Foreword by E.G.R. Taylor. London: George
      Philips & Sons, 1945. viii, 241 p.

> Good background to an ongoing problem in Yugoslav-Italian
> relations. See particularly section on post-World War I claims
> and settlement.

1122 Moraca, Pero. THE LEAGUE OF COMMUNISTS OF YUGOSLAVIA:
      A BRIEF HISTORICAL SURVEY. Belgrade: Medjunarodna politika, 1966.
      73 p.

> The most concise Yugoslav version of LCY history available in
> English. Includes impact of expulsion from the Cominform on
> party institutional evolution. Author a researcher for the
> Workers Movement Research Institute in Belgrade.

1123 Neal, Fred Warner. TITOISM IN ACTION: THE REFORMS IN YUGO-
      SLAVIA AFTER 1948. Berkeley and Los Angeles: University of Cali-
      fornia Press, 1958. xi, 331 p. Black and white illus.

> Based on both Yugoslav sources and personal observations.
> Useful for understanding the changes brought about as a result
> of the Soviet-Yugoslav split in 1948, thereby showing the
> domestic repercussions of Yugoslav foreign policy. Includes
> postscript specifically dealing with the foreign policy direc-
> tions taken after the split until the post-1965 period.

1124 Omrcanin, Ivo. DIPLOMATIC AND POLITICAL HISTORY OF CROATIA.
      Philadelphia: Dorrance, 1972. 252 p.

1124a Palmer, Stephen E., Jr., and King, Robert R. YUGOSLAV COMMU-
NISM AND THE MACEDONIAN QUESTION. Hamden, Conn.: Shoe
String Press, 1971. vii, 247 p. Maps.

See no. 381.

1125 Pavlowitch, Stevan K. YUGOSLAVIA. Nations of the Modern World
Series. New York: Praeger, 1971. 461 p.

An attempt to place contemporary Yugoslavia in the context of
historical trends and the various political cultures making up
the Yugoslav state. A good general reference.

1126 Petrovic, Gajo. MARX IN THE MID-TWENTIETH CENTURY. New
York: Doubleday, 1967. 237 p. Paperbound.

A Yugoslav philosopher's reinterpretation of Marx in light of
contemporary developments. A useful contribution to works
by East European philosophers available in English. Useful
for an understanding of the interaction of philosophy and
politics both as a part of the Yugoslav political process and
in the broader sphere of East European interparty relations.
Author a member of the Praxis school of Marxist humanism.

1127 Petrovich, Michael B. "The Significance of Yugoslav 'Heresy'." In
THE FUTURE OF COMMUNISM IN EUROPE, edited by R.V. Burks,
pp. 19-69. Detroit: Wayne State University Press, 1968.

Analysis of Yugoslav doctrine, economic reforms, and policy
dilemmas with an eye to repercussions elsewhere in Eastern
Europe.

1127a _____. YUGOSLAVIA: A BIBLIOGRAPHIC GUIDE. Washington, D.C.:
Library of Congress, 1974. xi, 270 p.

1128 Popovic, Nenad D. YUGOSLAVIA: THE NEW CLASS IN CRISIS.
Syracuse, N.Y.: Syracuse University Press, 1968. xv, 240 p.

Well-documented study by a knowledgeable former senior official in Tito's government. Written with an extremely negative
bias.

1129 Pridonoff, Eric L. TITO'S YUGOSLAVIA. Introduction by Brodie E.
Ahlport. Washington, D.C.: Public Affairs Press, 1955. vii, 243 p.

A personal account of the author's experience as a State Department official and UN Relief and Rehabilitation Administration administrator in Yugoslavia during and immediately after
the second World War. Bitterly opposed to U.S. policy, but
a worthwhile look for students interested in the first stage of
Yugoslav communism.

1129a Prifti, Peter R. "The Communist Seizure of Power in Albania." Cambridge, Mass.: MIT Center for International Studies, August, 1974, 47 p. Mimeograph.

Indicates close contact of the Albanian guerrillas with their Yugoslav counterparts. Also shows extent of Yugoslav concern to aid the Albanian Communist efforts.

1130 _____. "Kosovo in Ferment." Cambridge, Mass.: MIT Center for International Studies, 1969. 37 p. Multilith.

A center monograph analyzing the riots that took place in the Albanian region of Yugoslavia during summer and fall of 1968. Important for students of Albanian-Yugoslav relations. Subsequently translated into German in ALBANIEN VORPOSTEN CHINAS, edited by Rolf Italiaander, pp. 221-43. Munich: Delp'sche Verlagsbuchandlung KG, 1970.

1130a Prpic, George J. THE CROATIAN PUBLICATIONS ABROAD AFTER 1939: A BIBLIOGRAPHY. Cleveland: Institute for Soviet and East European Studies, 1969. x, 66 p. Illus.

1131 _____. IRELAND, CROATIA, AND BANGLADESH. Arcadia, Calif.: American Croat., 1973. 38 p. Paperbound.

A monograph comparing the fate of the Croatian nation to that of Ireland and Bangladesh. Strongly nationalistic. Useful for students of nationalism, the role of non-state-nations in international politics, or the impact of emigré Croat activity on Yugoslav foreign relations; in this case particularly regarding Australia. Author a professor of history at John Carroll University, Cleveland, Ohio, and a member of its institute for Soviet and East European studies.

1132 Remington, Robin Alison. "Armed Forces and Society in Yugoslavia." In POLITICAL-MILITARY SYSTEMS: COMPARATIVE PERSPECTIVES, edited by Catherine McArdle Kelleher, pp. 163-91. Beverly Hills, Calif., and London: Sage Publications, 1974.

An analysis of civil-military relations in Yugoslavia. Deals with impact of the Brezhnev Doctrine justifying Soviet intervention in Czechoslovakia on Yugoslav strategic thinking, the turn to territorial defense units (TDUs), and the political implications of emigré guerrilla activity.

1133 _____. "Fundamental Forces Determining Post-Tito Yugoslavia." Paper prepared for the Washington Center of Foreign Policy Research Mediterranean Seminar, 26 May 1977. Washington, D.C.: Johns Hopkins University School of Advanced International Studies, forthcoming.

Focused on domestic-foreign policy linkages.

1134 _____. "Yugoslavia and European Security." ORBIS 17 (Spring 1973): 197-226.

A detailed analysis of the domestic and international developments influencing the Yugoslav preferences for a European Security Conference. Discusses attempts at influence building in Europe, reaction to the Brezhnev Doctrine, the theory of "all peoples' deterrence," and the Yugoslav platform for the 1975 Helsinki conference on European Security and Cooperation.

1135 Roberts, Adam. NATIONS IN ARMS: THE THEORY AND PRACTICE OF TERRITORIAL DEFENSE. London: Chatto and Windus for the International Institute for Strategic Studies, 1976. 288 p.

Chapters 5 and 6 deal with the Yugoslav version of territorial defense in its political context. Particularly valuable for students concerned with the implications of military strategy for foreign policy in cross-systems analysis.

1136 Roberts, Walter R. TITO, MIHAILOVIC AND THE ALLIES, 1941-1945. New Brunswick, N.J.: Rutgers University Press, 1973. xv, 406 p.

One of the few comprehensive studies of this period, showing the impact of Allied policies, or sometimes the lack of them, on the outcome in Yugoslavia during and after World War II.

1137 Rogel, Carole. "Prepordovci: Slovene Students for an Independent Yugoslavia, 1912-1914." CANADIAN SLAVIC STUDIES 5 (Summer 1971): 196-212.

1138 Rubinstein, Alvin Z. "The Evolution of Yugoslavia's Mediterranean Policy." INTERNATIONAL JOURNAL 27 (Autumn 1972): 528-45.

Discusses Yugoslav increased policy concern with the Mediterranean in the context of growing Soviet naval power in the region and the decline of nonalignment as a factor in international politics. Sees the long-term objective as a denuclearized, neutralized Mediterranean.

1139 _____. "Whither Yugoslavia?" CURRENT HISTORY 65 (May 1973): 202-7.

Discussion of the continuity of Yugoslav foreign policy in the context of the drive for domestic reform and reorganization of the League of Communists (LCY) following the "Croatian events" of 1971.

1140 Rusinow, Dennison I. "Crisis in Croatia." AMERICAN UNIVERSITY FIELD STAFF (AUFS) REPORTS 19 (June-September 1972): 17, 20, 23, 24.

One of the best analyses of complex circumstances and issues
surrounding the 1971-72 Croatian crisis. Four-part series.

1141 _____ . "Ghosts that Haunt Yugoslavia's Foreign Policy." AUFS RE-
PORTS 15 (February 1968): 1-9.

1142 _____ . "The 'Macedonian Question' Never Dies." AUFS REPORTS
15 (March 1968): 1-16.

1143 _____ . "A Note on Yugoslavia: 1972." AUFS REPORTS 19 (July
1972): 1-14.

Continuing domestic-foreign policy spin-offs from the December
1971 Croatian crisis.

1144 _____ . "Ports and Politics in Yugoslavia." AUFS REPORTS 11 (April
1964): 1-24.

Illustrates the relationship of intercommunity competition for
development projects to international relations.

1145 _____ . "Tito Between Neo-Cominform and Neo-Alignment." AUFS
REPORTS 15 (February 1968): 1-13.

1146 _____ . "Trade and Aid at the Halfway Point in Developing Yugoslavia."
AUFS REPORTS 11 (February 1964): 1-24.

1147 _____ . "Whatever Happened to the 'Trieste Question'?" AUFS RE-
PORTS 16 (January 1969): 1-22.

Sensitive summary and updating of Yugoslav-Italian tensions
over Trieste in the context of cold war politics.

1148 _____ . "The Yugoslav Concept of 'All National Defense.'" AUFS RE-
PORTS 19 (November 1971): 1-10.

1149 _____ . THE YUGOSLAV EXPERIMENT, 1948-1974. London and Berkeley,
Calif.: Royal Institute of International Affairs and University of California
Press, 1977. xxi, 410 p.

1150 _____ . "Yugoslavia: 1969." AUFS REPORTS 16 (August 1969): 1-
14.

An update on the political scene and the continuing impact of
the invasion of Czechoslovakia on Yugoslav domestic and foreign policy priorities.

1151 _____ . "Yugoslavia and Stalin's Successors, 1968-1969." AUFS RE-PORTS 16 (August 1969): 1-13.

Emphasis on Belgrade's reaction to the invasion of Czechoslovakia.

1152 _____ . "Yugoslavia Reaps the Harvest of Coexistence." AUFS REPORTS 11 (January 1964): 1-20.

1153 Samardzija, Milos, and Klein, George. "A Perspective View of Self-Management in a Socialist Context." STUDIES IN COMPARATIVE COMMUNISM 14 (July-August 1971): 141-68.

Analysis of the problems and possibilities for self-management in European socialist countries with emphasis on the Yugoslav experience.

1154 Sharp, Samuel L. "The Yugoslav Experiment in Self Management: Soviet Criticism." STUDIES IN COMPARATIVE COMMUNISM 14 (July-October 1971): 169-78.

Analysis of a key element of tension in Soviet-Yugoslav relations showing the problems raised by Belgrade's alternative to the Soviet model from Moscow's perspective.

1154a Shoup, Paul. COMMUNISM AND THE YUGOSLAV NATIONAL QUESTION. New York: Columbia University Press, 1968. 308 p.

A classic study of the interaction of Communist theory and the problem of a multiethnic society. Shows the influence of Soviet, Comintern thinking on the Yugoslav party prior to 1941. Analysis of postwar period also has important international considerations, particularly concerning relations of Yugoslav, Bulgarian, and Greek Communists on the issue of Macedonia.

1155 _____ . "The National Question in Yugoslavia." PROBLEMS OF COMMUNISM 21 (January-February 1972): 18-29.

A good background survey that also deals with the impact of the constitutional amendments of 1971 on rising national tensions. Unfortunately, appears to have already been in press when the crisis of November-December "events in Croatia" took place.

1156 _____ . "Yugoslavia's National Minorities Under Communism." SLAVIC REVIEW 22 (March 1963): 64-81.

A basic survey of Yugoslav Communists' attempts to deal with ethnic reluctance to accept the party's program for national integrations.

1157 _____. "Yugoslavia Today." PROBLEMS OF COMMUNISM 17 (July-October 1969): 67-77.

1158 _____. "The Yugoslav Revolution: The First of A New Type." In THE ANATOMY OF COMMUNIST TAKEOVERS, edited by Thomas T. Hammond, pp. 244-72. New Haven, Conn., and London: Yale University Press, 1975. Paperbound.

1159 Silberman, Laurence. "Yugoslavia's 'Old' Communism." FOREIGN POLICY 26 (Spring 1977): 3-27.

> Sharp criticism of U.S. foreign policy towards Yugoslavia by a former American ambassador to Belgrade.

1160 Singleton, Fred [B.]. TWENTIETH CENTURY YUGOSLAVIA. New York: Columbia University Press, 1976. xiv, 346 p. Paperbound.

> Emphasis primarily domestic. Particularly good background regarding implications of the economic nationalism in 1960s and 1970s.

1161 Singleton, Fred [B.], and Topham, Anthony. WORKERS CONTROL IN YUGOSLAVIA. London: Fabian Society, 1963. 32 p.

1162 Slijepcevic, Djoko M. THE MACEDONIAN QUESTION: THE STRUGGLE FOR SOUTHERN SERBIA. Translated by James Larkin. Munich: American Institute for Balkan Affairs, 1959. 266 p.

> A Serbian interpretation of historical development of the Macedonian question from the sixth century until 1950. A carefully researched, but strongly biased study. Primarily Serbian and German sources.

1163 SOME YUGOSLAV PAPERS PRESENTED TO THE EIGHTH WORLD CONGRESS OF THE I.S.A. Ljubljana, Yugoslavia: Univeristy of Ljubljana, 1974. 363 p. Paperbound.

> A selection of papers presented to the eighth world congress of the International Sociological Association held in Toronto, August 1974. Particularly useful to scholars studying the impact of massive outmigration of Yugoslav workers on Yugoslav relations with the host countries. Two papers dealing with Yugoslav workers in West Germany.

1164 Stanojevic, Tihomir, ed. JOSIP BROZ TITO: SELECTED SPEECHES AND ARTICLES 1941-1961. Zagreb, Yugoslavia: Naprijed, 1963.

> An extremely useful collection of key statements by the Yugoslav leader covering the war years, the 1948 split with Moscow,

and outlining the preferred Yugoslav version of nonalignment as well as important domestic developments. Unfortunately, not easily available outside of Yugoslavia.

1164a Stojanovic, Svetozar. BETWEEN IDEALS AND REALITY: A CRITIQUE OF SOCIALISM AND ITS FUTURE. Translated by Gerson S. Sher. New York: Oxford University Press, 1973. xvii, 222 p. Paperbound.

1165 Sturmthal, Adolf. WORKERS COUNCILS: A STUDY OF WORKPLACE ORGANIZATION ON BOTH SIDES OF THE IRON CURTAIN. Cambridge, Mass.: Harvard University Press, 1964. x, 217 p.

An interesting comparative analysis of workers councils as a part of the political process with chapters on both Yugoslavia and Poland.

1166 Supek, Rudi. "The Statist and Self-Managing Models of Socialism." In OPINION-MAKING ELITES IN YUGOSLAVIA, edited by Allen H. Barton et al., pp. 295-315. New York: Praeger, 1973.

A valuable theoretical analysis of alternative models of socialism based on Soviet and Yugoslav experience. Written by a Yugoslav professor of sociology at the University of Zagreb, Yugoslavia, who is also editor of the journal PRAXIS.

1167 Tomasevich, Jozo. WAR AND REVOLUTION IN YUGOSLAVIA: 1941-1945: THE CHETNIKS. Stanford, Calif.: Stanford University Press, 1975. 508 p.

An objective study of Mihailovich and the Chetniks. Makes use of Italian and German as well as Yugoslav sources.

1168 _____. "Yugoslavia During the Second World War." In CONTEMPORARY YUGOSLAVIA: TWENTY YEARS OF SOCIALIST EXPERIMENT, edited by Wayne S. Vucinich, pp. 59-119. Berkeley and Los Angeles: University of California Press, 1969.

A good survey of complex domestic and international developments that contributed to the Communist-led partisan victory, setting the stage for Tito's postwar consolidation of power.

1169 Tomasic, Dinko A., with assistance of Joseph Strmecki. NATIONAL COMMUNISM AND SOVIET STRATEGY. Washington, D.C.: Public Affairs Press, 1957. viii, 222 p.

An analysis of Yugoslav communism with emphasis on the significance of Titoism within the broader framework of the international Communist movement and Soviet intentions.

1170 Vucinich, Wayne S., ed. CONTEMPORARY YUGOSLAVIA: TWENTY
YEARS OF SOCIALIST EXPERIMENT. Berkeley and Los Angeles: University of California Press, 1969. xi, 441 p.

> A collection of scholarly essays on both domestic and interna-
> tional aspects compiled from conference papers presented in
> 1965.

1171 _____. "Interwar Yugoslavia." In CONTEMPORARY YUGOSLAVIA:
TWENTY YEARS OF SOCIALIST EXPERIMENT, edited by Wayne S.
Vucinich, pp. 3-59. Berkeley and Los Angeles: University of Cali-
fornia Press, 1969.

> Insight into exacerbation of Yugoslav ethnic hostilities due to
> rising international tensions. Subsection on Yugoslav foreign
> relations between the two world wars.

1171a Weiner, Myron. "The Macedonian Syndrome: An Historical Model of
International Relations and Political Development." WORLD POLITICS
23 (July 1971): 665-83.

1172 Winner, Irene. A SLOVENE VILLAGE: ZEROVNICA. Providence,
R.I.: Brown University Press, 1971. xiv, 267 p. Black and white illus.

1172a YUGOSLAVIA'S WAY: PROGRAM OF THE LEAGUE OF YUGOSLAV
COMMUNISTS. Translated by Stoyan Pribechevich. New York: All
Nations Press, 1958. xxii, 263 p.

> The best English language text of the program finally accepted
> by the League of Communists (LCY) seventh congress, the draft
> version of which set off the second Soviet-Yugoslav dispute in
> April 1958.

1173 Zalar, Charles. YUGOSLAV COMMUNISM: A CRITICAL STUDY.
Foreword by Thomas J. Dodd. Washington, D.C.: Government Printing
Office, 1961. xii, 387 p.

> Analysis by a former Yugoslav diplomat, who has subsequently
> worked in the Library of Congress research. Examination rang-
> ing from a brief history of the party, to the partisan struggle,
> consolidation of Communist power, imitation of the Soviet
> model, and subsequent isolation following the split with the
> Soviet Union in 1948. One of the more comprehensive works
> on the early years of Tito's communism.

1174 Zaninovich, M. George. "The Case of Yugoslavia: Delineating Political Culture in a Multi-Ethnic Society." STUDIES IN COMPARATIVE
COMMUNISM 4 (April 1971): 58-70.

> Discussion of the political cultures of Yugoslavia from the

perspective of the need for an analytical model flexible enough
to encompass Yugoslav political variables crucial to both domestic and foreign policy making.

1175 _____ . THE DEVELOPMENT OF SOCIALIST YUGOSLAVIA. Foreword
by Jan F. Triska. Baltimore, Md.: Johns Hopkins Press, 1968. xxi,
182 p. Paperbound.

Considers Yugoslav communism both from the perspective of its
unique attributes and as a potential model for other East European countries. Also deals with impact of Soviet-Yugoslav
split on domestic political processes. Part of the integration
and community building in Eastern Europe series.

1176 _____ . "Yugoslav Party Evolution: Moving Beyond Institutionalization."
In AUTHORITARIAN POLITICS IN MODERN SOCIETY: THE DYNAMICS
OF ONE PARTY SYSTEMS, edited by Samuel P. Huntington and Clement
H. Moore, pp. 484-505. New York: Basic Books, 1970.

1177 Zimmerman, William. "National-International Linkages in Yugoslavia: The
Political Consequences of Openness." In POLITICAL DEVELOPMENT IN
EASTERN EUROPE, edited by Jan F. Triska and Paul [M.] Cocks, pp. 334-
64. New York: Praeger, 1977.

A provocative analysis of the social and political consequences
of Yugoslavia's mass labor migration. Valuable insight into
the interaction of domestic and foreign policy considerations.
Also indicates extent to which Yugoslavia has become integrated into the European labor market. Originally an APSA
paper, New Orleans, 1973.

1178 _____ . "The Tito Legacy and Yugoslavia's Future." PROBLEMS OF
COMMUNISM 26 (May-June 1977): 33-49.

1179 Zukin, Sharon. BEYOND MARX AND TITO: THEORY AND PRACTICE
IN YUGOSLAV SOCIALISM. New York and London: Cambridge University Press, 1975. ix, 302 p.

A stimulating participant-observer study of Yugoslav self-management. Relevant for cross-systems analysis of experiments
with worker participation both in respect to content and methodology.

B. ECONOMIC BACKGROUND; FOREIGN TRADE

1180 Bicanic, Rudolf. ECONOMIC POLICY IN SOCIALIST YUGOSLAVIA.
Foreword by Michael Kaser. New York: Cambridge University Press,
1973. vii, 254 p.

Posthumously published study of a well-known Yugoslav economist who taught at Zagreb University, Yugoslavia. Academi-
cally sound as well as readable for nonspecialists.

1181 Bogosavljevik, Milutin. THE ECONOMY OF YUGOSLAVIA. Belgrade,
Yugoslavia: Prosveta, 1961. 114 p.

A Yugoslav collection of economic and industrial statistics.

1182 Bombelles, Joseph T. ECONOMIC DEVELOPMENT OF COMMUNIST
YUGOSLAVIA 1947-1964. Stanford, Calif.: Hoover Institution, 1968.
xi, 219 p.

1183 Clark, Cal. "Yugoslav Trade and Foreign Policy." SOUTHEASTERN
EUROPE 1, part 2 (1974): 173-91.

1184 Dimitrijevic, D., and Macesich, George. MONEY AND FINANCE IN
CONTEMPORARY YUGOSLAVIA. New York: Praeger, 1973. xviii,
261 p.

A book for specialists dealing with comparative economic
theory rather than for students of Yugoslavia.

1185 Dirlam, Joel B., and Plummer, James L. AN INTRODUCTION TO THE
YUGOSLAV ECONOMY. Columbus, Ohio: Charles E. Merrill, 1973.
ix, 259 p.

Emphasis on changes in the Yugoslav economic system since
1965, with a separate chapter on "the international dimension."
A good general survey based on field research in the country.
Dirlam at the University of Rhode Island; Plummer with the
U.S. Agency for International Development.

1186 Djodan, Sime. THE EVOLUTION OF THE ECONOMIC SYSTEM OF
YUGOSLAVIA AND THE ECONOMIC POSITION OF CROATIA. New
York: reprinted from the JOURNAL OF CROATIAN STUDIES, 1973.
102 p.

A monograph presenting the Croatian nationalist position that
Croatia is economically exploited within the present Yugoslav
state, but using largely insystem arguments to attempt to im-
prove the situation. Valuable for any student of the Yugoslav
national question and its implications for Yugoslav internal and
external security. Author expelled from the Croatian League
of Communists on charges of national deviations in 1971; arrested in January 1972.

1187 Dubey, Vinod. YUGOSLAVIA: DEVELOPMENT WITH DECENTRALIZA-
TION. Baltimore, Md., and London: Johns Hopkins Press, 1975. xiv,
490 p.

Report of a mission sent to Yugoslavia by the World Bank.
Focus on economic and political determinants of development
in the Yugoslav system. Useful reference to students of modernization, comparative political development, or Communist
systems.

1188 Farkas, Richard P. YUGOSLAV ECONOMIC DEVELOPMENT AND PO-
LITICAL CHANGE: THE RELATIONSHIP BETWEEN ECONOMIC MAN-
AGERS AND POLICY-MAKING ELITES. New York: Praeger, 1975.
x, 133 p.

Concerned with impact of the Yugoslav experiment on other
Socialist systems as well as domestic implications for public
policy.

1188a Freedman, Robert O. ECONOMIC WARFARE IN THE COMMUNIST
BLOC: A STUDY OF SOVIET ECONOMIC PRESSURE AGAINST YUGO-
SLAVIA, ALBANIA, AND COMMUNIST CHINA. New York: Praeger,
1970. xvi, 192 p.

1189 Hamilton, F.E. Ian. YUGOSLAVIA: PATTERN OF ECONOMIC AC-
TIVITY. New York: Praeger, 1968. xvi, 384 p.

A detailed economic analysis by a British scholar, in part
based on research conducted in Yugoslavia during 1959-60.
Includes a chapter on foreign trade and tourism. Extensive
Yugoslav sources.

1190 Hocevar, Toussaint. THE STRUCTURE OF THE SLOVENE ECONOMY
1848-1963. New York: Studia Slovenica, 1965. 277 p.

A useful background for understanding both the role of economic factors in ethnic politics and the importance of foreign
trade and capital in Yugoslav development.

1191 Horvat, Branko. BUSINESS CYCLES IN YUGOSLAVIA. Translated by
Helen M. Kramer. White Plains, N.Y.: International Arts and Sciences
Press, 1971. x, 259 p.

See chapter 11 on the cycle of exports and imports and the
influence of international trade.

1192 _____. "Yugoslav Economic Policy in the Post-War Period: Problems,
Ideas, Institutional Developments." THE AMERICAN ECONOMIC RE-
VIEW 61 (June 1971) Supplement: 71-161.

Covers economic reforms, planning, decentralization, self-
management at the enterprise level, market, and prices. Includes section on foreign trade.

1193 Macesich, George. YUGOSLAVIA: THE THEORY AND PRACTICE OF DEVELOPMENT PLANNING. Charlottesville: University of Virginia Press, 1964. ix, 227 p.

Detailed analysis of contemporary Yugoslav economy. Useful to students of comparative planning and development. Author a professor of economics at Florida State University.

1194 Milenkovitch, Deborah D. PLAN AND MARKET IN YUGOSLAV ECONOMIC THOUGHT. New Haven, Conn.: Yale University Press, 1971. x, 323 p.

A specialized study of Yugoslav planning with the unusual advantage of being written in language understandable to readers who are not economists. Includes a brief discussion of Marx on plan and market as well as a useful comparative analysis of the economics of socialism in the USSR.

1195 Pejovich, Svetozar. THE MARKET PLANNED ECONOMY OF YUGOSLAVIA. Minneapolis: University of Minnesota Press, 1966. xii, 160 p.

Primarily of interest to other economists. Data on importance of American aid to the Yugoslav economy after 1949.

1196 Radin, George. ECONOMIC RECONSTRUCTION IN YUGOSLAVIA: A PRACTICAL PLAN FOR THE BALKANS. Preface by James Shotwell. New York: King's Crown Press, 1946. xii, 161 p.

An imaginative attempt to apply American techniques to the building back of Yugoslav agricultural productivity after wartime destruction in the hope of finding a model applicable to other Balkan areas. Author an authority on agricultural economics.

1197 Sacks, Stephen R. ENTRY OF NEW COMPETITORS IN YUGOSLAV MARKET SOCIALISM. Berkeley: Institute of International Studies, University of California, 1973. 141 p. Paperbound.

Particularly interesting for students of the Yugoslav economy concerned with joint ventures involving foreign capital. By an economist for economists. Based on field work in Yugoslavia.

1198 Stojanovic, Radmila, ed. YUGOSLAV ECONOMISTS ON THE PROBLEMS OF A SOCIALIST ECONOMY. White Plains, N.Y.: International Arts and Sciences Press, 1964. 175 p.

1199 Sukijasovic, Miodrag. YUGOSLAV FOREIGN INVESTMENT LEGISLATION AT WORK. New York: Oceana Publications, 1970. 178 p.

Specialized account.

1200 Tomasevich, Jozo. PEASANTS, POLITICS, AND ECONOMIC CHANGE
IN YUGOSLAVIA. Stanford, Calif.: Stanford University Press, 1955.
xii, 743 p.

> An exhaustive work dealing with Yugoslav economics and agri-
> culture. Considerable information on the impact of interna-
> tional developments on Yugoslav economic options.

1201 Waterston, Albert. PLANNING IN YUGOSLAVIA: ORGANIZATION
AND IMPLEMENTATION. Baltimore, Md.: Johns Hopkins Press, 1962.
ix, 109 p.

1201a Wilczynski, Jozef. SOCIALIST ECONOMIC DEVELOPMENT AND RE-
FORMS: FROM EXTENSIVE TO INTENSIVE GROWTH UNDER CENTRAL
PLANNING IN THE USSR, EASTERN EUROPE AND YUGOSLAVIA.
New York: Praeger, 1972. xvii, 350 p.

C. SOVIET-YUGOSLAV DISPUTES, 1948 AND 1958

1202 Armstrong, Hamilton F. TITO AND GOLIATH. New York: Macmillan,
1951. xi, 312 p.

> A somewhat journalistic analysis of the 1948 split between
> Tito and Stalin and its repercussions in other East European
> states. Written by a former editor of FOREIGN AFFAIRS.
> Excellent for a general reader.

1203 Bass, Robert, and Marbury, Elizabeth, eds. THE SOVIET-YUGOSLAV
CONTROVERSY 1948-1958: A DOCUMENTARY RECORD. Introduction
by Hans Kohn. New York: Prospect Books, 1959. xix, 225 p.

> A collection of key documents of the Soviet-Yugoslav dispute
> with helpful introductory essays. Valuable for understanding
> the ideological implications of the split.

1204 Benes, Vaclav [L.], et al., eds. THE SECOND SOVIET-YUGOSLAV
DISPUTE. Bloomington: Indiana University Press, 1959. xlii, 272 p.

> A documentary of the period from April to June 1958 during
> the second deterioration in Soviet-Yugoslav relations. Gen-
> eral introductions put the documents in historical and political
> context.

1205 Clissold, Stephen, ed. YUGOSLAVIA AND THE SOVIET UNION, 1939-
1973: A DOCUMENTARY SURVEY. New York: Oxford University Press,
1975. xxiii, 318 p.

> Introduction and documents. Unfortunately, relies heavily on
> excerpts.

1206 Deakin, F.W.D. THE EMBATTLED MOUNTAIN. London and New York: Oxford University Press, 1971. xx, 284 p. Illus.

A dramatic, personal account by a member of the first British mission to Tito's partisan headquarters in 1943.

1207 Dedijer, Vladimir. THE BATTLE STALIN LOST: MEMOIRS OF YUGO-SLAVIA 1948-1953. New York: Viking Press, 1971. x, 341 p. Paperbound.

An important addition to memoir literature of the 1948 Soviet-Yugoslav crisis. Deals with both causes and consequences of the split for Yugoslav foreign policy. Author a participant at the top levels of Yugoslav government and party during the years he describes.

1208 _____. TITO. New York: Simon and Schuster, 1953. vii, 443 p.

A detailed biography of Tito written by one of the Yugoslav president's oldest comrades, a high-ranking partisan during World War II. After the war, author a member of Parliament and then of the Yugoslav delegation to the United Nations. Subsequently was in disfavor for his support of Djilas. Book particularly strong on Yugoslav Communist relations with the Soviets, other Communist parties, and the British during World War II. Important also for Belgrade's version of the 1948 split with Moscow and initial repercussions at the highest levels of the Yugoslav party.

1208a Deutscher, Isaac. STALIN: A POLITICAL BIOGRAPHY. 2d ed., rev., enl. New York: Oxford University Press, 1967. xvi, 603 p. Paperbound.

Insights into the role of personality in the Soviet-Yugoslav 1948 split. See also no. 131.

1209 Djilas, Milovan. CONVERSATIONS WITH STALIN. New York: Harcourt, Brace, 1962. 211 p. Paperbound.

An account of three meetings with Stalin in 1944, 1945, and 1948 by one of the key partisan leaders during the war. Author also one of the four top party leaders until his disgrace in 1954. Fascinating both as background to the Soviet-Yugoslav 1948 break and for insights into Yugoslav-Albanian relations during and immediately after World War II.

1209a _____. THE NEW CLASS: AN ANALYSIS OF THE COMMUNIST SYSTEM. New York: Praeger, 1957. vii, 214 p. Paperbound.

The theoretical basis for author's conclusion that rather than creating a classless society, communism produced another level of class structure. Includes analysis of "national communism."

In 1956, was sentenced to ten years in prison for expressing these ideas which remain at the center of many more contemporary criticisms.

1210 Farrell, R. Barry. YUGOSLAVIA AND THE SOVIET UNION 1948-1956. Hamden, Conn.: Shoe String Press, 1956. vii, 220 p.

Introductory analysis of Soviet-Yugoslav relations plus seventeen documents. Although many of these documents also in other collections, some of the speeches by high-ranking Yugoslav officials not easily available.

1211 Halperin, Ernst. THE TRIUMPHANT HERETIC: TITO'S STRUGGLE AGAINST STALIN. Translated from the German by Ilsa Barea. New York: British Book Service, 1958. 324 p.

One of the best analyses of the Soviet-Yugoslav split, its background, and consequences for other East European countries. Author, at the time, a journalist who had worked in Eastern Europe. Now teaches in the political science departments of Boston University and the Fletcher School of Law and Diplomacy.

1212 THE SOVIET-YUGOSLAV DISPUTE, TEXT OF THE PUBLISHED CORRESPONDENCE. London and New York: Royal Institute of International Affairs, 1948. 79 p.

Full text of the letters exchanged between the CPSU and Yugoslav Communist party as well as the YCP and Cominform statements at the time of Yugoslavia's expulsion from that organization. These documents have since been included in other English language collections.

1213 Ulam, Adam [B.]. TITOISM AND THE COMINFORM. Cambridge, Mass.: Harvard University Press, 1952. viii, 243 p.

An academic analysis of Titoism as a political philosophy set in the context of the 1948 Soviet-Yugoslav dispute. Emphasis on the role played by the Cominform as a multilateral organization of European Communist parties, subsequent impact of these events and the Yugoslav model on other East European regimes.

1214 WHITE BOOK ON AGGRESSIVE ACTIVITIES BY THE GOVERNMENTS OF THE USSR, POLAND, CZECHOSLOVAKIA, HUNGARY, ROUMANIA, BULGARIA AND ALBANIA TOWARDS YUGOSLAVIA. Belgrade: Ministry of Foreign Affairs, 1951. 481 p.

The official Yugoslav documentation of the pressures and hostile actions against Yugoslavia by the Soviet Union and other

East European Communist states following the break with the Cominform in June 1948. A valuable reference for Stalin's method of dealing with defiance on the part of a small, ideologically like-minded ally.

D. THE NONALIGNED ALTERNATIVE

1215 Acimovic, Ljubivoje, ed. NONALIGNMENT IN THE WORLD TODAY. Belgrade: Institute of International Politics and Economics, 1969. 274 p.

A collection of papers from an international symposium on Nonalignment in Novi Sad, Yugoslavia, 16-18 January 1969; includes summary of the symposium discussion. A valuable reference with statements by both scholars and Yugoslav policy makers.

1216 Bebler, Anton. "The Military Aspects of Non-Alignment." In SOME YUGOSLAV PAPERS PRESENTED TO THE EIGHTH WORLD CONGRESS OF THE I.S.A., pp. 25-43. Ljubljana, Yugoslavia: University of Ljubljana, 1974.

A concise, contemporary analysis of the military importance of nonalignment for Yugoslav foreign policy.

1217 Christman, Henry M. NEITHER EAST NOR WEST: THE BASIC DOCUMENTS OF NON-ALIGNMENT. New York: Sheed and Ward, 1973. ix, 206 p. Paperbound.

A collection of documents from the Belgrade Conference, 1961; the Cairo Conference, 1964; and the Lusaka Conference, 1970. Includes excerpts of the speeches by heads of state and the final declaration or program. Useful reference for those interested in the nonaligned alternative to bipolar models of international relations.

1218 Griffith, William E. "Yugoslavia." In AFRICA AND THE COMMUNIST WORLD, edited by Zbigniew [K.] Brzezinski, pp. 116-41. Stanford, Calif.: Stanford University Press for the Hoover Institution, 1963.

1219 Johnson, A. Ross. "The U.S. Stake in Yugoslavia, 1948-1968." Southern California Arms Control and Foreign Policy Seminar, June 1972. v, 20 p.

Excellent summary. Discusses the alliance against Stalin and the ambivalence of U.S. policy toward Communist nonalignment. Concludes with an evaluation of both Washington's policy aims that considers the core policy more realistic than the instruments used in its implementation.

1220 _____ . "Yugoslavia and the Sino-Soviet Conflict: The Shifting Triangle, 1948-1974." STUDIES IN COMPARATIVE COMMUNISM 7 (Spring-
Winter 1974): 184-203.

A detailed survey of Yugoslavia's policy toward Russia and
China, including the attempt to apply Belgrade's philosophy
of nonalignment to this aspect of intra-Communist politics.

1221 Mates, Leo. NONALIGNMENT: THEORY AND CURRENT POLICY.
Dobbs Ferry, N.Y.: Oceana Publications, 1972. 543 p.

Originally published in Belgrade in 1971. An exhaustive
treatment of history, conceptualization, and political maneuvering of nonaligned nations from the late 1940s until the end
of the 1960s. By a former Yugoslav ambassador to the United
Nations who was for many years director of the Institute of
International Politics and Economics in Belgrade. Writes not
only as a scholar but as a diplomat often acting on the policies
he describes. An indispensable source for students of Yugoslav
foreign policy. Includes key nonaligned documents.

1222 Nord, Lars. NONALIGNMENT AND SOCIALISM: YUGOSLAV FOR-
EIGN POLICY IN THEORY AND PRACTICE. Stockholm: Raben and
Sjogren, distributors, 1974. 306 p.

An analytical study of how in specific cases Yugoslav security
interests and socialist goals do or do not dovetail with the
principles of nonalignment.

1223 Remington, Robin Alison. "Yugoslavia: Nonaligned Between Whom?"
BALKANISTICA: OCCASIONAL PAPERS IN SOUTHEAST EUROPEAN
STUDIES 1 (1974): 104-25.

Discusses the changing international context of Yugoslav nonalignment. Emphasis on the shift in target area from the third
world to Europe.

1224 Rubinstein, Alvin Z. "Reforms, Nonalignment and Pluralism." PROB-
LEMS OF COMMUNISM 17 (March-April 1968): 31-41.

Focuses on both domestic and foreign policy purposes served
by Yugoslav nonalignment. Sees an increasingly European
cast to Yugoslav policy despite Tito's enthusiasm for the closest
possible cooperation with Afro-Asian countries.

1225 _____ . YUGOSLAVIA AND THE NONALIGNED WORLD. Princeton,
N.J.: Princeton University Press, 1970. xv, 353 p.

A scholarly study of the evolution of Yugoslav foreign policy
from the split with Moscow in 1948 throughout the 1960s.
Crucial for students of nonalignment in theory or practice, or

of Yugoslav relations with the third world. Contains a good discussion of Yugoslav diplomacy in the United Nations, also a valuable case study of Yugoslavia-United Arab Republic contacts.

1226 Vukadinovic, Radovan. "European Security: A Yugoslav View." SOUTHEASTERN EUROPE 2, part 2 (1975): 154-60.

1227 _____. "Small States and the Policy of Nonalignment: The Yugoslav Position." SOUTHEASTERN EUROPE 1, part 2 (1974): 202-12.

APPENDIX

Appendix

BASIC BOOKS

Bass, Robert, and Marbury, Elizabeth, eds. THE SOVIET-YUGOSLAV CON-
TROVERSY 1948-1958: A DOCUMENTARY RECORD. Introduction by Hans Kohn.
New York: Prospect Books, 1959. xix, 225 p.

Beck, Carl, et al., eds. COMPARATIVE POLITICAL LEADERSHIP. New York:
David McKay, 1973. xi, 319 p. Paperbound.

Bender, Peter. EAST EUROPE IN SEARCH OF SECURITY. Baltimore, Md.:
Johns Hopkins Press, 1972. x, 144 p. Paperbound.

Bromke, Adam. POLAND'S POLITICS: IDEALISM V. REALISM. Cambridge,
Mass.: Harvard University Press, 1967. x, 316 p.

Bromke, Adam, and Rakowska-Harmstone, Teresa, eds. THE COMMUNIST STATES
IN DISARRAY 1965-1971. Minneapolis: University of Minnesota Press, 1972.
vii, 363 p.

Bromke, Adam, and Strong, John W., eds. GIEREK'S POLAND. New York:
Praeger, 1973. 219 p.

Bromke, Adam, and Uren, Philip E., eds. THE COMMUNIST STATES AND THE
WEST. New York and London: Praeger and Pall Mall Press, 1967. x, 242 p.

Brown, J[ames]. F. BULGARIA UNDER COMMUNIST RULE. London; Washington, D.C.; New York: Praeger, 1970. ix, 339 p.

_____. THE NEW EASTERN EUROPE: KHRUSHCHEV ERA. New York:
Praeger, 1966. vii, 306 p.

Brzezinski, Zbigniew K. THE SOVIET BLOC: UNITY AND CONFLICT. Rev.
ed. Cambridge, Mass.: Harvard University Press, 1971. xviii, 599 p. Paperbound.

Burks, R.V. THE DYNAMICS OF COMMUNISM IN EASTERN EUROPE. Princeton, N.J.: Princeton University Press, 1961. xii, 244 p.

Campbell, John C. TITO'S SEPARATE ROAD: AMERICA AND YUGOSLAVIA IN WORLD POLITICS. New York: Harper and Row for the Council on Foreign Relations, 1967. viii, 180 p.

Clissold, Stephen, ed. YUGOSLAVIA AND THE SOVIET UNION, 1939-1973: A DOCUMENTARY SURVEY. New York: Oxford University Press, 1975. xxiii, 318 p.

Davis, Lynn Etheridge. THE COLD WAR BEGINS: SOVIET-AMERICAN CONFLICT OVER EASTERN EUROPE. Princeton, N.J.: Princeton University Press, 1974. x, 427 p.

Davison, W. Phillips. THE BERLIN BLOCKADE: A STUDY IN COLD WAR POLITICS. Princeton, N.J.: Princeton University Press, 1958. 423 p.

Denitch, Bogdan Denis. THE LEGITIMATION OF A REVOLUTION: THE YUGOSLAV CASE. New Haven, Conn., and London: Yale University Press, 1976. xi, 254 p.

Djilas, Milovan. CONVERSATIONS WITH STALIN. New York: Harcourt, Brace, 1962. 211 p. Paperbound.

Dobrin, Bogoslav. BULGARIAN ECONOMIC DEVELOPMENT SINCE WORLD WAR II. New York: Praeger, 1973. xv, 185 p.

Farrell, R. Barry, ed. POLITICAL LEADERSHIP IN EASTERN EUROPE AND THE SOVIET UNION. Chicago: Aldine, 1970. xiv, 359 p. Paperbound.

Fejto, Francois. A HISTORY OF THE PEOPLE'S DEMOCRACIES: EASTERN EUROPE SINCE STALIN. Harmondsworth, Engl.: Penguin Books, 1974. 586 p. Paperbound.

Fischer-Galati, Stephen [Z.]. THE NEW RUMANIA: FROM PEOPLE'S DEMOCRACY TO SOCIALIST REPUBLIC. Cambridge, Mass.: MIT Press, 1967. ix, 126 p.

Fleron, Frederic J., Jr., ed. COMMUNIST STUDIES AND THE SOCIAL SCIENCES: ESSAYS ON METHODOLOGY AND EMPIRICAL THEORY. Chicago: Rand McNally, 1971. xiii, 481 p. Paperbound.

Gati, Charles, ed. THE INTERNATIONAL POLITICS OF EASTERN EUROPE. New York: Praeger, 1976. xii, 309 p. Paperbound.

_____. THE POLITICS OF MODERNIZATION IN EASTERN EUROPE: TEST-ING THE SOVIET MODEL. New York: Praeger, 1974. xvii, 389 p.

Gitelman, Zvi Y. THE DIFFUSION OF POLITICAL INNOVATION: FROM EASTERN EUROPE TO THE SOVIET UNION. Beverly Hills, Calif.: Sage Publications, 1972. 59 p. Paperbound.

Golan, Galia. THE CZECHOSLOVAK REFORM MOVEMENT: COMMUNISM IN CRISIS 1962-1968. London: Cambridge University Press, 1971. viii, 349 p.

_____. REFORM RULE IN CZECHOSLOVAKIA: THE DUBCEK ERA 1968-1969. London and New York: Cambridge University Press, 1973. vii, 327 p.

Griffith, William E. ALBANIA AND THE SINO-SOVIET RIFT. Cambridge, Mass.: MIT Press, 1963. xv, 407 p. Paperbound.

Gryzbowski, Kazimierz. THE COMMONWEALTH OF SOCIALIST NATIONS: ORGANIZATIONS AND INSTITUTIONS. New Haven, Conn.: Yale University Press, 1964. xvii, 300 p.

Hamm, Harry. ALBANIA--CHINA'S BEACHHEAD IN EUROPE. Translated by Victor Anderson. New York: Praeger, 1963. x, 176 p.

Hiscocks, Richard. POLAND: BRIDGE FOR THE ABYSS? AN INTERPRETA-TION OF DEVELOPMENTS IN POSTWAR POLAND. London: Oxford University Press, 1963. viii, 359 p.

Hoptner, J.B. YUGOSLAVIA IN CRISIS, 1934-1941. New York: Columbia University Press, 1962. xvi, 328 p.

Ionescu, Ghita. THE BREAK-UP OF THE SOVIET EMPIRE IN EASTERN EUROPE. Baltimore, Md.: Penguin, 1965. 168 p. Paperbound.

_____. COMMUNISM IN RUMANIA 1944-1962. New York: Oxford University Press, 1964. xvi, 378 p.

Jackson, George D. COMINTERN AND PEASANT IN EASTERN EUROPE. New York: Columbia University Press, 1966. ix, 330 p.

Jelavich, Charles, and Jelavich, Barbara. THE BALKANS. Englewood Cliffs, N.J.: Prentice Hall, 1965. xi, 148 p.

Johnson, A. Ross. THE TRANSFORMATION OF COMMUNIST IDEOLOGY: THE YUGOSLAV CASE 1945-1953. Cambridge, Mass.: MIT Press, 1972. ix, 269 p.

Johnson, Chalmers, ed. CHANGE IN COMMUNIST SYSTEMS. Stanford, Calif.: Stanford University Press, 1970. xiii, 368 p. Paperbound.

Jowitt, Kenneth. REVOLUTIONARY BREAKTHROUGHS AND NATIONAL DE-VELOPMENT: THE CASE FOR RUMANIA, 1944-1965. Berkeley and Los Angeles: University of California Press, 1971. 317 p.

Kanet, Roger E. SOVIET AND EAST EUROPEAN FOREIGN POLICY: A BIB-LIOGRAPHY OF ENGLISH AND RUSSIAN LANGUAGE PUBLICATIONS 1967-1971. Santa Barbara, Calif., and Oxford: ABC-Clio Press, 1974. xvi, 208 p.

Kaser, Michael. COMECON. London: Oxford University Press, 1965. 203 p.

_____. COMECON: INTEGRATION PROBLEMS OF PLANNED ECONOMIES. 2d ed. London: Oxford University Press, 1967. vi, 215 p. Illus.

King, Robert R. MINORITIES UNDER COMMUNISM: NATIONALITIES AS A SOURCE OF TENSION AMONG BALKAN COMMUNIST STATES. Cambridge, Mass.: Harvard University Press, 1973. vii, 326 p.

King, Robert R., and Dean, Robert W., eds. EAST EUROPEAN PERSPECTIVES ON EUROPEAN SECURITY AND COOPERATION. New York: Praeger, 1974. xxi, 254 p.

Kinter, William R. and Klaiber, Wolfgang. EASTERN EUROPE AND EURO-PEAN SECURITY. Foreword by William E. Griffith. New York: Dunellen, 1971. xix, 303 p. Paperbound.

Krisch, Henry. GERMAN POLITICS UNDER SOVIET OCCUPATION. New York: Columbia University Press, 1974. xii, 312 p.

Kulski, W.W. GERMANY AND POLAND: FROM WAR TO PEACEFUL RELA-TIONS. Syracuse, N.Y.: Syracuse University Press, 1976. xii, 336 p.

Lauter, Geza Peter, and Dickie, Paul M. MULTINATIONAL CORPORATIONS AND EAST EUROPEAN SOCIALIST ECONOMIES. New York: Praeger, 1975. xxi, 137 p.

Lippmann, Heinz. HONECKER AND THE NEW POLITICS OF EUROPE. Trans-lated by Helen Sebba. New York: Macmillan, 1972.

Littell, Robert, ed. THE CZECH BLACK BOOK. New York: Avon Books, 1969. x, 318 p. Paperbound.

Loebl, Eugen. STALINISM IN PRAGUE: THE LOEBL STORY. Introduction by Herman Starobin. New York: Grove Press, 1969. 327 p.

Marer, Paul. POSTWAR PRICING AND PRICE PATTERNS IN SOCIALIST FOREIGN TRADE, 1946-1971. Bloomington: International Development Research Center, Indiana University, 1972. iv, 102 p. Paperbound.

Mates, Leo. NONALIGNMENT: THEORY AND CURRENT POLICY. Dobbs Ferry, N.Y.: Oceana Publications, 1972. 543 p.

Mensonides, Louis J., and Kuhlman, James A., eds. THE FUTURE OF INTERBLOC RELATIONS IN EUROPE. New York; Washington, D.C.; London: Praeger, 1974. xiv, 217 p.

Miller, Marshall Lee. BULGARIA DURING THE SECOND WORLD WAR. Stanford, Calif.: Stanford University Press, 1975. xii, 290 p.

Montias, John Michael. ECONOMIC DEVELOPMENT IN COMMUNIST RUMANIA. Cambridge, Mass.: MIT Press, 1967. xiv, 327 p.

Morrison, James F. THE POLISH PEOPLE'S REPUBLIC. Integration and Community Building in Eastern Europe Series. Foreword by Jan F. Triska. Baltimore, Md.: Johns Hopkins Press, 1968. xiii, 160 p. Paperbound.

Nagy, Imre. ON COMMUNISM: IN DEFENCE OF THE NEW COURSE. Foreword by Hugh Seton-Watson. New York: Praeger, 1957. xliv, 306 p.

Nord, Lars. NONALIGNMENT AND SOCIALISM: YUGOSLAV FOREIGN POLICY IN THEORY AND PRACTICE. Stockholm: Raben and Sjogren, distributors, 1974. 306 p.

Oren, Nissan. BULGARIAN COMMUNISM: THE ROAD TO POWER, 1934-1944. New York: Columbia University Press, 1972. xii, 288 p.

_____. REVOLUTION ADMINSTERED: AGRARIANISM AND COMMUNISM IN BULGARIA. Baltimore, Md.: Johns Hopkins Press, 1973. xv, 204 p. Paperbound.

Palmer, Stephen E., Jr., and King, Robert R. YUGOSLAV COMMUNISM AND THE MACEDONIAN QUESTION. Hamden, Conn.: Shoe String Press, 1971. vii, 247 p. Maps.

Remington, Robin Alison. THE WARSAW PACT: CASE STUDIES IN COMMUNIST CONFLICT RESOLUTION. Cambridge, Mass.: MIT Press, 1971. xix, 268 p. Paperbound.

Roberts, Henry L. EASTERN EUROPE: POLITICS, REVOLUTION, AND DI-PLOMACY. New York: Knopf, 1970. xii, 324 p.

Robinson, William F. THE PATTERN OF REFORM IN HUNGARY: A POLITI-CAL, ECONOMIC AND CULTURAL ANALYSIS. New York: Praeger, 1973. xvi, 467 p.

Rothschild, Joseph. EAST CENTRAL EUROPE BETWEEN TWO WORLD WARS. Seattle: University of Washington Press, 1974. xvii, 240 p. Paperbound.

Rubinstein, Alvin Z. YUGOSLAVIA AND THE NONALIGNED WORLD. Princeton, N.J.: Princeton University Press, 1970. xv, 353 p.

Schaefer, Henry Wilcox. COMECON AND THE POLITICS OF INTEGRATION. New York: Praeger, 1972. xiv, 200 p.

Schick, Jack M. THE BERLIN CRISIS 1958-1962. Philadelphia: University of Pennsylvania Press, 1971. xix, 266 p.

Seton-Watson, Hugh. THE EAST EUROPEAN REVOLUTION. 3d ed. New York: Praeger, 1956. xix, 435 p. Illus. Paperbound.

_____ . NATIONALISM AND COMMUNISM: ESSAYS, 1946-1963. New York: Praeger, 1964. x, 253 p.

Shoup, Paul. COMMUNISM AND THE YUGOSLAV NATIONAL QUESTION. New York: Columbia University Press, 1968. 308 p.

Sinanian, Sylva, et al., eds. EASTERN EUROPE IN THE 1970'S. New York: Praeger, 1972. ix, 260 p.

Skilling, H. Gordon. COMMUNISM, NATIONAL AND INTERNATIONAL: EASTERN EUROPE AFTER STALIN. Toronto: University of Toronto Press, 1964. ix, 168 p. Paperbound.

_____ . CZECHOSLOVAKIA'S INTERRUPTED REVOLUTION. Princeton, N.J.: Princeton University Press, 1976. xvi, 924 p. Paperbound.

Slusser, Robert M. THE BERLIN CRISIS OF 1961: SOVIET AMERICAN RELA-TIONS AND THE STRUGGLE FOR POWER IN THE KREMLIN, JUNE-NOVEMBER 1961. Baltimore, Md.: Johns Hopkins Press, 1973. xvi, 509 p. Paperbound.

Staar, Richard F., ed. YEARBOOK ON INTERNATIONAL COMMUNIST AF-FAIRS. Stanford, Calif.: Hoover Institution Press, 1966-- .

Stehle, Hansjakob. THE INDEPENDENT SATELLITE: SOCIETY AND POLITICS IN POLAND SINCE 1945. Translated by O.J.S. Thompson. New York; Washington, D.C.; London: Praeger, 1965. xi, 361 p.

Stern, Carola [pseud.]. ULBRICHT: A POLITICAL BIOGRAPHY. Translated by Abe Farbstein. New York; Washington, D.C.; London: Praeger, 1965. xi, 231 p.

Sugar, Peter F., and Lederer, Ivo J., eds. NATIONALISM IN EASTERN EUROPE. Seattle: University of Washington Press, 1969. vii, 465 p. Paperbound.

Szporluk, Roman, ed. THE INFLUENCE OF EAST EUROPE AND THE SOVIET WEST ON THE USSR. New York: Praeger, 1975. x, 258 p.

Taborsky, Edward. COMMUNISM IN CZECHOSLOVAKIA 1948-1960. Princeton, N.J.: Princeton University Press, 1961. xii, 628 p.

Tanter, Raymond. MODELLING AND MANAGING INTERNATIONAL CONFLICTS: THE BERLIN CRISES. Beverly Hills, Calif.: Sage Publications, 1974. 272 p.

Tigrid, Pavel. WHY DUBCEK FELL. London: Macdonald, 1971. 229 p.

Tomasevich, Jozo. WAR AND REVOLUTION IN YUGOSLAVIA: 1941-1945: THE CHETNIKS. Stanford, Calif.: Stanford University Press, 1975. 508 p.

Triska, Jan F., ed. COMMUNIST PARTY-STATES: COMPARATIVE AND INTERNATIONAL STUDIES. Indianapolis, Ind.: Bobbs-Merrill, 1969. xxxv, 302 p.

Ulam, Adam [B.]. TITOISM AND THE COMINFORM. Cambridge, Mass.: Harvard University Press, 1952. viii, 243 p.

Vali, Ferenc A. RIFT AND REVOLT IN HUNGARY: NATIONALISM VERSUS COMMUNISM. Cambridge, Mass.: Harvard University Press, 1961. xi, 590 p.

Vucinich, Wayne S., ed. CONTEMPORARY YUGOSLAVIA: TWENTY YEARS OF SOCIALIST EXPERIMENT. Berkeley and Los Angeles: University of California Press, 1969. xi, 441 p.

Wettig, Gerhard. COMMUNITY AND CONFLICT IN THE SOCIALIST CAMP: THE SOVIET UNION, EAST GERMANY AND THE GERMAN PROBLEM 1965-1972. Translated by Edwina Moreton and Hannes Adomeit. New York: St. Martin's Press, 1975. xiv, 161 p.

Whetten, Lawrence L. GERMANY'S OSTPOLITIK: RELATIONS BETWEEN THE FEDERAL REPUBLIC OF GERMANY AND THE WARSAW PACT COUNTRIES. London: Oxford University Press, 1971. x, 244 p.

Windsor, Philip. GERMANY AND THE MANAGEMENT OF DETENTE. London: Chatto and Windus for the Institute for Strategic Studies, 1971.

Windsor, Philip, and Roberts, Adam. CZECHOSLOVAKIA 1968: REFORM, REPRESSION AND RESISTANCE. New York: Columbia University Press for Institute of Strategic Studies-London, 1969. vii, 199 p. Paperbound.

Wolfe, Thomas W. SOVIET POWER AND EUROPE, 1945-1970. Baltimore, Md.: Johns Hopkins Press, 1970. x, 534 p. Paperbound.

Wolff, Robert Lee. THE BALKANS IN OUR TIME. Cambridge, Mass.: Harvard University Press, 1956. xxi, 618 p.

Zaninovich, M. George. THE DEVELOPMENT OF SOCIALIST YUGOSLAVIA. Foreword by Jan F. Triska. Baltimore, Md.: Johns Hopkins Press, 1968. xxi, 182 p. Paperbound.

Zartman, I. William, ed. CZECHOSLOVAKIA, INTERVENTION AND IMPACT. New York: New York University Press, 1970. xiv, 127 p.

Zinner, Paul E. COMMUNIST STRATEGY AND TACTICS IN CZECHOSLOVAKIA, 1918-1948. New York: Praeger, 1963. 264 p.

_____. REVOLUTION IN HUNGARY. New York: Columbia University Press, 1962. xiii, 380 p.

_____, ed. NATIONAL COMMUNISM AND POPULAR REVOLT IN EASTERN EUROPE: A SELECTION OF DOCUMENTS ON EVENTS IN POLAND AND HUNGARY, FEBRUARY-NOVEMBER 1956. New York: Columbia University Press, 1956. xx, 561 p. Paperbound.

INDEXES

AUTHOR INDEX

This index is alphabetized letter by letter. In addition to authors, it includes all editors, compilers, and translators cited in this text. Numbers, except where preceded by "p.," refer to entry numbers.

A

Acimovic, Ljubivoje 1215
Aczel, Tamas 891-92
Adams, Arthur E. 389-90
Adams, Jan S. 390
Adenauer, Chancellor Konrad 828, 833
Adizes, Ichak 1052
Adomeit, Hannes 813, p. 223
Agostin, Istvan 391
Ahlport, Brodie E. 1129
Ainsztein, Reuben 122
Allemann, Fritz Rene 820
Almond, Gabriel A. 37, 92, 108, 115
Alton, Thad Paul 392-93, 493, 624a, 846
Amacher, Ryan C. 394
Andersen, Victor 143, 575, p. 219
Anderson, Albin T. 826
Anderson, Evelyn 755
Anderson, Neal 920
Aptheker, Herbert 893
Armstrong, Anne 821
Armstrong, Hamilton F. 1202
Arnez, John A. 1053
Ashton, E. B. 817
Aspaturian, Vernon V. 193-95
Atlantic Council of the United States 306

Aubrey, Henry G. 489
Ausch, Sandor D. 395-96, 846a
Auty, Phyllis 123, 1054-57
Avakumovic, Ivan 1058

B

Bain, Leslie B. 894
Baker, James C. 286
Bako, Elemer 1
Balassa, Bela A. 847
Bannan, Alfred 124
Barany, George 362
Barber, Noel 895
Barea, Ilsa 1121
Bares, Victor 756
Baring, Amulg 816
Bark, Dennis L. 822
Barker, E. 1059
Barker, Elisabeth 1060
Barros, James 603
Barton, Allen H. 38, 1061, 1166
Bass, Elizabeth 196
Bass, Robert 39, 196, 1203, p. 217
Bauman, Zygmunt 40, 197
Baylis, Thomas A. 757-58
Bebler, Anton 1216
Beck, Carl 41-42, 51, 87, 257, 485, 1086, p. 217
Beer, Francis A. 553
Beke, Laszlo 896
Bender, Peter 494-95, 759

Author Index

Author Index

Author Index

Author Index

TITLE INDEX

This index is alphabetized letter by letter. Numbers, except where preceded by "p.," refer to entry numbers. Titles of articles and journals are not included. In some cases titles have been shortened.

A

B

Title Index

Title Index

SUBJECT INDEX

This index is alphabetized letter by letter. Numbers refer to entry numbers, except where preceded by "p." Underlined numbers refer to main entries on the subject.

Subject Index

International relations
bibliography, reference works, text-
    books 1-27
in the cold war <u>154-92</u>, 245,
    1037, p. 218
comparative studies of 37-121
economic development and 50, 55,
    192, <u>259a-304</u>, 311, 357,
    361, <u>936</u>, 1070, 1183
historical background to 122-53
institutional approaches to 28-36
introduction to pp. xi-xvi
in the post-Stalinist era 193-361
by country
    Albania 580, 585, 596-97
        with the Balkan countries 578,
            587
        with China 569, 574-77, 581,
            583-84, 600, p. 219
        with the USSR 569, 571, 574-
            77, 581, 583-84, 586-87,
            589, 591-92, 599, 601,
            1188a, p. 219
        with the West 578
        with Yugoslavia 572, 581,
            583, 1117b, 1129a-30
    Austria, with Yugoslavia 1053
    Austro-Hungary, with the Balkan
        countries 598
    Balkan countries 50
        with Albania 578, 587
        with Austro-Hungary 598
        with Bulgaria 620
        with Italy 598
        with the USSR 139, 209, 373
        with Yugoslavia 594
    Bulgaria 608
        with Great Britain 619
        with the USSR 609, 613-14,
            617-18, 620
        with Yugoslavia 381
    China 228, <u>352-61</u>, 1107
        with Albania 569, 574-77,
            581, 583-84, 589, 591, 600,
            p. 219
        with Germany, East 360, 793,
            806
        with Rumania 1008, 1014,
            1016, 1018, 1032-33, 1042
        with the USSR 199, 202, 251,
            309, 352, 355-57, 361, 531,

574, 984, 1008, 1014,
    1016, 1018, 1032-33,
    1188a, p. 219
        with the U.S. 589
        with Yugoslavia 1220
    Czechoslovakia 65, 502, 625
        with China 630
        with Germany, East 768,
            812a
        with Germany, post-World
            War II 643
        with Germany, pre-World
            War II 629, 643
        with Poland 632, 948
        with the USSR 101, 213, 217,
            251, 253, 258, 357, 376-
            77, 387, 538, 545, 549,
            554, 559, 583, 587, 626,
            630, 635, <u>669-754</u>
        with the U.S. <u>665</u>
    France, with Rumania 1009
    Germany, East 112, 338, 340,
        521, 759, 764-65, 767, 774,
        795a, 798, 811, 817, 842,
        p. 223
        with China 360, 806
        with Czechoslovakia 768,
            812a
        with Germany, West 168,
            322, 326, 342, 759-61,
            768-69, 785, 795, 805,
            814-14a, 834, 839
        with Hungary 866
        with Poland 749, 775, 787
        with the USSR 755-56, 762,
            770, 781, 784, 785a, 789,
            793, 796, 802, 804, 807,
            813-14, 815, 843
        with the U.S. 839
    Germany, post-World War II
        313
        with Czechoslovakia 643
        with the USSR 178, 829
        with the U.S. 154, 164
    Germany, pre-World War II
        with Czechoslovakia 629,
            643
        with Hungary 850, 852, 865
        with Poland 141, 812, 957
    Germany, West 166, 225,

Q

R

Radio Free Europe 323, 347
Rajk, Laszlo 883, 1108
Rakosi, Matyas 897, 901
Rankovic, Alexander 1065, 1112
Recessions, in Czechoslovakia (1962–65) 669–70
Recreation, attitudes of youth toward 242
Regional development 47, 429
  in the Balkan countries 139
Religion 200
  in Albania 590
  in the Balkan countries 139
  See also Catholic Church
Reparations. See World War II, reparations
Resource allocation 294, 393, 428
  relationship to defense and foreign policy 55
Revolutions, Communist 112, 221
  history of 143
Romania. See Rumania
Roosevelt, Franklin D. 165
Rumania 79, 606, 745, <u>1004–51</u>, p. 218, p. 219, p. 220
  antisemitism in 233
  bibliography 7
  commerce of 607, 1040, 1044
  consumption indexes of 460
  economics of 361, 422, 429, 461, 1032, 1040, 1048a–49, p. 221
  ethnic groups in 380, 1023, 1040
  industry in 478
  international relations of 502, 521, 1011, 1019, 1026, 1029a, 1036, 1048
    with China 1008, 1014, 1016, 1018, 1032–33, 1042
    with France 1009
    with Germany, West 1006
    with Hungary 1023
    with the Middle East 1006
    with the USSR 156, 356–57, 496, 498, 1004, 1006–8, 1016, 1018, 1021, 1024, 1027–29, 1032–33, 1035, 1037, 1043, 1047, 1112–14

  military and security considerations 532, 536, 540
  nationalism and polycentrism in 236, 356, 380, 1009, 1017, 1029, 1045
  politics and domestic relations of 78, 962a, 1009, 1025, 1028, 1034, 1044
  social development and change in 216, 1049
  See also Transylvania
Russia. See Union of Soviet Socialist Republics

S

Scaff, Adam 213
Science. See Technology
Serbia, political institutions of 1084, 1162
Serbs 1113. See also Chetnik movement
Sino-Soviet dispute. See China, international relations of, with the USSR; Union of Soviet Socialist Republics, international relations of, with China
Slovakia, history of 649, 653
Slovaks 363a, 365, 387, 627a, 654, 675, 722
Slovaks in the U.S. 658
Slovenes in Yugoslavia 1137
Slovenia
  economics of 1190
  Hitler and 1093
  political history of 1053
Social change and conditions 11, 26, 136, 216, 218, 313, 382
  comparative studies of 38, 70, 86, 94
  economic integration and 466
  among youth 242
  by country
    Albania 580, 584, 588, 593
    Balkan countries 139
    Czechoslovakia 641, 743
    Germany, East 788, 792
    Poland 86, 934, 947, 962,